L^{THE}OOKOUT

A History of Signal Hill

James E. Candow

Canada Council for the Arts Conseil des Arts du Canada   Canada   Newfoundland Labrador

We gratefully acknowledge the financial support of the Canada Council for the Arts, the Government of Canada through the Canada Book Fund (CBF), and the Government of Newfoundland and Labrador through the Department of Tourism, Culture and Recreation for our publishing program.

Cover Design by Todd Manning
Cover Image: Signal Hill and The Narrows from Fort Townshend, ca. 1795.
Anonymous. Source: Anne S.K. Brown Military Collection, Brown University Library
Layout by Joanne Snook-Hann
Printed on acid-free paper

Published by
CREATIVE PUBLISHERS
an imprint of CREATIVE BOOK PUBLISHING
a Transcontinental Inc. associated company
P.O. Box 8660, Stn. A
St. John's, Newfoundland and Labrador A1B 3T7

Printed in Canada by:
TRANSCONTINENTAL INC.

Library and Archives Canada Cataloguing in Publication

Candow, James E.
The lookout : a history of Signal Hill / Jim Candow.

Includes bibliographical references and index.
ISBN 978-1-897174-71-5

 **Mixed Sources**
Product group from well-managed forests, controlled sources and recycled wood or fiber
www.fsc.org Cert no. SW-COC-000952
FSC © 1996 Forest Stewardship Council

1. Signal Hill National Historic Site (St. John's, N.L.)-- History. 2. Historic sites--Newfoundland and Labrador-- St. John's. 3. Fortification--Newfoundland and Labrador-- St. John's. 4. Signals and signaling--Newfoundland and Labrador--St. John's. 5. Communications, Military-- History. I. Title.

FC2164.S5C36 2011   971.8'1   C2011-901877-2

THE LOOKOUT

A History of Signal Hill

James E. Candow

St. John's, Newfoundland and Labrador
2011

CONTENTS

I.   INTRODUCTION: IN FROM THE SEA 1

II.   FISH AND MEN'S LIVES 7
      The Newfoundland Fisheries and International Rivalry 7
      Settlement and Defence 11
      Iberville 19
      Establishment of an English Garrison 24
      Knock Two Times 27

III. MASTERS OF THE HILL 35
      St. John's and the Placentia Garrison 35
      1762 and All That 40
      Dénouement and the Treaty of Paris 56

IV.   THE KEY OF THE HARBOUR 61
      The Incredible Expanding Defence Network 61
      Fort Impregnable 70
      The Last Waltz 75
      Between a Rock and a Hard Place 80

V.   A MIGHTY FONDNESS FOR FLAGS 93
      Changing of the Guard 93
      Once More with Feeling 97
      The Civilian Invasion 104
      Withdrawal of the Imperial Garrison 114

VI.   A BIG LOOKOUT 123
      The People's Hill 123
      Cabot Tower and the Man in the Moon 129
      Who Stopped the Gun? 140
      Transatlantic Connections 145
      Keeping Time 162

VII. CANADA'S FRONT DOOR 169
      Reservists and Frontiersmen 169
      Cable, Wireless, and the Warden of the Watch Tower 184
      Hands across the Water 195

VIII. CONCLUSION: THIS VERY COMMENDABLE,
      NATIONAL MOVEMENT 219

      About the Author 236

      Acknowledgements 237

      Bibliographical Note 240

      Index 243

INTRODUCTION: IN FROM THE SEA

"You cannot expect to sail in unless the wind be in from the sea...."
James Cook, 1762

There are many Signal Hills in the world, even a city of Signal Hill in Los Angeles County, California. The name's appeal is no surprise, for signalling speaks to a basic human trait—the need to communicate. But the Signal Hill that overlooks St. John's, Newfoundland is the only one to have been declared a national historic site, an honour derived from its unique place in Canada's military and communications histories.

The hill is first and foremost a physical entity, and that physicality has profoundly affected its human history. It is located on the Signal Hill Peninsula, which is bound on the north by Quidi Vidi Harbour, River, and Lake, on the east by St. John's Bay and the Atlantic Ocean, and on the south by The Narrows, the name of the channel that connects the bay and St. John's Harbour.[1] Although people refer to

Fig. 1: Signal Hill and Area.

---

[1] As with Signal Hill, there is more than one Narrows; the best known, in North America at least, separates Brooklyn and Staten Island.

hill and peninsula interchangeably, Signal Hill is, strictly speaking, the peninsula's most elevated section, which comprises a ridge trending north-northeast for 365 metres, averaging 64 metres in width, and ranging from 152 to 160 metres above sea level. The apex occurs in the northernmost section and is known today as Ladies' Lookout, a corruption of the hill's original name.

To the east and south the hill rises nearly vertically from the water, but the southeast ascent is interrupted fifty metres above sea level by Ross's Valley. Geologists call this a "hanging valley" because the glacier that carved it melted prematurely, leaving it at a different height from the valley floor that lies beneath The Narrows.[2] Ross's Valley is strewn with erratics, rounded boulders that the glacier scooped up as it moved and deposited when it melted. From here to the summit the ascent is again almost vertical. The decline from the summit to the westward, while initially steep, is broken about ninety metres above sea level by another hanging valley, George's Valley. Its major features are George's Pond, which like the valley is the result of glacial action, and Gibbet Hill, which spikes to a height of 119 metres in the valley's southwest corner. At Gibbet Hill's western foot lies Deadman's Pond, beyond which the hill falls off again until merging with the city.

Geologically, Signal Hill is composed of purplish red and grey or greenish grey sandstones and conglomerates.[3] In the early nineteenth century the hill was densely covered in fir and spruce, much of which disappeared thanks to erosion after trees were felled for firewood and building material, or to make way for military structures.[4] Erosion on Gibbet Hill was hastened by its use as a quarry, and on the summit by attempts to make the western face steeper and thus more daunting to attackers. Other signs of human impact include Scottish heather, a legacy, perhaps, of its use as bed stuffing by British soldiers who lived on the hill. In the animal kingdom, green frogs and snowshoe hares are among the hill's main introduced species. All is not foreign. George's Pond, for example, is home to a colony of herring gulls, who perhaps because they are native to the place act as though they own it. And from the summit can be seen more creatures of the ocean, including gannets, puffins, humpback whales, and those modern glacial remnants, icebergs.

---

[2] A. F. King, "History of the Rocks and Scenery in and near Signal Hill National Historic Park," *Memorial University of Newfoundland Geology Report 6* (St. John's, 1972), p. 10.
[3] R. H. Picher, *Road Materials Survey in the Province of Newfoundland in 1951* (Ottawa, 1952), p. 4.
[4] The National Archives [Great Britain] (hereafter TNA): Public Record Office (hereafter PRO), Colonial Office 194 (hereafter C. O. 194), Colonial Office and Predecessors: Newfoundland Original Correspondence, Vol. 44, fols. 146-57, "Report upon the defences of St. Johns [sic] Newfoundland," 13 July 1805.

The hill cannot be fully understood without knowledge of its relationship to The Narrows and the harbour. At approximately one kilometre in length, The Narrows is framed on the north by Signal Hill and opposite by the Southside Hills, which attain a maximum height of 232 metres. Although the seaward entrance between North and South heads is 302 metres across, the channel tapers to only 174 metres between the navigational hazards of Chain and Pancake rocks, then widens as it merges with the harbour. The latter is a modest 1,920 metres long with a maximum width of 640 metres, and at one time shrunk almost to a point at its western extremity. The harbour's relative smallness has long been offset by its sheltered location and excellent anchorage.

The tightness of The Narrows, the sharpness of the angle between it and the harbour, and the height disparity between the opposing hills all combined to cause major headaches in the age of sail. A southwest wind, for example, would carry vessel and crew half way up The Narrows and then abruptly blow in their face. As the great navigator James Cook discovered in 1762: "You cannot expect to sail in unless the wind be in from the sea, when this is not the case, ships endeavour to shoot into the narrows as far as they can; come to an anchor and afterwards warp in."[5] But the same natural factors that were trouble for sailors were a boon to the port's defenders and to the operators of its signalling service.

Geography has given Newfoundland a stature in international affairs out of all proportion to its small population. It is also fundamental to Signal Hill's story. If we exclude Greenland, which is politically European but physically North American, then Newfoundland is North America's most easterly land mass. This enabled its fisheries to be integrated into the western European economy, and thus to become factors in international rivalries, hence the fortifications on Signal Hill and in The Narrows. Geography also thrust Signal Hill into the forefront of modern communications, first as the site of Guglielmo Marconi's attempt to span the Atlantic Ocean by wireless telegraphy, and later as the eastern terminus of transatlantic telegraph cables. During the first and second world wars Newfoundland's position as North America's easternmost flank made it the hub of hemispheric defence, again with repercussions for the hill and The Narrows.

---

[5] Cited in Andrew David, "James Cook's 1762 Survey of St. John's Harbour and Adjacent Parts of Newfoundland," *Terrae Incognitae*, Vol. 30 (1998), p. 69. See also Jean M. Murray (ed.), *The Newfoundland Journal of Aaron Thomas: Able Seaman in HMS Boston* (London, 1968), p. 49. To warp a ship is to move it gradually with a heavy rope (that is, a warp) attached to a fixed object, such as an anchor or buoy, by using the ship's windlass or capstan.

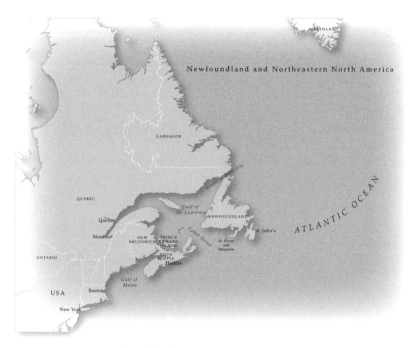

Fig. 2: Newfoundland and Northeastern North America.

The military and communications themes that help to define the hill are closely related, often to the point of inseparability. Early communications such as heliographs, smoke signals, and talking drums were employed, perhaps even invented, to warn of an enemy's approach. In other words, they served a military function. Over the centuries, as fighting forces grew larger and their tools more advanced, their coordination required increasingly sophisticated forms of communication.[6] Recently and perhaps most famously, the United States Department of Defense played a leading role in the creation of the internet, the most formidable communications network in human history. The development of more complex ways of communicating and waging war was much in evidence on Signal Hill, and there as elsewhere was part of a broader cultural shift by which the traditional world gave way to the modern one.

Signal Hill's story is a vivid reminder that the local, the national, and the international all form part of the whole. The word "national"

---

[6] Martin van Creveld, *Technology and War: From 2000 B.C. to the Present* (New York, 1989), p. 38.

has special significance here, since Newfoundland did not join the Canadian confederation until 1949.[7] Prior to that it had a separate existence and, with due allowance for its chequered constitutional development, was a nation in its own right. The same military and communications themes that figure in Signal Hill's story also loom large in Newfoundland's embrace of Canadian nationhood. Moreover, the hill and its most prominent building, Cabot Tower, have been imbued with multiple meanings down through the years, some of them national in scope. Those meanings reflect both the people who invented them and the times in which they lived.

---

[7] In 2001 the province's name was officially changed to Newfoundland and Labrador. Because this book deals mostly with events before 2001, I have employed the old name throughout. I occasionally use the words "Newfoundland and Labrador," but in a geographical context, not a political one.

CHAPTER

☙ II ❧

FISH AND MEN'S LIVES

"It's no fish ye're buying—it's men's lives." Sir Walter Scott, *The Antiquary* (Edinburgh, 1816)

THE NEWFOUNDLAND FISHERIES AND INTERNATIONAL RIVALRY

It is now an accepted fact that the first European settlement in North America was established by the Norse around AD 1000 at L'Anse aux Meadows, Newfoundland, at the northern entrance to the Strait of Belle Isle in sight of the Labrador coast.[1] The settlement, which served as a gateway to further explorations southward, lasted no more than a decade. Sustained European interest in Newfoundland and Labrador had to wait until after 1497, when Venetian navigator Zuan Caboto (John Cabot) made landfall while searching for a western sea route to Asia on behalf of the English Crown. Although the most recent informed opinion places the landfall on Newfoundland's northeast coast between Bonavista and Twillingate, others have used the available evidence to argue for landfalls from Labrador to Maine.[2] At the time, the landfall's whereabouts were not as important as news that Cabot had found a sea so full of fish that they could be caught "not only with the net, but in baskets let down with a stone."[3] As a pioneer, Cabot might have been expected to stretch the truth, and some who followed him definitely did, notably Sir Richard Whitbourne, who in 1620 wrote wistfully of meeting a mermaid in St. John's Harbour. But Cabot was so well regarded that European fishermen were soon beating a path to the coastal waters of Newfoundland and eastern Canada.

If, as the saying goes, "Timing is everything," then Cabot's could not have been better. The plagues and famines of the fourteenth century, which killed over a quarter of all Europeans, had been followed by unprecedented growth. By 1500 the continent's population had recovered to an estimated 81.8 million, and it would

---

[1] The definitive work is Birgitta Linderoth Wallace, *Westward Vikings: The Saga of L'Anse aux Meadows* (St. John's, 2006).

[2] The best account of the landfall debate is Peter E. Pope, *The Many Landfalls of John Cabot* (Toronto, 1997). The argument for a landfall between Bonavista and Twillingate is made in Trevor Kenchington, "On John Cabot: An Hypothesis," *Argonauta*, Vol. 16, No. 1 (Jan. 1999), pp. 17-32.

[3] James A. Williamson, *The Cabot Voyages and Bristol Discovery under Henry VII* (Cambridge, 1962), p. 210.

soar to 115.3 million by 1700.[4] With no shortage of mouths to be fed, the discovery of a major new food source was bound to be welcomed. The chief markets for dried, salted cod (saltfish) from Newfoundland and Labrador were the Catholic countries of western Europe and the Mediterranean. Religion's influence on saltfish consumption has probably been overrated, since the Protestant countries of western Europe were also big consumers of fish, especially herring. Even so, among Catholics meat was taboo during Lent and other Holy Days totalling more than a third of the year in the Middle Ages, and this was bound to encourage fish consumption.[5] Demand later spread to the Caribbean, where African slaves formed a captive market for inferior grades of saltfish that Europeans refused to eat except during dire shortages—hence the expression "refuse fish."

Fig. 3: "La Pesche des Morues Vertes et Seches, sur le Grand Banc et aux Costes de Terre Neuve" (The Green and Dry Fisheries on the Grand Bank and on the Coasts of Newfoundland), by Nicolas Guérard. Detail from Nicolas de Fer's wall map of North America (1698). Source: Library and Archives Canada/Nicolas Guérard/NMC-026825/2. It is no accident that this, the first thorough depiction of European fishing operations in Newfoundland, comes from France. No other European country has had a longer presence in the northwest Atlantic fisheries.

---

[4] Roger Mols, "Population in Europe 1500-1700,"in Carlo M. Cipolla (ed.), *The Fontana Economic History of Europe: The Sixteenth and Seventeenth Centuries* (London, 1974), Vol. 2, p. 38.
[5] Jean-Louis Flandrin and Massimo Montanari (eds.), *Food: A Culinary History from Antiquity to the Present* (New York, 1999), p. 261; Albert C. Jensen, *The Cod* (New York, 1972), p. 5.

Despite claims to the contrary, England was a relatively minor player in the Newfoundland fisheries until the 1570s, when the West Country (the southwest counties) got seriously involved.[6] Previously, most Europeans in Newfoundland were from Spain, Portugal, and above all France, whose fishermen were making regular trips by 1508, maybe as early as 1504. Even by today's standards the late-sixteenth-century transatlantic cod fishery was impressive, employing some 500 vessels and 12,000 fishermen, to say nothing of the untold shipwrights, chandlers, weavers, shoemakers, sail makers, rope makers, and others whose incomes depended on this vast enterprise. Total yearly catches ranged between 150,000 and 200,000 tonnes (live weight), and the sky, not the ocean, was the limit, or so people thought at the time. Fur, sugar, coffee, cotton, and tobacco would follow in due course, but for France and England alike, cod came first, and so did Newfoundland and Labrador.

With an industry this broad in economic scope, it was only a matter of time before Newfoundland became a factor in international rivalries. Englishman Bernard Drake's capture of some sixteen Portuguese fishing vessels off its shores in 1585 was both a setback for Portugal and a sign of things to come.[7] Happily for England, the Spanish Newfoundland fishery, which was dominated by the Basque Country, was about to implode. This had various causes, but the main one was probably the extended diversion of men and ships into the Spanish navy during the course of wars with England (1580-1604) and France (1595-1598).[8] By the early seventeenth century Spain and Portugal played trivial roles in the production end of the Newfoundland fisheries, but they were (and would remain) vital as markets for saltfish made by French and English fishermen, who now had the run of the place.

For most of the seventeenth century the French and the English obeyed an unwritten code for sharing the spoils in Newfoundland and Labrador. The English Shore extended southward from Bonavista past Trinity and Conception bays, then down the east coast of the Avalon Peninsula to Cape Race (There was some intermingling of French and English fishermen in Trepassey Bay after 1650). Despite its relatively modest length, the English Shore was the closest part of the island to

---

[6] The classic—and erroneous—argument for English primacy before 1570 is D. W. Prowse, *A History of Newfoundland from the English, Colonial, and Foreign Records* (London, 1895), pp. 15-18.

[7] *Dictionary of Canadian Biography* (hereafter *DCB*) (Toronto, 1966), Vol. 1, "Drake, Sir Bernard."

[8] Michael M. Barkham, "French Basque 'New Found Land' Entrepreneurs and the Import of Codfish and Whale Oil to Northern Spain, c. 1580 to c. 1620: The Case of Adam de Chibau, Burgess of Saint-Jean-de-Luz and 'Sieur de St. Julien'," *Newfoundland Studies*, Vol. 10, No. 1 (Spring 1994), pp. 2-6.

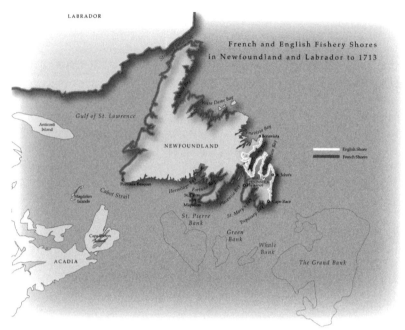

Fig: 4: French and English Fishery Shores in
Newfoundland and Labrador to 1713.

Europe, an advantage that enabled shorter outward trips, quicker
start-ups, earlier departures to market (where the first fish always
commanded top price), and timely payment in the form of bullion
(gold and silver), bills of exchange, fruit, salt, wine, or olive oil. The
better-established French fishery occupied so much of the
Newfoundland coastline that it is impossible to speak of a single
shore. The French worked the south coast from Trepassey Bay
westward to Hermitage Bay (including St. Pierre and Miquelon), the
west coast (where French Basques dominated), the northeast coast
(Petit Nord) down to Notre Dame Bay, and the Labrador side of the
Strait of Belle Isle. The catch from these shores—about 100,000
metric tonnes (live weight) annually during the seventeenth
century—was on balance twice as large as the English catch, and
France's offshore fishery on the Grand Banks added another 50,000
tonnes to the disparity.[9] The enormous extent of the French realm
makes a mockery of claims that Newfoundland, by virtue of Sir
Humphrey Gilbert's planting the flag in St. John's in 1583, was

---

[9] Peter E. Pope, "The Scale of the Early Modern Newfoundland Fishery," in David J.
Starkey and James E. Candow (eds.), *The North Atlantic Fisheries: Supply, Marketing and
Consumption, 1560-1990: Studia Atlantica 8* (Hull, 2006), pp. 26-27.

England's oldest colony.[10] Even if we ignore the fact that Gilbert left no colonists, the truth is that Newfoundland was shared territory, and it would stay that way, in certain respects, until 1904.

SETTLEMENT AND DEFENCE

Formal English colonies were established in Conception Bay and on the east coast of the Avalon Peninsula between 1610 and 1637. Sanctioned by the Crown and backed by private investors, they were business failures but did leave a rump of permanent inhabitants, some of whom spread to other areas. This may explain how, by 1625, settlers had appeared in St. John's, a place that until then had been the exclusive domain of migratory fishermen for a hundred years.[11] Unaccustomed as they were to sharing the spoils, the West Country merchants who underwrote the migratory fishery used their political connections to try and make life miserable for settlers. As a result, the colonizing grant of Sir David Kirke, resident governor between 1638 and 1651, was saddled with a clause prohibiting settlement within six miles of the coast. However, this and like measures down through the years were widely ignored and have been overrated as factors in Newfoundland's slow demographic growth. More influential was the tendency of residents to return to England when their Newfoundland careers were over, and of indentured servants to flee to New England aboard that colony's increasingly numerous trading vessels. There was also the exclusively male character of the early fishery workforce, which for obvious reasons inhibited growth by natural reproduction.[12] After the demise of the early colonies, the prevailing pattern was therefore one of "relatively invisible settlement without the fanfare of royal charters, the expense of colonization schemes, or, probably, any expectation of permanence."[13] The resident English population probably did not exceed 2,000 at any time during the seventeenth century.[14] While this may not sound like much, it compares favourably with Acadia (1,400) and Maine (2,000) in the same period.

---

[10] One of the earliest exponents of this myth was Daniel Woodley Prowse. See his *History of Newfoundland*, ch. 4.

[11] Gillian T. Cell, *English Enterprise in Newfoundland 1577-1660* (Toronto, 1969), p. 78; Alan G. Macpherson, "The Demographic History of St. John's, 1627-2001," in Alan G. Macpherson (ed.), *Four Centuries and the City: Perspectives on the Historical Geography of St. John's* (St. John's, 2005), pp. 1-2.

[12] This is the main argument of W. Gordon Handcock, *So longe as there comes noe women: Origins of English Settlement in Newfoundland* (St. John's, 1989).

[13] Cole Harris, *The Reluctant Land: Society, Space, and Environment in Canada before Confederation* (Vancouver, 2008), p. 139.

[14] Peter E. Pope, *Fish into Wine: The Newfoundland Plantation in the Seventeenth Century* (Chapel Hill, 2004), pp. 200-02.

The timing is hazy, but a few tiny French settlements—probably clusters of overwintering fishermen—seem to have taken root in Placentia Bay by 1650. English encroachment into the bay spurred the French Crown to establish the royal colony of Plaisance (in English, Placentia) in 1662.[15] This opened the door to further population growth in Placentia Bay as well as in Fortune and Hermitage bays and in the archipelago of St. Pierre and Miquelon, amounting in all to 640 people in 1687, of whom 308 lived in or near Plaisance.[16] The founding of Plaisance was part of a broader North American surge by France that included immigration schemes for New France and expansion of the fur trade into the Great Lakes and the Mississippi River Valley. This effort was less cohesive than it

Fig. 5: "The West Prospect of Placentia" and "A Draught of ye Harbour of Placentia," by Christian Lilly, 1693. Source: From the collection of the James Ford Bell Library, University of Minnesota. Placentia's undeserved reputation as "the Gibraltar of North America" can be traced to the ineffectiveness of the English naval officers who tried to take it.

---

[15] The standard work is Nicolas Landry, *Plaisance (Terre-Neuve) 1650-1713: Une colonie française en Amérique* (Sillery, QC, 2008).
[16] Olaf Uwe Janzen, "The French Presence in Southwestern and Western Newfoundland Before 1815," in André Magord (ed.), *Les Franco-Terreneuviens de la péninsule de Port-au-Port: Évolution d'une identité franco-canadienne* (Moncton, 2002), pp. 32-39; Pope, *Fish into Wine*, p. 210.

sounds, and many of the imperial goals for Plaisance emerged only with the passage of time.[17] The immediate aims were to stop English expansion along the south coast, and to create a port of refuge for the Grand Banks fishing fleet and for metropolitan vessels travelling between France, Acadia, and New France. Strategically, Plaisance was meant to flank the seaward approaches to Acadia and New France in wartime, a fine theory but meaningless without a permanent naval force, which it never got. Still, the French were the first to appreciate Newfoundland's strategic value vis-à-vis the North American mainland, a theme of great significance in its history.

Although from the outset Plaisance had a small garrison (and eventually fortifications), later accounts of it as "the Gibraltar of North America" were ludicrous.[18] The soldiers mutinied during their first winter on the island, and their replacements eked out a living only by working as fishermen. Perception being more influential than reality, the martial presence worried the island's English settlers, especially those in St. John's, which with 150 residents in the 1660s was the largest community on the English Shore. Pleas for offsetting fortifications fell on deaf ears, in part because of official concern that defences would attract more settlers, who would in turn compete against the migratory fishery. Also, the government saw the migratory fishery as a training ground for naval recruits, and more colonists in Newfoundland might spell trouble for the Royal Navy.[19] The navy's peacetime strength of 4,000 swelled to over 20,000 in wartime, mainly thanks to fishermen being pressed—hence "press gangs"—into naval service.[20] England was an ambitious island nation with overseas colonies and an expanding global commerce, and a strong navy was critical to its prosperity. Anything that threatened that navy was not going to be popular. Besides, the navy already gave some protection to the Newfoundland fisheries in the form of convoys (in peacetime, usually a couple of ships) that escorted West Country ships to and from the island, or from Newfoundland to Iberian and Mediterranean

---

[17] This is the central argument in James Pritchard, *In Search of Empire: The French in the Americas, 1670-1730* (Cambridge, 2004).

[18] Prowse, *History of Newfoundland*, p. 181.

[19] Gerald S. Graham, "Newfoundland in British Strategy from Cabot to Napoleon," in R. A. MacKay (ed.), *Newfoundland: Economic, Diplomatic, and Strategic Studies* (Toronto, 1946), pp. 252-53. On the English fisheries as a training ground, see Robb Robinson, "The Effective Use of Scarce Resources: The British Government and Fish, Fishermen and Fishing Vessels," in David J. Starkey *et al.* (eds.), *Fish, War and Politics in the North Atlantic Fisheries, 1300-2003: Studia Atlantica 7* (Vlaardingen, 2005), pp. 100-12.

[20] J. D. Davies, "A Permanent National Maritime Fighting Force 1642-1689," in J. R. Hill (ed.), *The Oxford Illustrated History of the Royal Navy* (Oxford, 1995), p. 64.

markets.[21] None of this was especially helpful for residents, but for now it was all they were getting.

The English settlers had more worries than just the French. Relations with their own countrymen in the migratory fishery were prickly, and there were counter-charges of destruction of settlers' property and of fishermen's gear and facilities.[22] Migrants and residents alike had to be on the lookout for a third type of Englishman, the pirate. Pirates were more interested in gold and silver from Mexico and South America than in fish from Newfoundland, but they did visit Newfoundland to obtain food, supplies, and crews for their ships.[23] Two of the most famous were Peter Easton, who in 1612 robbed thirty fishing vessels in St. John's Harbour and conscripted 100 fishermen in Conception Bay, and Henry Mainwaring, who in 1614 "recruited" 400 men from the English Newfoundland fleet.

Although piracy was so serious that it briefly curbed interest in settlement, it was hardly the biggest challenge to the English fisheries. That distinction belonged to the Islamic privateers of Morocco and the Ottoman regencies of Algiers, Tripoli, and Tunisia.[24] Long characterized as pirates, they were actually privateers—individuals authorized by their governments to prey on foreign shipping—and therefore no different from Bernard Drake or other English adventurers of the era. With their singular talent for mangling foreign languages, the English employed various names to describe these privateers: Barbary pirates (after the Berber people of North Africa), Sallee rovers (after the Moroccan city of Salé), or the generic Turks (because of the Ottoman connection). Whatever they were called, their goals were the same: to attack foreign shipping and to confiscate their cargoes and crews, enslaving the latter or seeking ransom for their release. Ranging throughout the Mediterranean and along Europe's Atlantic coast, they captured some 20,000 Britons during the seventeenth and eighteenth centuries, with

---

[21] Sari R. Hornstein, *The Restoration Navy and English Foreign Trade, 1674-1688: A Study in the Peacetime Use of Sea Power* (Aldershot, UK, 1991), pp. 47-52, and "The English Navy and the Defense of American Trade in the Late Seventeenth Century," in Clark G. Reynolds (ed.), *Global Crossroads and the American Seas* (Missoula, 1988), pp. 105-10; Cell, *English Enterprise*, p. 121. For details of convoy organization in wartime, see William R. Miles, "The Royal Navy and Northeastern North America, 1689-1713" (Unpublished MA thesis, St. Mary's University, Halifax, NS, 2000), pp. 150-55. The Newfoundland convoy was inaugurated in 1649, but the start-up date for the Mediterranean convoys is unclear. However, English convoys to the Italian port of Livorno, a key distribution centre for Newfoundland saltfish, were first noted in 1651. See Gigliola Pagano de Divitiis (Stephen Parkin, trans.), *English Merchants in Seventeenth-Century Italy* (Cambridge, 1997), p. 56.
[22] Cell, *English Enterprise*, pp. 74-75.
[23] Olaf Uwe Janzen, "The Problem of Piracy in the Newfoundland Fishery in the Aftermath of the War of the Spanish Succession," in Poul Holm and Olaf Janzen (eds.), *Northern Seas Yearbook 1997: Association for the History of the Northern Seas* (Esbjerg, 1998), pp. 60-61.
[24] Linda Colley, *Captives: Britain, Empire, and the World, 1600-1850* (New York, 2002), pp. 43-44.

the bulk of the seizures occurring between 1600 and 1640. The English system of assigning naval vessels to accompany merchantmen—including ones bearing Newfoundland saltfish—into the Mediterranean was a direct result of the privateering plague.

To give themselves a fighting chance against pirates and privateers, fishing and trading vessels bound for Newfoundland or for market tended to carry a few cannons. The picture ashore is less clear. Claims made after the fact that Sir David Kirke erected forts and distributed fifty-six guns between Ferryland, Bay Bulls, St. John's, and other English harbours seem dubious; even if true, the guns would have been useless unless placed in actual defence works, for which there is no evidence.[25] St. John's pretty well rolled over when a Dutch squadron under Admiral Michiel de Ruyter attacked during the Second Anglo-Dutch War (1665-67), fought because of English efforts to oust the Dutch from the international carrying trade.[26] The harbour was unusually quiet in June 1665—there were only two ships, which De Ruyter promptly seized—likely because most of the migratory fishermen had been pressed into naval service. De Ruyter found only six unmounted eight-pounder guns at unspecified locations, and these, like the two ships, were unmanned, every living soul having disappeared into neighbouring woods. Before fleeing, however, the residents had managed to lay a "cable" of thick hemp rope across The Narrows to snarl the rudders of the enemy ships, a good idea in principle but not in practice, as De Ruyter's flagship easily broke through. In England and elsewhere, cable was a standard element in the harbour defence repertoire of the period.[27] This, the earliest record of its use in St. John's, would not be the last.

Despite the lack of opposition, De Ruyter is alleged to have said that "if there had been but six guns mounted in St. John's, he would not have adventured in."[28] This echoed the words of contemporaries who felt that the harbour's natural features, especially the tunnel-like entrance flanked by precipitous hills, were so advantageous that the

---

[25] "A Brief Narrative concerning Newfoundland, by John Downing," in Prowse, *History of Newfoundland*, pp. 205-06.

[26] Dicky Glerum Laurentius, "A History of Dutch Activity in the Newfoundland Fish Trade from about 1590 till 1680" (Unpublished MA thesis, Memorial University of Newfoundland, St. John's, 1960), pp. 64-71; Bert den Boggende, "Raid on St. John's," *The Beaver*, Vol. 83, No. 5 (Oct./Nov. 2003), pp. 22-25.

[27] Norman Longmate, *Island Fortress: The Defence of Great Britain 1603-1945* (London, 1991), p. 10.

[28] TNA:PRO, Colonial Office 1 (hereafter C. O. 1), Privy Council and Related Bodies: America and West Indies, Colonial Papers (General Series), Vol. 22, Deposition of John Raynor, late Deputy Governor in Newfoundland, 13 Jan. 1668. Dates have been adjusted where necessary to conform to the modern Gregorian calendar, adopted by France in 1582 and by Great Britain in 1752. Prior to 1752, dates in the original British sources are eleven days earlier than French dates for the same events.

place could easily be made invincible. In 1665 (presumably after the Dutch raid) and 1667 the Devon-based trader Christopher Martin attempted to give teeth to these claims by landing a few guns from his ships and placing them in two earthen forts.[29] Martin was also present in August 1673 (Third Anglo-Dutch War, 1672-74) when a Dutch squadron led by Captain Nicholas Boes destroyed at least 150 ships along the English Shore.[30] Martin landed six guns from the *Elias Andrews* and, with the support of fewer than thirty men, stood his ground while Boes sized things up, concluded that the danger to his ships was real, and sheered off in search of easier prey. Two years later Henry Southwood drew the first detailed map of St. John's Harbour.[31] It shows two defences in The Narrows: North Fort, situated on the north side at what later became known as Chain Rock Point; and South Fort, on the opposite side, roughly midway between today's Anchor

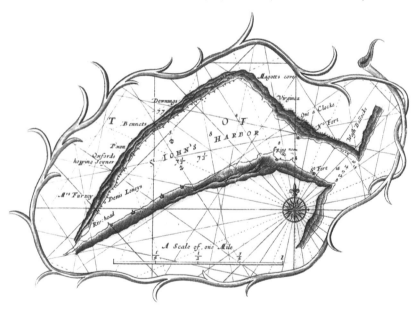

Fig 6: Map of St. John's Harbour, 1675, by Henry Southwood. Source: Library and Archives Canada/Atlas maritimus, or A collection of sea-charts: describing the coasts, capes, bays, rivers, roads, & ports ... of the whole world/AMICUS 26306140/Plate 45. This, the oldest known map of St. John's, shows the early Narrows defences.

---

[29] Prowse, *History of Newfoundland*, p. 175.
[30] Donald G. Shomette and Robert D. Haslach, *Raid on America: The Dutch Naval Campaign of 1672-1674* (Columbia, SC, 1988), pp. 204-05.
[31] William Gilbert, " 'Ye Strength of Ye Place': Defence Works in the St. John's Narrows, 1638-1778," *Newfoundland and Labrador Studies*, Vol. 25, No. 2 (Fall 2010), pp. 197-216.

Point and South Head. It is reasonable to assume that these were the sites that Martin had used.

Despite talk during the 1680s of sending a governor and fortifying St. John's, there was no change, not even after England joined the War of the League of Augsburg (or Nine Years War) (1689-97) to stop French expansion on the European continent. More wary than ever of Plaisance, the inhabitants of St. John's declared in 1691 that they had "raised a small work according to the best of our judgments for our present defence, where we have a few guns; but we are in want of powder, shot, and other materials."[32] Things improved slightly in September 1693 when a large English naval squadron unexpectedly anchored in nearby Bay Bulls.[33] Commanded by Rear-Admiral Sir Francis Wheler, the squadron had left England in January with ambitious plans to drive the French from the Caribbean island of Martinique, then to proceed to New England to organize an expedition against New France, and finally to have a go at French settlements and fishing ships in Newfoundland on the homeward leg.[34] The Caribbean episode fizzled out amid organizational chaos and tropical illness, whereupon Wheler sailed for Boston in hopes of mounting the New France expedition. When that proved impossible because of time constraints, he left for Newfoundland. Arriving off Plaisance on 28 August with twenty-four ships, he spent a few days trading cannon fire with the French before deciding that the defences were so strong and his men so weak that it was pointless to continue. By then his scouts had returned from Bay Bulls, which they had identified as a place big enough

Fig. 7: "The Town of St. John" [St. John's], by Christian Lilly, 1693. Source: From the collection of the James Ford Bell Library, University of Minnesota. With Lilly's help, the residents of St. John's expanded the defences from The Narrows into the inner harbour.

---

[32] TNA:PRO, C. O. 1, Vol. 68, "The inhabitants of St. John's, Newfoundland, to Captain Stephen Akarman," 26 Oct. 1691.
[33] Olaf Uwe Janzen, "New Light on the Origins of Fort William at St. John's, Newfoundland, 1693-1696," *Newfoundland Quarterly*, Vol. 83, No. 2 (Fall 1987), pp. 24-31.
[34] K. A. J. McLay, "Sir Francis Wheler's Caribbean and North American Expedition, 1693: A Case Study in Combined Operational Command during the Reign of William III," *War in History*, Vol. 14, No. 4 (2007), pp. 383-407; Pritchard, *In Search of Empire*, pp. 348-49; *Oxford Dictionary of National Biography* (hereafter *ODNB*) (Oxford, 2004-08), "Wheler, Sir Francis."

Fig. 8: "Prospect of St. John's from the Sea," by Christian Lilly, 1693. Source: From the collection of the James Ford Bell Library, University of Minnesota. One of the two town forts laid out by Lilly appears in the centre. The old south-side Narrows battery is also visible, and a sentry appears to have been posted at South Head.

to accommodate the ships, and where everyone could get some much-needed rest before going home.

The people of St. John's took advantage of the squadron's presence by petitioning Wheler for help with the town's defences. The admiral offered the services of his engineer, Captain Christian Lilly, under whose direction the residents began to erect a square redoubt on a small hill on the north side of the harbour, looking directly out The Narrows. Lilly marked lines for an even larger redoubt closer to the harbour and "within Musquett reach" of the first, naming the two, respectively, Fort William and Fort Mary (after the reigning monarchs, William III and Mary II). Turning his attention to The Narrows, he recommended getting rid of the south-side battery, which he called Old Fort (possibly Henry Southwood's South Fort), in favour of a position opposite at Piggs Point (possibly Southwood's North Fort), where The Narrows cable was stored. That was as far as things had got when Wheler's hapless squadron left for England.

In their meetings with Lilly the residents had stressed that they did not fear naval attack so much as "the Indians and the French together coming from Placentia overland to destroy and burn their habitations."[35] But if Plaisance was strong enough to thwart a twenty-four-ship Royal Navy squadron—it had also beaten off a smaller squadron in 1692—why had the French not bothered St. John's? The simple answer is that the Plaisance garrison was too small to mount an attack. Indeed, its courageous resistance against Wheler likely would have crumbled if the admiral had kept up the pressure for a few more days. Things began to change in 1694 when a small privateering squadron set out from Bayonne to commit mischief along the English Shore.[36] After a failed attack on Ferryland in early September, the privateers headed north to St. John's, where like Boes in 1673 they took one look at the Narrows defences, thought better of it, and went home via Plaisance.

---

[35] Cited in Janzen, "Origins of Fort William," p. 27.
[36] Pritchard, *In Search of Empire*, pp. 349-57.

IBERVILLE

In the winter of 1696-97 the French hammer finally came down in the form of a joint land and sea campaign designed to drive the English from Newfoundland.[37] The pivotal figure was New France's greatest warrior, thirty-five-year-old Pierre Le Moyne d'Iberville et d'Ardillières, who had proposed the campaign in 1692. The going would be tough in winter, but with the English population at its lowest point, fewer men would be needed for the job. Preoccupied with

Fig. 9: Ex-voto dit de Pierre Le Moyne d'Iberville. Anonyme. (Votive offering by Pierre Le Moyne d'Iberville. Anonymous.) Source: Le Musée de Sainte Anne. Iberville's Newfoundland campaign of 1696-97 was a only a temporary setback for the English fisheries. In the long run, however, it fed anti-French sentiment in Newfoundland.

[37] Guy Frégault, *Iberville le conquérant* (Montréal, 1944), pp. 209-35; Nellis M. Crouse, *Lemoyne d'Iberville: Soldier of New France* (Ithaca, 1954), pp. 118-38; Alan F. Williams, *Father Baudoin's War: D'Iberville's Campaigns in Acadia and Newfoundland 1696, 1697* (St. John's, 1987), pp. 24-56, 119-38; Pritchard, *In Search of Empire*, pp. 350-51; Janzen, "Origins of Fort William," p. 29; *DCB* (Toronto, 1969), Vol. 2, "Le Moyne d'Iberville et d'Ardillières, Pierre," and "Monbeton de Brouillan, Jacques-François."

fighting in Hudson Bay, Iberville was unable to focus on the Atlantic coast until 1696, arriving in Plaisance that September, fresh off a victory at Fort William Henry in Pemaquid, Maine. His fearsome band of 124 men included regular soldiers and handpicked volunteers from New France, along with Abenaki and Mi'kmaq warriors, the former led by Chief Nescambiouit.[38] Despite Iberville's reputation, overall responsibility had been assigned to the Governor of Plaisance, the irascible Jacques-François de Monbeton de Brouillan, who was also in charge of the campaign's naval component, a single ship bearing a

Fig. 10: The French Campaign of 1696-97.

---

[38] *DCB*, Vol. 2, "Nescambiouit."

hundred soldiers and volunteers from Plaisance. There were supposed to have been eight more ships crewed by privateers from Saint-Malo, but these had all left for France after an earlier cruise along the English Shore ended in disagreement between Brouillan and the privateer captains, who apparently refused his order to force The Narrows.[39] (That was the problem with privateers. They trod a fine line between adventure and profit, and adventure was sometimes not worth the bother). News of this development enraged Iberville, for whom Brouillan and the privateers were supposed to have waited, and Iberville's men took to calling Brouillan's "the jokers from Plaisance." Still, Brouillan's September sortie had brought destruction to Renews, Fermeuse, Bay Bulls, and Ferryland, making for less opposition this time around.

Brouillan sailed from Plaisance on 29 October in the *Profond* with food and supplies for Iberville's men, with whom he was to rendezvous at Renews. Iberville's group, which included chaplain Abbé Jean Baudoin, left on 1 November and took a route some 100 kilometres long through the frozen bogs and snow-covered woods of the southern Avalon, winter having come earlier than usual. Veering off track, they ran out of food and emerged ten days later not at Renews but at Ferryland, thirteen kilometres to the north. They were so famished that they butchered and ate a dozen horses, who, until they became dinner, had been Ferryland's only remaining inhabitants. Iberville would need a full stomach when he reached Renews a day or two later, for Brouillan now wanted a bigger share of the spoils than what he and Iberville had agreed to in Plaisance. Moreover, a reconnaissance party that Brouillan had sent northward had managed to capture and then lose an English settler, who hastened to St. John's to warn of the French approach, thus removing the element of surprise. Rather than jeopardize the campaign, Iberville ceded the governor a bigger share, and in a spirit of "unfriendly neutrality" they returned to the business at hand.[40]

On 23 November the patchwork army piled aboard some sloops and sailed for Bay Bulls, forty kilometres south of St. John's, where they disembarked later that day. Wisely, they had decided to approach by land, and although this meant another march, it was better than hurling themselves into the jaws of The Narrows. On the twenty-sixth they met skirmishers near Petty Harbour, only fourteen kilometres

---

[39] Frégault, *Iberville*, p. 217; James Pritchard, " 'Le Profit et La Gloire': The French Navy's Alliance with Private Enterprise in the Defense of Newfoundland, 1691-1697," *Newfoundland Studies*, Vol. 15, No. 2 (Fall 1999), p. 168.
[40] Crouse, *Lemoyne d'Iberville*, p. 126.

from their goal, and easily brushed them aside. The next day it snowed so heavily that they had to mark time, but on the twenty-eighth they got away for good. As the advance party came within sight of St. John's, it encountered gunfire from a group of between eighty and ninety inhabitants hiding behind boulders in a burnt wood. The civilians did the best they could, but nearly half of them were killed after the main body caught up and joined the battle, their arrival having been delayed so that Abbé Baudoin could absolve them of their sins. In addition to absolution, Brouillan gained some much-needed respect from the Canadiens when he showed fearlessness during the assault.

The panic-stricken English survivors retreated down the Southside Hills and took refuge as best they could, some in an unnamed fort at the head of the harbour, others in Forts William and Mary, and a third group in a ketch that was anchored in the harbour. The wind being favourable—that is, westerly—these last weighed anchor and escaped through The Narrows, apparently bound for Carbonear. The rest were not so lucky. Those who had holed up in the anonymous fort and in Fort Mary surrendered without a fight, yielding as prisoners thirty-three men and unspecified numbers of women and children. The remaining 200 or so residents, including their leader, known to history only by his surname "Miners," were completely surrounded in Fort William, or as the residents called it, King William's Fort. Although this was the best of the three works, it lacked ammunition to withstand a siege, which the French now got ready to mount, first by burning every house in the fort's vicinity, then by sending word to Bay Bulls to bring up the mortars. The mood inside the fort could not have been helped by the uncommonly cold weather, or by the heavy snow that fell all day on the twenty-ninth. The next day, a lone male brandishing a white flag walked tentatively through the gates to see about possible terms of surrender. After Miners requested twenty-four hours to ponder Brouillan's terms, the French decided to speed his deliberations by sending one of their prisoners, an unfortunate soul named William Drew, toward the fort minus his scalp and bearing a message that they "would serve them all in like manner if they did not surrender."[41] This they did in short order, after which they were loaded aboard two vessels and deported to England.[42]

With the big prize in the bag, Brouillan and his men returned to Plaisance. Iberville's, on the other hand, spent the rest of the winter and most of the spring torching English settlements in Conception

---

[41] TNA:PRO, C. O. 194, Vol. 1, fols. 50-51, Affidavit of Philip Roberts *et al.*, received 25 Jan. 1697.
[42] Williams, *Father Baudoin's War*, pp. 48-49.

and Trinity bays, failing to take only Carbonear Island. They eventually fell back on Plaisance, from which Iberville sailed on 8 July for his old haunts in Hudson Bay. Almost exactly nine years later, while leading an expedition in the Caribbean, he died suddenly from an unknown illness. Although he was gone, his name lived on, and not just because of Abbé Baudoin's unlikely claim that he introduced English settlers to a new type of footwear—the snowshoe. Anglo-Newfoundland historians would later belittle Iberville's achievements, blasting him for cruelty and describing his Canadien and First Nation accomplices in terms that would be deemed racist today.[43] Iberville's ruthlessness is not in dispute. He and his men killed 200 civilians and deported another 471 (380 to England, 91 to France), women and children among them. They also seized more than 190,000 quintals of saltfish and destroyed the physical infrastructure of the English Newfoundland fisheries.[44] But to imply that the French or anyone else had a monopoly of extreme violence defies both history and common sense. War is a siren call to atrocity, and few if any cultures have been immune to the temptation, witness Anglo-Newfoundland icon Sir Humphrey Gilbert, who also killed women and children, and who used decapitation to terrorize the queen's enemies in Ireland.[45]

For all of its outward success, the French effort was a failure in that it did not achieve its aim of driving the English from Newfoundland, at least not permanently. For that, an army of occupation would have been necessary, and France was not about to provide one; indeed, the whole point of campaigning in winter was that it would take fewer men. There was, then, an irreconcilable gap between the objective and the resources that France could spare for it. On the English side, the campaign proved that the inhabitants of St. John's had been right to fear an overland attack from Plaisance. Limited though their means were, they had attempted to forestall it by erecting the unnamed fort in the town's west end, which might have done the trick with a garrison or proper armament. While the French raid underscored the town's vulnerability via the back door, it gave further evidence of the threat that The Narrows posed to anyone trying to enter by the front. Even

---

[43] The classic example is Prowse, *History of Newfoundland*, pp. 214-20. For proof that the demonization of Iberville continues, see George A. Rose, *The Ecological History of the North Atlantic Fisheries* (St. John's, 2009), p. 230.
[44] Frégault, *Iberville*, p. 231; Pritchard, *In Search of Empire*, p. 351; Williams, *Father Baudoin's War*, p. 25, p. 38, p. 44. The English quintal, or hundredweight, was 50.8 kilograms/112 pounds. The French quintal was four percent lighter. The saltfish taken by Iberville would have had a live weight of 47,500 tonnes.
[45] *DCB*, Vol. 1, "Gilbert, Sir Humphrey."

without a garrison, no enemy had made it through that bottleneck since De Ruyter in 1665, and while no one knew it at the time, he would be the last to do so.

ESTABLISHMENT OF AN ENGLISH GARRISON

Among West Country merchants the French campaign prompted calls for the establishment of small fortifications in St. John's, Ferryland, and Fermeuse.[46] This went against the grain of the merchants' anti-settlement stance, which to a certain extent had always been for public consumption only, because while they decried settlement on the one hand, they nurtured it on the other. They knew that settlers were necessary to safeguard the gear and equipment that were left behind after each fishing season, and they welcomed the profits to be had from selling provisions to settlers, for which they usually received payment in fish that, if all went well, could be sold for additional gain at market. To them, the prodigious amount of saltfish that Iberville made off with was a major loss. They also profited from the fares of indentured servants who worked for residents and travelled to and from Newfoundland on the fishing ships, and of bye-boat keepers, men who kept a few boats in Newfoundland and who also came and went with the fleet.[47] Iberville's campaign raised the troubling possibilities that, without settlers, the passenger traffic might wither on the vine, the supply trade might be lost to the pesky New Englanders, and the migratory fishery might default to the French. The West Country merchants were no different from other capitalists for whom profit was the name of the game, and they would continue to invoke the horrors of settlement whenever it suited their purposes. Their desire to have it both ways meant that they were willing to accept some residents— the magic number being bandied about was 1,000—to protect their own interests.

In March 1697 a reduced migratory fleet departed for Newfoundland accompanied by thirteen warships under the command of Captain John Norris. On board were also 760 soldiers led by Colonel John Gibson, who in partial compliance with the West Countrymen's

---

[46] Charles Burnet Judah, Jr., *The North American Fisheries and British Policy to 1713* (Urbana, IL, 1933), p. 161; John J. Murray, "Anglo-French Naval Skirmishing off Newfoundland, 1697," in John J. Murray (ed.), *Essays in Modern European History* (Bloomington, IN, 1951), pp. 73-84.

[47] Keith Matthews, "The West of England-Newfoundland Fishery" (Oxford University, unpublished PhD thesis, 1968), pp. 267-68.

demands were about to establish a garrison in St. John's.[48] It would be one of only a handful of English garrisons in North America in the period, and the first in present-day Canada. The men arrived off the harbour on 17 June, taking care to enter only after they were sure the French had gone. Inside, in a scene common along the English Shore, they found only two or three merchant ships, "with some very few inhabitants, but all the Houses & Stages destroyed."[49] The troops disembarked three days later and hurriedly built some crude barracks and an equally crude hospital before starting the strenuous work of erecting a new fort and Narrows batteries.[50] These were in varying degrees of completion on 28 August when an imposing French squadron of ten warships came into view in St. John's Bay. Commanded by André, marquis de Nesmond, it had been sent to engage Norris's

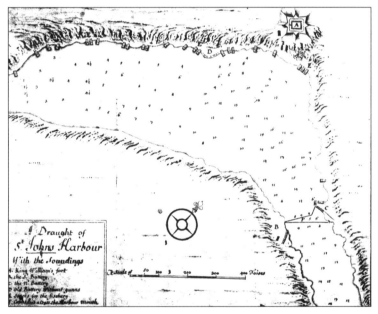

Fig. 11: "A Draught of St. John's Harbour," 1698. Source: Library and Archives Canada/NMC-65. On this, the first plan of St. John's after the establishment of an English garrison, "A" indicates King William's Fort, and "D" an "Old Battery Without gunns," possibly the original King William's Fort laid out by Lilly in 1693. "B" and "C" represent new Narrows defences, and "F" the Narrows cables, which were made of stout hemp rope.

---

[48] Miles, "The Royal Navy and Northeastern North America," p. 67.
[49] TNA:PRO, C. O. 194, Vol. 1, fols. 173-83, "Narrative relating to the Expedition to Newfoundland…," by Colonel John Gibson, 1697.
[50] John Childs, "Secondary Operations of the British Army during the Nine Years' War, 1688-1697," *Journal of the Society for Army Historical Research*, Vol. 73, No. 294 (Summer 1995), p. 97.

squadron and to prevent English fishermen from getting re-established in their old haunts. Norris had no intention of venturing out of port, hoping instead to draw Nesmond in, to which end he had aligned his ships, broadsides facing seaward, behind two barriers, one of chain and one of cable, spanning The Narrows.[51] Meanwhile 400 of Gibson's men were divided between two earthen batteries diagonally opposite each other in The Narrows. After a token exchange of fire the French ships stood to for the remainder of the day. Recognizing an invitation to commit suicide when he saw one, Nesmond wisely withdrew during the night.

The first official fortifications of St. John's had passed their initial test. Whether their existence would have spurred a broader recovery of the English Newfoundland fisheries became moot after the Treaty of Ryswick ended the war on 20 September 1697. Norris and Gibson would not have known of that agreement when they sailed for home on 17 October. The only thing that mattered to them was the certain knowledge that Nesmond, who had made two subsequent passes off The Narrows, was no longer in Newfoundland waters. Behind them they left new defences and a garrison of 263 officers and men, plus thirty-six men deemed too weak to survive the Atlantic crossing. (The shortage of supplies had been so dire that the whole force was on reduced rations for most of their time in St. John's, and relief came mainly from impounding the cargoes of merchant vessels unlucky enough to wander into port). In The Narrows, North and South batteries, sometimes grandly described as "forts," were finished except for stone or brick facing to prevent erosion from surf and tide. The north-side work sported five guns, its south-side counterpart nine. King William's Fort was situated flush in the heel of the harbour, east of the old civilian fort of the same name; meant for sixteen guns, it was not quite finished in mid-October.[52] If the French reappeared, four guns were to be fired from the fort to summon the civilians of St. John's and nearby Quidi Vidi, along with any soldiers living outside the fort's walls if their permanent barracks were not yet completed.[53]

There was no resident fishery to speak of on the English Shore in 1697, and only a handful of migratory crews ventured out with that year's convoy. However, there was such a remarkable recovery in 1698 that it was hard to believe the French had ever been there. In St. John's

---

[51] Clements R. Markham (ed.), *Life of Captain Stephen Martin 1666-1740* (London, 1895), p. 30.

[52] Janzen, "Origins of Fort William," p. 29; Markham, *Captain Stephen Martin*, p. 32.

[53] TNA:PRO, C. O. 194, Vol. 1, fols. 173-83, "Narrative relating to the Expedition to Newfoundland...," by Colonel John Gibson, 1697.

the population seems to have completely rebounded, although there were many unfamiliar faces, the raid having created openings for newcomers by ruining established interests.[54] The rapid turnaround showed just how easy it was to rebuild the fishery infrastructure, a key factor in the survival of an industry that even then was nearly two hundred years old.

KNOCK TWO TIMES

Nations invariably rise at the expense of others, and for now and a good time afterward France and England did so at the expense of Spain. The War of the Spanish Succession (1702-13) arose from concern by England and its allies that the accession to the Spanish throne of Philippe d'Anjou, grandson of Louis XIV, might lead to an integrated Franco-Spanish empire with France calling all the shots. In Newfoundland, despite the presence of the St. John's garrison, the war played out along lines strikingly similar to the previous one. It began deceptively well for the English in 1702, thanks to a late-summer pass along the south coast by a squadron under Captain John Leake that captured or destroyed fifty-one French fishing vessels.[55] Leake avoided Plaisance, and in 1703 the Royal Navy reverted to form with another botched attempt on the French capital, this one under the command of Vice-Admiral John Graydon, a man familiar with Newfoundland from his stint in 1701 as naval commodore and governor (as the commodores were unofficially known since the 1670s).[56] Like Wheler, Graydon reached Newfoundland via the Caribbean, where many of his men also became sick. Three of the squadron's thirty-three ships arrived off Petit Plaisance on 24 August 1703, lingering until two French warships appeared, whereupon they left to rejoin the main squadron in St. Mary's Bay. Owing to the lateness of the season, the emaciated condition of his men, and his exaggerated sense of Plaisance's strength, Graydon accepted the advice of a council of war and returned to England. For his less than stellar performance he was hauled before a House of Lords committee and dismissed from the navy.

If France's reliance on privateers was in some respects an admission of weakness—where, after all, was the French navy?—these were still a

---

[54] Macpherson, "Demographic History of St. John's," pp. 4-5.
[55] *ODNB*, "Leake, Sir John."
[56] *ODNB*, "Graydon, John"; *DCB*, Vol. 2, "Auger de Subercase, Daniel d' "; Jean-Pierre Proulx, "The Military History of Placentia: A Study of the French Fortifications," *History and Archaeology 26* (Ottawa, 1979), p. 45.

problem for the English. Plaisance's privateers were a cosmopolitan lot who included Mi'kmaq warriors from Cape Breton Island and adventurers from France (especially Saint-Malo), Acadia, New France, and Plaisance itself.[57] Between them they brought 102 prizes into Plaisance during the course of the war. Predictably, some of these were carrying saltfish, but others were laden with provisions and manufactured goods from England and New England, and tobacco from Virginia.[58] There is evidence to suggest that Plaisance's privateers emulated their Acadian cousins and ventured to the New England coast in search of booty.[59] Whether they did or not, Plaisance was awash in prize money, and privateering came to rival the fisheries in economic importance.

There were two notable French land campaigns, both patterned after Iberville's, although the need for any campaign at all speaks to the futility of Iberville's accomplishments and to the resilience of the English fisheries and settlement. The first was launched in mid-January 1705 when some 400 men led by the Governor of Plaisance, Daniel d'Auger de Subercase, struck off in a northeasterly direction across the Avalon Peninsula.[60] Although larger than Iberville's force, its makeup was similar, consisting of forty Canadiens and forty Abenaki warriors, among them two veterans of Iberville's campaign, Lieutenant Jacques Testard de Montigny and Chief Nescambiouit, whose presence was deemed so essential that Subercase sent a ship to New France to fetch them. For a while it looked as though the campaign might not happen at all, for unlike in 1696-97 the weather was mild and rainy. Although Nature eventually complied with a mid-January freeze, the lack of snow caused the men to abandon their sleds and most of their snowshoes, and to lug everything on their backs. This was a mistake, because as they were nearing Bay Bulls the snow came down like a curtain. Some sixty centimetres fell during the next forty-eight hours, stopping the marchers in their tracks and giving them plenty of time to regret their impulsiveness. They took out their frustrations on Bay

---

[57] *DCB*, Vol. 2, "Auger de Subercase, Daniel d'."
[58] Nicolas Landry, "Les activités de course dans un port colonial français: Plaisance, Terre-Neuve, durant la guerre de Succession d'Espagne, 1702-1713," *Acadiensis*, Vol. 34, No. 1 (Automne 2004), p. 61; Nicolas Landry, "Portrait des activités de course à Plaisance, Terre-Neuve 1700-1715," *La Société Historique Acadienne: Les Cahiers*, Vol. 33, Nos. 1 et 2 (mars-juin 2002), p. 78.
[59] Donald F. Chard, "The Impact of French Privateering on New England, 1689-1713," *American Neptune*, Vol. 35, No. 3 (July 1975), p. 160.
[60] Robert Le Blant, "Daniel d'Auger de Subercase: Gouverneur de Plaisance (1703-1705)," *Nova Francia* 7 (Paris, 1932), pp. 1-80; *DCB*, Vol. 2, "Auger De Subercase, Daniel D' "; Proulx, "Military History of Placentia," pp. 45-46; *Collection de Manuscrits contenant Lettres, Mémoires, et autres Documents Historiques relatifs à la Nouvelle France....* (Québec, 1883), Vol. 1, pp. 605-06.

Bulls on the twenty-fifth and Petty Harbour on the twenty-ninth, and fully intended to attack St. John's on the first of February. However, the near impossibility of making orderly headway in the deep snow meant that only the advance guard made it into town that day, and they were not up to taking a well-defended town by themselves.

St. John's was not the same place that had fallen to Iberville eight years ago. True, the winter population had stagnated at around 300, reflecting both the loss of the Spanish saltfish market (Spain now being in the enemy camp) and labour shortages caused by Royal Navy press gangs.[61] But years of hard work and bringing out building stone from England had transformed the defences, especially at Fort William (as it was now called), North Battery (completed in stone), and on the south side of The Narrows, where South Battery had been replaced by an imposing timber and masonry structure known as the South Castle.[62] The defence of these works fell to a garrison that had shrunk to approximately eighty men of the Independent Company under the temporary command of Lieutenant John Moody. The incumbent, Captain Thomas Lloyd, had gone to England to defend himself— successfully, as it turned out—against charges of improper conduct.[63] In addition to a couple of other minor batteries in The Narrows, there was an enormous boom of timbers connected by a chain stretching from the castle, which housed the capstan mechanism for raising and lowering it, to a rock jutting out of the water in front of North Battery, where it was fastened to a ring bolt, or at least would be if the project could ever be finished.[64] Garrison engineer John Roope complained in December 1704 that a mere eight to ten days would be enough to complete the boom, then in its second year of construction, but he had been unable to persuade Moody to detach enough men for a work party. On a more positive note, the signalling system had been upgraded by removing the lookouts from Fort William, where their presence had made little sense, and stationing them on "either of the Hills," from which, on spotting the enemy, they were to "give notice by Firing a Small cannon or Paterero, and hoisting the Colours, if Weather permit, and Discharging as many Musketts as Saile shall be Discovered, which shall be Answered at the Fort by Hoisting the

[61] Matthews, "West of England-Newfoundland Fishery," pp. 283-87.
[62] *Documents Historiques relatifs à la Nouvelle France*, Vol. 1, p. 610; TNA:PRO, C. O. 194, Vol. 3, fols. 417-21, "Mr. Jackson the Ministers Repn. of the State of the Garrison, the State of the Trade and the abuses committed therein," received 13 Feb. 1705.
[63] James E. Candow, "The British Army in Newfoundland, 1697-1824," *Newfoundland Quarterly*, Vol. 79, No. 4 (Spring 1984), p. 22; *DCB*, Vol. 2, "Lloyd, Thomas."
[64] Gilbert, "Defence Works in the St. John's Narrows," pp. 206-07; TNA:PRO, C. O. 194, Vol. 3, fol. 121B, Roope to Board of Trade and Plantations, 19 Dec. 1704.

Colours, and returning as many Small Shott."[65] The code's use of flags ("the Colours") to denote an enemy's nationality reflects naval influence, which makes sense given the Royal Navy's place in Anglo-Newfoundland affairs. Naval signalling was still in its infancy and therefore simplistic, but the most vital signals—those denoting an enemy's presence—had been around since at least the fourteenth century.[66] As for the hills on which the lookouts were posted, their exact locations are unknown, but it is extremely likely that one of them was the eminence later called Signal Hill. Certainly, by 1711 Signal Hill had been identified by its original name and function: The Lookout.[67]

As reassuring as all this was, there were shortcomings, one so obvious that it even caught the attention of garrison chaplain the Reverend John Jackson, who told a House of Commons committee that Fort William was "very ill situated having a Hill in the front & Rear to com[m]and it, w[hi]ch as it is very disadvantagious [sic] to the Gar[r]ison, so it is of necessity advantagious [sic] to the Enimy [sic]."[68] This was a revealing comment whose veracity would be borne out in due course, but the more pressing problem was the lack of any works oriented toward the landward, something that the town's civilian defenders had tried to address during the previous decade. The French, after finally sorting out their logistical issues, took full advantage and trudged unopposed over the Southside Hills. They had not, however, counted on the stiff defence offered by troops commanded by Moody at Fort William and by Acting Lieutenant Robert Latham of the Royal Engineers at the South Castle.[69] Although the French occupied the town for all of February, took 200 prisoners, and destroyed boats, flakes, stages, and 120 houses, neither military action nor diplomacy could induce the surrender of Fort William and the South Castle.[70] Exasperated and fearing the arrival of the migratory fishing fleet and, more to the point, its naval escorts, Subercase decided to return to Plaisance in early March and to send Montigny, Nescambiouit, and their men northward to rain destruction on the

---

[65] TNA:PRO, C. O. 194, Vol. 3, fols. 315-18, "A Relation of the Most Material Occurrences and Transactions at St. John's and parts Adjacent in Newfoundland during the Administration of Lieut. John Moody from and after ye 12th day of September 1704...."
[66] Daniel R. Headrick, *When Information Came of Age: Technologies of Knowledge in the Age of Reason, 1700-1850* (Oxford, 2000), p. 206.
[67] TNA:PRO, C. O. 194, fols. 74-85, "A report Containing an Extract of a Journal to NEWFOUNDLAND...," by Col. C. Lilly, 1711.
[68] TNA:PRO, C. O. 194, Vol. 3, fols. 417-21, "Mr. Jackson the Ministers Repn. of the State of the Garrison, the State of the Trade and the abuses committed therein," received 13 Feb. 1705.
[69] *DCB*, Vol. 2, "Moody, John" and "Latham, Robert."
[70] *DCB*, Vol. 2, "Campbell, Colin."

rest of the English Shore, which they did pretty well according to script, right down to their failure to take Carbonear Island. This was partially offset by the surrender of Bonavista, which had gone untouched in 1697 because Iberville ran out of time. Subercase, who would be rewarded with the governorship of Acadia, predicted that the English fisheries would be idled for the rest of the war.[71] However, his campaign produced no more in the way of lasting effects than Iberville's. Of the 1,200 prisoners who were taken, almost all were released because of the impossibility of feeding them, the exceptions being some eighty men who were taken to Plaisance and put to work on the fortifications.[72]

In the immediate aftermath of the campaign, relations between St. John's and Plaisance were strangely civil and included the routine exchange of prisoners captured by privateers and naval vessels.[73] Nonetheless, the temperature began to rise in 1707 when the British mounted a joint army/navy expedition up the northeast coast, ruining the Petit Nord fishery for the year. Despite the setback, the French fisheries continued to operate throughout the war, erratically to be sure, and in defiance of government edicts to try and confine them to Placentia Bay, but often with good results. Indeed, France's Newfoundland fisheries were more productive in the war-dominated years 1695-1714 than in the peaceful ones 1715-34.[74]

The smallness of the Plaisance garrison discouraged further attacks on St. John's, that is, until the stars accidentally aligned in the late fall of 1708. The occasion was the nearly simultaneous arrival in Plaisance of four vessels: one from France, two from New France, and most importantly of all, the privateer frigate *Vénus*, commanded by Louis Denys de La Ronde, which had succumbed to contrary winds while working back to Port-Royal, Acadia with two prizes in tow.[75] Sensing a golden opportunity, Governor Philippe Pastour de Costebelle enlisted La Ronde's support for an effort against St. John's. Between them they cobbled together about 170 men, including settlers, sailors, soldiers, fishermen, and privateers. Under the leadership of Lieutenant Joseph de Monbeton de Brouillan, *dit* Saint-Ovide, nephew of the former governor, they got away on 14 December, bound overland for St. John's

[71] Proulx, "Military History of Placentia," p. 46.
[72] *DCB*, Vol. 2, "Auger de Subercase, Daniel d'."
[73] *DCB*, Vol. 2, "Pastour de Costebelle, Philippe."
[74] Laurier Turgeon, "Pour une histoire de la pêche: le marché de la morue à Marseille au XVIIIe siècle," *Histoire sociale/Social History*, Vol. 14, No. 28 (Nov. 1981), pp. 307-10.
[75] *DCB*, Vol. 2, "Pastour de Costebelle, Philippe"; *DCB* (Toronto, 1974), Vol. 3, "Denys de La Ronde, Louis."

in the knowledge that La Ronde would bring the *Vénus* around with food and munitions. By now it was understood that trying to force The Narrows was a non-starter, and the men followed the usual route over the Southside Hills, from which they fell upon St. John's shortly before dawn on New Year's Day 1709.

So unexpected was their arrival that they took Fort William in just over an hour, thus sealing the fate of the so-called New Fort, immediately below it, which contained a horde of civilians.[76] The South Castle surrendered the following day, bringing the total number of prisoners, military and civilian, to about 800, a number that reflected the presence of people from nearby communities who, ironically, had decided to winter in St. John's because they thought it would be safer.[77] In mid-February Saint-Ovide gave the civilians a tough choice: they could submit to his ransom demands, payable in money or in the form of the first fish of the upcoming season, or he would burn their property and deport them to New France. Saint-Ovide's hopes of permanently occupying St. John's did not find favour with Costebelle, who ordered him to withdraw to Plaisance no later than the end of March.[78] Before doing so, Saint-Ovide proceeded to destroy the military works, but only after removing the guns and ammunition for transportation back to Plaisance. The South Castle proved remarkably stubborn and had to be blown up, and the much vaunted but still unfinished Narrows boom was dismembered.[79] The bewildered garrison and its commanding officer, the controversial Thomas Lloyd, were conveyed to New France, although Lloyd was subsequently sent to France, where, true to form, he would die from wounds allegedly sustained in a duel.[80] Half a dozen community leaders were temporarily imprisoned in Plaisance as guaranties for the ransom payments. All were back in St. John's by 26 June, even though one of them, merchant William Keen, still owed Costebelle 35,000 livres.[81]

In the wake of this latest disaster, the British made no attempt to re-establish the St. John's garrison. Captain Joseph Taylor,

---

[76] Prowse, *History of Newfoundland*, pp. 268-71.
[77] For the number of prisoners, see *DCB*, Vol. 2, "Pastour de Costebelle, Philippe." On St. John's as a haven, see C. Grant Head, *Eighteenth Century Newfoundland: A Geographer's Perspective* (Toronto, 1976), pp. 56-59; Handcock, *Origins of English Settlement*, p. 45.
[78] Proulx, "Military History of Placentia," p. 49.
[79] TNA:PRO, C. O. 194, Vol. 4, fols. 358-59, "Memorial from Captain Moody relating to the future Governmt. & Security of Newfoundland," received 14 May 1709.
[80] *DCB*, Vol. 2, "Lloyd, Thomas"; *Collection de Manuscrits contenant Lettres, Mémoires, et autres Documents Historiques relatifs à la Nouvelle France....* (Québec, 1884), Vol. 2, p. 506.
[81] Gerald S. Graham (ed.), *The Walker Expedition to Quebec, 1711* (London, 1952), p. 240.

commodore in 1709, helped some civilians to erect a new Fort William, and before sailing in October appointed merchant John Collins—whose patriotism had been stoked by his captivity in Plaisance—as governor and commander in chief of the "Fort and harbour of St. John's," an arrangement that continued to the end of the war.[82] Small numbers of residents and migratory fishermen stood guard at the fort, augmented by sailors from naval vessels when these were in port.[83] Talk of installing a garrison in Ferryland was dropped after Captain Josiah Crowe, the commodore in 1711, told his superiors that St. John's was more important, "it being the Metropolis of this Island and lying just in the Center of Trade."[84]

Although French privateers had their most productive year in 1711, this was the same year in which British privateers from St. John's and elsewhere seized an estimated one-third of all supplies bound for Plaisance.[85] French sources speak of a British naval blockade of Plaisance, but there were only half a dozen Royal Navy vessels in Newfoundland waters, and they were spread along the entire English Shore. The impact of British privateers may have made it feel like a blockade existed, but none did. To make matters worse, a number of supply ships coming from Quebec were lost in a storm on the St. Lawrence River that same summer.[86] The surrender of the Acadian capital of Port-Royal to British and New England troops in October 1710 had enhanced Plaisance's importance to France, and in 1711 the arrival of two companies previously based in Port-Royal brought the garrison's strength to an all-time high of 250 men. It was, however, too late to make a difference. Preliminary peace negotiations began in the fall of 1711, and in April 1713 the Treaty of Utrecht brought the war to a close.

---

[82] Prowse, *History of Newfoundland*, pp. 270-71. The rank of commodore denoted a senior captain in charge of a small squadron.

[83] Miles, "The Royal Navy and Northeastern North America," p. 169.

[84] TNA:PRO, C. O. 194, Vol. 5, fols. 29-30, Crowe to Board of Trade, 31 Oct. 1711.

[85] *DCB*, Vol. 2, "Pastour de Costebelle, Philippe"; Landry, "Les activités de course," pp. 61-62; Proulx, "Military History of Placentia," p. 50; Miles, "The Royal Navy and Northeastern North America," pp. 169-70.

[86] Graham, *Walker Expedition*, p. 239.

MASTERS OF THE HILL

"We remained masters of the hill, and were obliged to remain on it without a mouthful of food or drink of any sort, until morning of the second day after we started, when a British Colonel came on the hill, and applauded us very highly for our exploit and success, and said we should have some refreshment." David Perry, *Recollections of an Old Soldier: The Life of Captain David Perry* (Windsor, Vermont, 1822)

ST. JOHN'S AND THE PLACENTIA GARRISON

While the terms of the Treaty of Utrecht underscored the extent to which the war had been about carving up the Spanish empire, the agreement also profoundly affected Newfoundland. Britain's acquisition of Gibraltar and Minorca from Spain extended its economic and strategic reach in Iberia and the western Mediterranean, which was music to the ears of West Countrymen and Newfoundlanders, for whom these were prime market areas. Those same parties were equally pleased by France's recognition of British

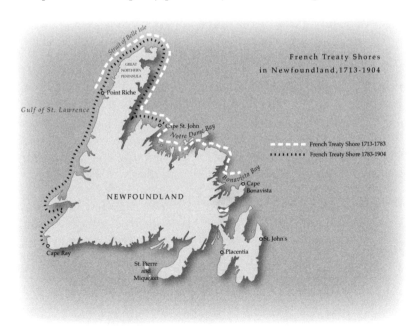

Fig 12: French Treaty Shores in Newfoundland, 1713-1904.

sovereignty over Acadia and Newfoundland, and by its promise to abandon Plaisance and the rest of its south-coast settlements. But there was a rub. France kept Île Royale (Cape Breton Island) and other islands in the Gulf of St. Lawrence, and its fishermen were given rights to catch and dry fish, although not to settle, along the northeast coast of Newfoundland from Cape Bonavista to the tip of the Great Northern Peninsula—a stretch that included the all-important Petit Nord—and down the west coast to Point Riche. Since the treaty did not affect France's Grand Banks fisheries, the French negotiators had ensured the survival of their country's North American fisheries, along with the usual benefits that flowed from them.

For practical reasons, the deportation of the French residents of Plaisance, henceforth known as Placentia, was not completed until September 1714.[1] A few diehards swallowed their Gallic pride and swore an oath of allegiance to the Crown in order to stay, but the rest were relocated to English Harbour (Havre à l'Anglais) in southeastern Île Royale.[2] The profits from fishing and privateering in wartime Placentia were ploughed into the new colony, which became the fortress town of Louisbourg. Fishing was Île Royale's economic mainstay, with annual saltfish production ranging between 120,000 and 160,000 quintals during the 1720s and 1730s, or about one-third of the French catch in the northwest Atlantic.[3] Louisbourg became an entrepôt with links to New France and the French Caribbean, and enjoyed an active peacetime trade with New England, where jealous men eyed its rise to prominence and bided the time till they could do something about it.

In the short term the evacuation of Placentia had a negative impact on the military fortunes of St. John's. Blinded by their futile attempts to take Placentia, and mindful of the proven vulnerability of St. John's, the British chose to re-establish their garrison not in St. John's but in the old French capital, a decision that might have made sense had it not flown in the face of local realities. Old habits die hard, especially among fishermen, and for this and other reasons the British were slow to move into the south coast; it was mid-century before catches at Placentia approximated those of the French regime.[4] Things were considerably different in St. John's. Its harbour offered excellent anchorage and better shelter than any other place along

---

[1] Jean-Pierre Proulx, "Placentia: 1713-1811," *History and Archaeology 26* (Ottawa, 1979), p. 118.
[2] Ch. De la Morandière, *Histoire de la Pêche Française de la Morue dans l'Amérique Septentrionale (Dès Origines à 1789)* (Paris, 1962), 3 vols, Vol. 1, p. 507.
[3] B. A. Balcom, *The Cod Fishery of Isle Royale, 1713-58* (Ottawa, 1984), p. 50.
[4] Head, *Eighteenth Century Newfoundland*, pp. 58-59.

that stretch of the coast, and could accommodate between 200 and 250 sail.[5] This and its proximity to "The Great Bank" (known later as The Grand Bank) caused it to dominate the British bank fishery that emerged after 1713, eventually to become the backbone of the migratory effort. There was also activity in the service sector, epitomized by a growing number of public houses, or taverns. As Josiah Crowe had already noted, St. John's was roughly in the middle of the old English Shore, and this made it the perfect place for trading vessels to drop off goods and provisions and to acquire return cargoes, and for fishing vessels to rendezvous before leaving for home or market in convoy.[6] For the same reason, St. John's was already headquarters for the naval vessels that accompanied the migratory fleet, and in 1729 the naval commodore was formally made governor during his time on the station. Thereafter the navy became deeply involved in the island's unique system of government, a role aided and abetted by the town's central location.[7] Given all this, it made no sense that the only garrison on the island should be in Placentia, but there it was, and nothing much would be done about it until another war came along and turned things right side up.

The trouble arose from a clause in the Treaty of Utrecht that had given Britain a thirty-year monopoly to supply slaves to Spain's American colonies. Not satisfied with the proceeds from this lucrative trade, the British also took to smuggling with those same colonies.[8] Spain understandably took umbrage and began to exercise its right to search British ships, in the course of which, in 1731, a zealous coastguard officer from Havana lopped off one of the ears of merchant captain Robert Jenkins. Seven years later, at the urging of warmongers in the House of Commons, Jenkins displayed his pickled ear before Parliament, a stunt that had the desired effect, leading as it did to a declaration of war against Spain in 1739. The War of Jenkins's Ear (1739-48) was subsumed in the War of the Austrian Succession (1740-48), the name assigned to the multiple conflicts that were triggered by the death of Austrian Emperor Charles VI in October 1740, and the subsequent refusal of France and Prussia to recognize his daughter Maria Theresa as his heir. Broadly speaking, the war pitted France,

---

[5] Head, *Eighteenth Century Newfoundland*, pp. 8-9, p. 186; Matthews, "West of England-Newfoundland Fishery," p. 317; TNA:PRO, C. O. 194, Vol. 5, fols. 29-30, Crowe to Board of Trade, 31 Oct. 1711; and Vol. 29, fols. 36-44, "The Report of Captn. Hugh Debbieg," 18 Oct. 1769.

[6] Head, *Eighteenth Century Newfoundland*, pp. 152-53, p. 186; Matthews, "West of England-Newfoundland Fishery," p. 488.

[7] The definitive study of naval government is Jerry Bannister, *The Rule of the Admirals: Law, Custom, and Naval Government in Newfoundland, 1699-1832* (Toronto, 2003).

[8] Reed Browning, *The War of the Austrian Succession* (New York, 1995), p. 21.

Spain, and Prussia against Britain, Austria, and the Netherlands; while the bulk of the fighting took place in Europe, it also spilled over into India and the Americas.

The outbreak of war gave France preferred status in the Spanish saltfish market, raising the ire of not only the West Country, but also New England, whose bank fishery had now spread to the Scotian Shelf.[9] With Louisbourg likely in mind, a group of concerned merchants petitioned the British government to fortify St. John's "for the Security of this Valuable Trade and Nursery of Seamen."[10] Their plea was partially answered in 1741 when the governor, Captain Thomas Smith, convened a meeting in the St. John's courthouse and agreed to have his men build a fort if the residents would share the work. On this basis Fort St. George was erected just below the ruins of Fort William. It was a modest affair consisting of ten 18-pounder guns and partially stockaded earthen walls surrounding a wooden guardhouse and a brick powder magazine.[11] There was no garrison at first, but Smith rectified this in 1743 by leaving behind a force of eighty-five marines, which was nearly three times the number of troops then at Placentia.[12] The commanding officer there, Captain Joseph Gledhill, complained about the weak state of the garrison and the possibility of an attack from Louisbourg.[13] But he was also unnerved by the growing numbers of indentured servants from Ireland who were wintering in Placentia, where they allegedly outnumbered Englishmen by a ratio of ten to one.

Gledhill must have said all the right things, because the British government ordered major new defences for St. John's and Placentia, and modest ones for Ferryland, Carbonear, and Trinity. The need for these was cast in doubt when an expedition of Royal Navy ships and 5,500 New Englanders captured Louisbourg in 1745, a dazzling achievement that portended the future military might of the United States of America. But construction continued, with decidedly mixed results. At Placentia the blandly named New Fort proved overly ambitious and was never finished.[14] By 1748 St. John's boasted a four-

---

[9] Olaf Uwe Janzen, "The Illicit Trade in English Cod into Spain, 1739-1748," *International Journal of Maritime History*, Vol. 8, No. 1 (June 1996), p. 8.
[10] TNA:PRO, C. O. 194, Vol. 10, fols. 112-14, "The humble Petition of the Merchants of London in behalf of themselves and all others Fishing in and Trading to Newfoundland," n.d.
[11] TNA:PRO, C. O. 194, Vol. 11, fols. 41-44, "Letter from Captn. Smith, Governor of Newfoundland, dated at Lisbon ye 19th of Decbr. 1741."
[12] TNA:PRO, C. O. 194, Vol. 12, fols. 12-15, "4 Orders of Council, dated the 19th of July 1744 in relation to the Fortifying and Defence of Newfoundland."
[13] Proulx, "Placentia: 1713-1811," p. 138.
[14] Proulx, "Placentia: 1713-1811," p. 137.

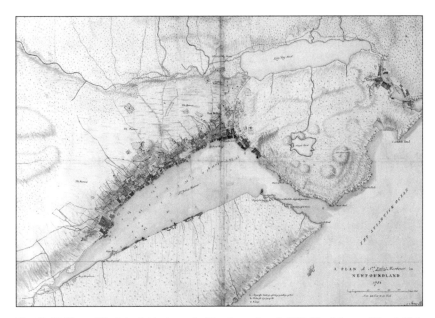

Fig. 13: "A Plan of St. John's Harbour in Newfoundland, 1751," by Edmond Scott Hylton and James Bramham. Source: © The British Library Board, Shelf Mark Maps K.Top.119.104. Signal Hill is denoted by its original name, "The Lookout." In addition to showing the new Fort William, this plan includes an early cartographic mention of "Chain Rock," as well as the first use of "George's Pond," Cuckold's Head," and "Cuckold's Head Cove" (soon to be shortened to "Cuckold's Cove").

gun battery at the mid-way point of the south side of The Narrows, while closer to the harbour mouth, near the site of the former South Castle, construction was proceeding on a six-gun battery with a powder magazine and barracks for thirty men. The latter would shortly be abandoned when it was discovered that it had been oriented in the wrong direction.[15] More significant than either of the Narrows batteries was the presence of a new Fort William on the same site as its namesakes from 1697 and 1709. A square-shaped work for thirty guns, it incorporated Fort St. George (variously known as Fort George, George's Battery, or the Lower Fort), to which it was joined by a covered way (a deep trench providing cover to men passing between the works). Fort William was not the only connection with the past. A plan of St. John's Harbour in 1751 depicts a signal mast atop The Lookout, and if a signalling system existed so soon after the war, it is reasonable to assume it was re-established, along with the garrison,

<hr>

[15] TNA:PRO, C. O. 194, Vol. 12, fols. 72-73, "The State & Condition of Fort William in St. John's, Newfoundland, August ye 15th 1748," and Vol. 13, fols. 75-79, "A State of the Fortifications of Fort William and the other Forts or Batterys for the Defence of the Harbour of Saint Johns [sic] in Newfoundland," 28 Sept. 1752.

during the war itself. The same 1751 plan includes an early use of "Chain Rock" to denote the navigational hazard in front of the old North Battery site, and to which the chain of the Narrows boom had been affixed earlier in the century.

In 1749 St. John's boasted a garrison of 131 troops and 32 artillerymen. Trailing it in order of numerical importance were Placentia (65 troops and 25 artillerymen), Ferryland (18 artillerymen), Trinity (17 artillerymen), and Carbonear (11 artillerymen).[16] While St. John's had clearly regained military ascendancy within Newfoundland, the regional context was a different matter. By the Treaty of Aix-la-Chapelle (1748), Louisbourg had been returned to France, a move that caused such anger in New England that, the very next year, the British founded the naval base of Halifax as a buffer against Louisbourg. This had major implications for St. John's, because Halifax would eventually become the linchpin of British naval strategy in the northwest Atlantic.

1762 AND ALL THAT

During the War of the Austrian Succession the migratory fishery was weakened by the contraction of the Spanish saltfish market and by the impressment of fishermen into the Royal Navy. To cope with the resulting labour shortage, residents recruited indentured servants from southeast Ireland, much to the chagrin of Joseph Gledhill and his ilk.[17] In 1740 there had been 379 winter (or permanent) residents in St. John's and perhaps 3,500 in Newfoundland as a whole, or much as things had stood at the end of the previous century.[18] In 1754, on the eve of the next Anglo-French war, the resident population of St. John's had reached 915, and for Newfoundland as a whole had passed the 7,000 mark.[19] Larger both in absolute terms and as a proportion of

---

[16] TNA:PRO, C. O. 194, Vol. 12, "A Return of His Majesty's Troops in the several Garrisons in Newfoundland," 1749. In terms of the number of the communities that boasted garrisons, this would be the high-water mark in Newfoundland until the Second World War.
[17] Head, *Eighteenth Century Newfoundland*, pp. 92-93; John Mannion, "Irish Merchants Abroad: The Newfoundland Experience, 1750-1850," *Newfoundland Studies*, Vol. 2, No. 2 (Fall 1986), p. 129.
[18] Macpherson, "Demographic History of St. John's," p. 8; Handcock, *Origins of English Settlement*, p. 102, p. 82. Population had declined between 1711 and 1728, a period of widespread catch collapse in coastal waters, including the French treaty shore. Population figures from 1740 therefore reflect the recovery that began in 1728 and continued more or less without interruption until the American Revolution. See Matthews, "West of England-Newfoundland Fishery," p. 378; Jean-François Brière, "The French Fishery in North America in the 18th Century," in James E. Candow and Carol Corbin (eds.), *How Deep is the Ocean?: Historical Essays on Canada's Atlantic Fishery* (Sydney, NS, 1997), p. 60.
[19] Macpherson, "Demographic History of St. John's," p. 9; Head, *Eighteenth Century Newfoundland*, p. 82.

total population, St. John's was "very much the dominant Newfoundland settlement."[20] Still, its economic reach was not as pervasive as it would later become, and communities such as Placentia, Ferryland, Carbonear, and Trinity were regional centres—hence their garrisons—with direct ties to West Country and Irish merchants. Those merchants were slowly turning to the supply and passenger trades, and away from the old model of direct participation in fishing. Demographic growth was reflected in the output of the fisheries, where annual saltfish production rose from less than 100,000 quintals in the early 1720s to roughly 500,000 quintals in the late 1740s.[21] With output in the French northwest Atlantic fisheries fluctuating between 250,000 quintals and 400,000 quintals annually in the same period, there was no question about the continuing importance of the fisheries to imperial considerations.[22]

The underlying causes of the War of the Austrian Succession—enmity between Austria and Prussia and between Britain and France—had not been resolved by the peace. As tensions festered, Empress Maria Theresa of Austria rebuilt her army and made diplomatic moves to isolate Prussia. Such were the vagaries of European politics that by the time the dust settled in 1756 Britain backed Prussia and France supported Austria, the exact opposite of allegiances in the previous conflict. Thus the stage was set for the Seven Years' War, so-called because it officially lasted from 1756 to 1763. To say the least, it was an oddly-named war. In North America, Britain and France began fighting in 1754 in the disputed Ohio Valley, and Nova Scotia was dragged in the following year when officials in Halifax and Boston jointly launched the Acadian deportation. Britain subsequently achieved dominance in North America by the captures of Louisbourg and Fort Duquesne (1758), Quebec (1759), and Montreal (1760); elsewhere, triumphs in the battles of Lagos and Quiberon Bay (both in 1759) established British naval superiority for the remainder of the conflict.

After the so-called "year of victories" (1759), Newfoundland saltfish exporters did not have to give a second thought to the safety of shipping or to French competition in the marketplace. As a result, the resident population of St. John's passed the 1,000 mark and fisheries output rose to a record 564,000 quintals. Peace talks began in the spring of 1761 but broke down in September, largely because Secretary of State William Pitt opposed France's demands not only to retain its

---

[20] Head, *Eighteenth Century Newfoundland*, p. 152.
[21] Head, *Eighteenth Century Newfoundland*, p. 65; Matthews, "West of England-Newfoundland Fishery," p. 385.
[22] Turgeon, "Pour une histoire de la pêche," pp. 302-03.

fishery privileges in coastal Newfoundland but to extend them into the
Gulf of St. Lawrence, and even to regain Louisbourg as a base for
fishing in the gulf and on the Grand Banks.[23] It was a prickly issue
because both sides saw access to the fisheries as fundamental to France's
survival as a naval power. When a deal began to look unlikely, France
opened negotiations with Spain, leading to a secret convention by
which Spain agreed to enter the war on France's side if the fighting had
not stopped by 1 May 1762. The secret got out, and on 4 January 1762
Britain ended the sham by declaring war on Spain. Planning began at
once for an expedition against Cuba, which did not actually commence
until June. In the interim, British and Provincial (American colonial)
forces captured Martinique, St. Lucia, Grenada, and St. Vincent, leaving
Saint-Domingue as the only French possession in the Caribbean.

It was against this darkest of dark backdrops that France launched
a surprise raid against Newfoundland. The unlikely project was the
brainchild of Étienne-François de Stainville, duc de Choiseul, minister
of the army and the navy, and the same man who as foreign secretary
in 1761 had insisted on the inclusion of those fishing privileges in any
peace settlement. Choiseul now issued orders for naval captain and
expedition leader chevalier Charles-Henry-Louis d'Arsac de Ternay to
capture St. John's and to use it as a base for destroying the English
Newfoundland trade and fisheries, the whole of the operation to last
no more than one month, a schedule that would theoretically enable
his squadron to keep ahead of the Royal Navy.[24] If possible, Ternay was

---

[23] J. K. Hiller, "The Newfoundland Fisheries Issue in Anglo-French Treaties, 1713-1904," *Journal of Imperial and Commonwealth History*, Vol. 24, No. 1 (January 1996), p. 5; Jonathan R. Dull, *The French Navy and the Seven Years' War* (Lincoln, NE, 2005), pp. 194-95.

[24] Unless otherwise indicated, this account of the events of 1762 is based on Olaf Uwe Janzen "The French Raid upon the Newfoundland Fishery in 1762: A Study in the Nature and Limits of Eighteenth-Century Sea Power," in William B. Cogar (ed.), *Naval History: The Seventh Symposium of the U.S. Naval Academy* (Wilmington, DE, 1988), pp. 35-54, and "Newfoundland and British Maritime Strategy during the American Revolution" (Unpublished PhD thesis, Queen's University, Kingston, ON,1983); Maurice Linÿer de la Barbée, *Le Chevalier de Ternay: Vie de Charles Henry Louis d'Arsac de Ternay Chef d'escadre des armies navales 1723-1780* (Grenoble, 1972), 2 vols., Vol. 1, pp. 151-71; Georges Cerbelaud Salagnac, "La reprise de Terre-Neuve par les Français en 1762," *Revue française d'Histoire d'Outre-Mer*, Tome 63, No. 231 (1976), pp. 211-21; John Clarence Webster (ed.), *The Recapture of St. John's, Newfoundland in 1762 as described in the Journal of Lieut.-Colonel William Amherst, Commander of the British Expeditionary Force* (Privately printed, 1928); Evan W. H. Fyers, "The Loss and Recapture of St. John's, Newfoundland, in 1762," *Journal of the Society for Army Historical Research*, Vol. 11 (1932), pp. 179-215; C. H. Little (ed.), *The Recapture of Saint John's, Newfoundland: Dispatches of Rear-Admiral, Lord Colville 1761-1762* (Halifax, 1959). For the original of Amherst's journal, see LAC, R2856-0-8-E, Jeffery Amherst, 1st Baron Amherst and Family Fonds, Vol. 4, Captain William Amherst – recapture of St. John's, Newfoundland, 15 August – 19 October 1762. For a drama based loosely on the events of 1762, see Michael Cook, *Colour the Flesh the Colour of Dust* (Toronto, 1974). For a serviceable book-length treatment in French, see André de Visme, *Terre-Neuve 1762: Dernier combat aux portes de la Nouvelle France* (Montréal, 2005).

also to venture over to Île Royale to ravage the British fisheries that had sprung up there, but otherwise he was to re-cross the Atlantic and to dispense similar mayhem around Ireland and Scotland on his way home. Conceived as a raid and not as a conquest, it was quite a gamble, but then something extraordinary had to be done if French fortunes were going to change.

The men entrusted with the top-secret mission—all except Ternay believed they were going to Saint-Domingue—were an odd lot. At thirty-nine years of age, Ternay had only made captain in 1761 and had yet to lead a ship in action, but he had a reputation for fearlessness, which under the circumstances was likely to be useful. His modest squadron consisted of two battleships (*Robuste* and *Éveillé*), a frigate (*Licorne*), and a flute (*Garonne*), whose sailors were raw men drawn to

Fig. 14: Le chevalier Charles-Henry-Louis d'Arsac de Ternay. Source: Château de Ternay. Leader of the French force that occupied St. John's in the summer of 1762, Ternay lacked experience but made up for it in boldness.

the mission by offers of promotions if it succeeded. The navy's limitations were to be offset by the infantry, which consisted of thirty-one officers and 570 regulars belonging to four regiments (Beauvaisis, Marine, Penthièvre, and Montrevel) under the command of twenty-five-year-old Colonel Joseph-Louis-Bernard de Cléron, comte d'Haussonville, who was the duc de Choiseul's nephew. There were also an engineer, fifteen artillerymen and their officer, and, curiously, 161 Whiteboys, outlawed Irish radicals whom some Britons suspected of conspiring with France to plot an Irish rebellion.[25] Named after their white frocks and the white cockades that they sported on their headgear, the Whiteboys were coming along in hopes they could add to French strength in Newfoundland by recruiting among disaffected Irish Catholic servants. Their leader, who commanded the *Garonne*, went by the pseudonym Captain Clonard; his real name was Sutton, and although he came from Wexford, he had allegedly been born in Newfoundland. No precise numbers have ever been found for the ships' crews, but if we accept the word of seven men who later deserted to the British and whose testimony seems to have been accurate in most respects, the total French force was 870 men, which would put the number of seamen at a paltry ninety-two, a figure that accords with the general impression that the naval component was well below strength.[26]

There is some question as to whether Ternay's squadron, which sailed from Brest on 8 May, took advantage of a heavy fog to avoid detection by Royal Navy cruisers blockading the port. There is no question, however, that when the squadron passed the Cornwall coast three days later it was spotted by several Royal Navy vessels that were convoying merchantmen. The convoy escorts formed line for a fight, but the French ships declined and tacked off to the northward. Ternay was taking no chances with his unproven and undersized crews, nor did he want to jeopardize the mission by engaging in a potentially disastrous sideshow. Contrary winds meant that the French did not arrive off their rendezvous, Cape Broyle, until 20 June. Shortly before that the *Garonne* became separated from the rest of squadron, during which time Sutton and the Whiteboys amused themselves by pursuing an English merchantman, which managed to get away. When informed of this, Ternay surmised that the merchantman was probably bound for St. John's, meaning that he could anticipate a hot welcome there. Accordingly, he decided that the only way to retain the element of

---

[25] On the Whiteboys' origins, see James S. Donnelly, Jr., "The Whiteboy movement, 1761-5," *Irish Historical Studies*, Vol. 21, No. 81 (1978), pp. 20-54.
[26] Little, *Dispatches of Rear-Admiral, Lord Colvill*, p. 28.

surprise was to attack by land. In this roundabout manner he stumbled upon the surest way of taking the place.

Word did indeed reach St. John's, but it was garbled and did not come from the ship that eluded the *Garonne*. Instead, on the morning of the twenty-second, William Wood, master of the schooner *Squid*, arrived with news that, the day before, he had seen three unidentified men of war some eight leagues off the coast at latitude 47 degrees 20 minutes North (near Bay Bulls), and that a fourth, smaller vessel with them had fired on him. Since the warships flew no colours, Wood supposed they were Spanish. In this he was mistaken, but whoever they were, Captain Walter Ross, commanding officer of the St. John's garrison, knew he had a problem on his hands, and he now took what limited steps he could to address it. They were limited because, in the aftermath of the French defeats in North America, the works had been allowed to deteriorate and the garrison had been slashed from 350 men to about eighty. Spirits lifted when an estimated 370 residents and fishermen volunteered their services and received arms and ammunition from the military stores.

Of the three Royal Navy vessels assigned to the Newfoundland station that summer, only the frigate HMS *Syren* had arrived, but it was up the Southern Shore in Aquaforte.[27] The frigate HMS *Gramont* was expected any day in St. John's, and the last of the three to leave home, the battleship HMS *Antelope*, bearing the governor, Captain Thomas Graves, was still en route convoying a group of West Country fishing vessels. Ross therefore decided to send a vessel to Aquaforte to alert Captain Charles Douglas of the *Syren* about the unidentified squadron. The courier reached Aquaforte on the twenty-fourth, whereupon Douglas ordered two dozen marines to proceed to St. John's to reinforce Ross, dispatched a small vessel to intercept Graves and keep him from accidentally entering St. John's, and himself sailed for Halifax aboard *Syren*. There, on 1 July, he broke the news to Rear-Admiral Lord Alexander Colvill, the navy's Commander-in-Chief of North America.

The wheels were beginning to turn, although too slowly to make a difference in St. John's, where the element of surprise and the weak leadership of Walter Ross ensured an easy French victory. On the same day that Douglas was organizing in Aquaforte, Ternay's squadron put into Bay Bulls to disembark the infantry and the Whiteboys, who as soon as they got ashore began torching boats and fishing premises. They were careful, however, to spare the houses, and promised not to

---

[27] In local parlance, south is up and north is down.

harm the people, among whom Sutton began to recruit. At dawn the next day they marched on St. John's, and although it was tough going they reached the outskirts on Sunday the twenty-seventh. By then the *Gramont* had arrived in port, and its captain, Patrick Mouat, had improved Ross's odds by landing approximately 125 sailors and marines, who had taken positions in Fort William. (The marines from the *Syren*, who did not make it in time, ended up reinforcing the Royal Artillery detachment on the Isle of Boys, near Ferryland). Inexplicably, Ross would not allow the artillerymen to fire on the French, other than a couple of harmless rounds while they were out of range, and with no more opposition than that d'Haussonville's men closed to within 800 metres of the fort and took cover behind a hill. Shortly thereafter a lone French officer carrying a flag of truce poked his head above the crest of the hill and strode down to the fort. He was met, blindfolded, escorted through the gates, and taken into Ross's quarters, where a council of war soon took place. Lending credence to the military maxim that councils of war rarely vote to fight, Ross opted to surrender, supposedly because he thought the French had 1,500 men at their disposal. A distraught Mouat was reduced to tears, exclaiming: "My lads, you are all sold—I have ruined my character for ever coming into this damned place." Before the French took formal possession of the fort on the twenty-ninth, Mouat had his men spike the *Gramont's* guns and run her aground. The French eventually refitted her and gave command to one of the Whiteboys, known to posterity only by his pseudonym, M. de Séguiran. They also restored her original name, *Comtesse de Grammont*, for she had been a French privateer before being captured by the Royal Navy. She had come full circle.

According to his orders, Ternay ought to have spent the next month hunting British merchantmen and wreaking havoc on the inshore and bank fisheries, and possibly visiting Île Royale before high-tailing it back to Europe. But in a stunning about-face he decided instead to hunker down in St. John's and to send one of his officers, M. de Courval, back to France on an unidentified vessel (presumably a captured one) to request additional supplies. If these arrived by fall he would leave 350 infantrymen in St. John's and return to France himself, on the assumption that the British would not mount an expedition until at least the spring. Anticipating a worst-case scenario of attack by the remaining vessels of the Royal Navy's Newfoundland station, he ordered both an upgrade of the Fort William defences and the construction of a boom and flanking battery in The Narrows. This went against the wishes of his engineer, who pleaded for measures to defend against land-based attack, including occupying the high ground around Fort

William. Given that the French themselves had come by land, the engineer's advice was more than reasonable, but the inexperienced Ternay ignored it, at least for the time being. Thus began one of the strangest summers in Newfoundland's history, with the French ensconced in St. John's and the British in Placentia. The dance partners were still the same, but oh how their places had changed.

As it would be a while before any supplies could possibly arrive from France, Ternay set about finding food for his men. Guards were posted outside the merchants' stores in St. John's, and 150 men were put aboard vessels and sent to Trinity, Carbonear, and Harbour Grace to amass all the available livestock and provisions for forwarding to St. John's.[28] The marines from the *Syren* repulsed the group that Ternay sent south to Ferryland, but elsewhere the French had their way. They also invited Irish Catholics to join them, although it was puzzling that they should be adding to their strength while simultaneously trying to stockpile provisions—which may explain why a ship carrying 356 Irish Catholics left St. John's for France in July.[29]

The food situation definitely explains Ternay's decision to deport the captured soldiers, sailors, and marines, as well as all the Protestant residents of St. John's except seventy of the "principal People," who were kept as potential hostages.[30] During the month of July nearly a thousand men, women, and children were put aboard vessels and sent out The Narrows with vague instructions to make their way to mainland North America or Europe.[31] The following month, authorities in Halifax used the French capture of St. John's as an excuse to deport an additional 1,300 Acadians to Boston. However, the Massachusetts Assembly would have nothing to do with them and sent them back, thus ending the Acadian deportations, which in total had displaced 10,000 people.[32] Although different in nature and scale, the Newfoundland experience is a reminder that the agony of deportation was inflicted on civilians on both sides during the conflict. Moreover, this marked the second deportation of Anglo-Newfoundlanders, the first coming courtesy of Iberville.

---

[28] Gordon Handcock, "State-of-the-Art French Cartography in Eighteenth Century Newfoundland: The Work of Marc Antoine Sicre de Cinq-Mars," *Newfoundland Studies*, Vol.4, No. 2 (1988), p. 146-47.

[29] L. M. Cullen, "The Irish Diaspora of the Seventeenth and Eighteenth Centuries," in Nicholas Canny (ed.), *Europeans on the Move: Studies on European Migration, 1500-1800* (Oxford, 1994), pp. 114-15.

[30] Little, *Dispatches of Rear-Admiral, Lord Colvill*, p. 29.

[31] Linÿer de la Barbée, *Le Chevalier de Ternay*, Vol. 1, p. 158, states that there were 1,027 prisoners. If we deduct the seventy who were kept as hostages, there would have been 957 deportees.

[32] James E. Candow, *The Deportation of the Acadians* (Grand-Pré, NS, 2003), p. 6.

If Choiseul disapproved of Ternay's plan to hold St. John's through the winter, it did not show. To the contrary, when he learned of it in early August he realized that it might give him a badly needed bargaining chip at the peace talks. He therefore gave orders to get two supply ships ready to sail for St. John's. Like Ternay, however, he underestimated the British, because if the present war had proven one thing, it was that the British were not sluggish. Aside from some initial confusion, they were about to act true to form again.

In Halifax Colvill's first thought was that the unidentified ships were privateers, but his eagerness to sail against them was not shared by Lieutenant Governor Jonathan Belcher, who feared that Nova Scotia might be the enemy's next stop. By 24 July Colvill knew that the enemy forces were French and that they were planning to stay, but Belcher still refused to cooperate, as did the commanding officers of the Halifax and Louisbourg garrisons, who would not budge without orders from New York, headquarters of Major-General Sir Jeffery Amherst, the army's Commander-in-Chief of North America. Accordingly, Colvill figured that if he combined forces with the remaining ships of the Newfoundland squadron, the navy alone might be able to settle things by blockading St. John's.

Colvill left Halifax on 10 August aboard the flagship HMS *Northumberland* (whose master was James Cook) accompanied by HMS *Gosport* and the Massachusetts vessel *King George*. They arrived in Placentia on the fourteenth and were met by Captain Douglas of the *Syren* and by Governor Thomas Graves, whose own flagship, HMS *Antelope*, had gone there after Douglas's messenger intercepted it. Having thus grown to five ships, Colvill's squadron sailed on the twenty-second for St. John's via Ferryland and Bay Bulls. On the way they encountered a sloop and a schooner loaded with deportees, including many Irishmen, twenty-three of whom Colvill pressed into service to replace the marines he had left in Placentia and Ferryland. Perhaps relations between the French and the Irish were souring, for Colvill's new sailors told him that if he put into Bay Bulls, "numbers of their Countrymen" would join him. Based on this intelligence Colvill wasted two days in Bay Bulls, where "not a Man" came forward. Finally, on the twenty-fifth, the squadron assumed position outside The Narrows, aiming to seal the French in and prevent relief from reaching them, thereby forcing them to surrender or fight. The strategy paid immediate dividends when an armed schooner and its unsuspecting crew of thirty Frenchmen stumbled onto the scene and were collared after a brief chase.[33] Colvill's squadron, whose manpower would soon be strengthened by the addition of fifty volunteers from Conception Bay, then settled in for the tedious but potentially lethal business of blockade.

Major-General Amherst initially shared Belcher's belief that the enemy, whatever their identity, were only in Newfoundland as a prelude to attacking mainland North America. On 20 July, when he learned they were French, he saw no reason to change his mind, although he did send a vessel to Britain with word of what had happened in St. John's. (A squadron of four ships under Captain Hugh Palliser was dispatched from Britain on receipt of Amherst's message, but it did not reach St. John's until 20 September, by which time the French had surrendered.)[34] His disposition changed entirely after 8 August, when he finally understood not only that Newfoundland was the object, but that the French intended to winter there. He then immediately set about organizing a force to recapture St. John's, and sent word to Colvill of his intentions. He was under no illusions that the Nova Scotia garrisons would have to supply the bulk of the men, because he had virtually stripped New York and the adjacent colonies bare by sending 4,000 troops to assist in the siege of Havana. He was therefore only able to cobble together nineteen artillerymen and 191 "recovered" soldiers, so-called because they were overcoming wounds and tropical illnesses incurred in Martinique earlier that year. They came from assorted regiments, but Amherst grouped them into two companies of light infantry under Captain John Maxwell of the 15th Regiment and Captain Charles Macdonell of the 78th Regiment (Fraser's Highlanders).

To lead the expedition Amherst looked not merely to his own staff but to his own family, selecting his thirty-year-old brother, Lieutenant-Colonel William Amherst, who on 15 August sailed for Halifax aboard the transport *James*, accompanied by the recovered men and six other transports. In Halifax the younger Amherst picked up 915 men, over half of them Massachusetts Provincials, the rest members of the 1st (Royal) and 77th (Montgomerie's) regiments, together with a smattering of Royal Artillery. The next stop was Louisbourg, where he

---

[33] After the inhabitants of Carbonear and Harbour Grace complained to Colvill that the French were coming overland from St. John's to Portugal Cove and harassing people in Conception Bay, this same schooner was stationed in the bay.

[34] As sources differ on whether Palliser's squadron arrived on 19 or 20 September, I have chosen the date that appears in Amherst's journal. Of one thing, however, we can be certain: a recent claim that Palliser "commanded the squadron that took St. John's back from a French occupation in 1762" is nonsense. See Sean T. Cadigan, *Newfoundland and Labrador: A History* (Toronto, 2009), p. 64.

embarked 395 men of the 45th Regiment, for a final strength of 1,559 troops. Including the 1,500 sailors with Colvill off St. John's, the total British force was just over 3,000 men.[35] Although this was insignificant compared with the numbers involved in the captures of Louisbourg (27,000), Quebec (23,000), and Havana (12,000), the stakes were high because no one on the British side wanted the French to hold St. John's through the winter. The implications of their doing so were unknowable, but one thing was certain: they would not be good.

With his force now distributed among ten transports, Amherst left Louisbourg on 7 September. News of his impending arrival reached Colvill the next day by a sloop that Amherst had sent direct from Halifax. Whether because of impatience or frayed nerves, Colvill decided to take his squadron south to Cape Broyle to meet Amherst and work out a plan of attack. His shocking carelessness was not lost on Ternay, who had become alarmed by a rumour that 4,500 British troops were on their way. He saw Colvill's absence as a golden opportunity to escape, although he intended to leave 300 men behind to negotiate an honourable surrender or, if the rumour proved unfounded, to stay the winter. On 9 September, with the French warships loaded and about to leave, a favourable west wind suddenly changed to a northerly, meaning that no one was going anywhere. Meanwhile, up the Southern Shore, a recent deportee from St. John's had informed Colvill that the French were about to push off, and on receipt of this thunderbolt the wandering admiral scurried back to St. John's where, on the tenth, he was lucky to find Ternay still in port. Nonplussed, the chevalier had every intention of sailing as soon as wind conditions permitted, even if it meant risking an engagement. However, on the twelfth, after he saw Amherst's transports passing The Narrows on their way northward, he concluded that the enemy force was considerably smaller than the rumoured 4,500, and that this was a contest he could win. Accordingly, his men disembarked and got ready for battle.

The transports that Ternay had seen were heading north for good reason. Amherst had reached Petty Harbour on the eleventh and had promptly gone aboard *Northumberland* for a conference with Colvill, who in the course of waiting off St. John's had had plenty of time to size things up. One hopes that Colvill gave Amherst a fuller briefing than the one he later sent to Jeffery Amherst, whom he informed that Fort William "was fortified all round with new Works; and that a Redoubt or something like one was raised at the little Harbour of Kitty Witty

---

[35] Fyers, "Loss and Recapture of St. John's," p. 212.

[Quidi Vidi]. The old Battery at the south Side of the Harbour's mouth was repaired with additional Works, and a new one erected on the same side nearer the [harbour] Entrance." This was useful enough, but, to the senior Amherst at least, Colvill did not mention the Narrows boom, or the new north-side Narrows battery that commanded it, or the breastworks at Cuckold's Cove that were designed, like the unfinished defences at Quidi Vidi, to prevent a British landing. (Ternay had finally begun to listen to his engineer.) William Amherst had wanted to land at Quidi Vidi, but Colvill talked him out of it, noting that the French had anticipated this possibility by plugging Quidi Vidi Gut (the harbour's narrow entrance) with sunken boats. Colvill instead proposed Torbay "as the properest Place to land at: 'tis to the Northward of St. John's, about seven Miles [eleven kilometres] by land, and the Road pretty good." Amherst therefore made for Torbay on the twelfth, giving hope to Ternay in the process. Colvill and Douglas followed in *Northumberland* and *Syren* with a flotilla of navy boats and fishing shallops that would take the troops ashore after they disembarked from the transports. Leaving Douglas behind to work with Amherst, Colvill then rejoined the blockade.

That night a stiff wind blew out Tor Bay, causing some of the boats to become separated from the transports, but everything eventually

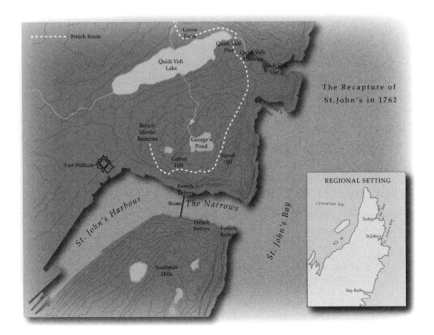

Fig. 15: The Recapture of St. John's in 1762.

got straightened away. The following morning the men disembarked and began rowing for shore as soon as Amherst gave the signal—a pendant hoisted from one of *Syren*'s boats. As they drew near they came under fire from about eighty French soldiers on nearby hills. The sniping had little effect, and the defenders fled toward St. John's as soon as enough men came ashore to challenge them. Within an hour Amherst gave the order to march on Quidi Vidi, whose harbour still appealed to him as the most convenient place to land supplies and artillery for the anticipated assault on Fort William. Contrary to Colvill's assurances, the road was merely a narrow path through marshes and thick woods, gradually giving way to open country, then narrowing again in more woods before ending at a farm known as "the Grove," on the northeast side of Quidi Vidi Pond (now Lake). Shortly after the men had entered the grove, they came under musket fire from enemy troops near Quidi Vidi Pass, an elevated position on the southeast side of the pond. These quickly retreated after two companies of light infantry forded the river and returned fire. Amherst then sent additional men to secure the pass, which commanded both Quidi Vidi and the ground toward Fort William.

On the fourteenth Amherst paused to survey the terrain and establish a hospital, and his men removed the sunken boats from the gut prior to unloading the stores and artillery that Douglas had brought from Tor Bay aboard the small boats. Whether he intended it from the outset or whether it emerged from his survey, Amherst reached the following conclusion: "The Signal Hill which overlooks this [Quidi Vidi] and the whole ground to the Fort, we must gain." Thus the appellation Signal Hill entered the historical record, replacing the name—The Lookout—that had been used since 1711. It is possible that Amherst was unaware of local usage and invoked a generic term reflecting the function performed on the hill, something that would have been obvious from the signal mast that crowned the summit. Sergeant David Perry of the Massachusetts Provincials, who left an account of his involvement in the campaign, used the generic "Flag-staff Hill."[36] Regardless, the name that would endure made its first appearance in Amherst's journal.

If William Amherst did christen Signal Hill, there would be no shame in its affiliation with an officer of his calibre. On 14 September 1762, one day short of a month after leaving New York, he had deposited 1,500 men on the doorstep of St. John's, ready to administer

---

[36] David Perry, *Recollections of an Old Soldier: The Life of Captain David Perry....* (Windsor, VT, 1822), p. 34.

the *coup de grâce* to its French occupiers. The man of action now ordered Captain Charles Macdonell to march his light infantry (one of the companies of recovered men, plus Colonel Jonathan Hoar's Massachusetts regiment) from the Grove to Quidi Vidi and, "so soon as the moon was up," to attack the enemy on Signal Hill. Ternay was about to pay the price for neglecting the high ground, although he tried to make amends by dispatching three companies of grenadiers under Lieutenant-Colonel Bellecombe with a cannon and a mortar to harass the British as they landed artillery and provisions at Quidi Vidi. Together with two pickets (small, advance bodies of detached troops) already on the hill, this brought the French strength there to approximately 300 men, or about 100 more than their enemy.

That evening, with an unidentified resident as their guide, Macdonell and the light infantrymen crept forward in single file and took positions practically under the noses of the French sentries. Whoever that resident was or how he came to be there, his participation enabled Amherst to exploit three of the cardinal principles of war: aggressive reconnaissance (in which the role of local knowledge is crucial); surprise (described by military historian Cyril Falls as "the most effective of all keys to victory"); and concentration (which when combined with surprise magnifies its impact).[37] Macdonell's men remained silent until the moment of attack on Wednesday the fifteenth, which Amherst described as "at peep of day" (sunrise, or roughly 6:30 a.m. in modern Newfoundland time). Luck also played a part, because a dense fog enabled a French-speaking infantryman named Peter Laford to fool one of the French sentries by responding convincingly when hailed. By this means, wrote Amherst, the attackers "got up a precipice where the men were obliged to shove one another up. The enemy gave them a fire and we never returned a shot, till we had gained the summit and these two Companies drove three Companies of the French Grenadiers and two pickets from the most advantageous ground I ever saw, — really, almost inaccessible."

Known to posterity as the Battle of Signal Hill, it was over in minutes. Casualties were modest on both sides, the British suffering four or five killed and roughly twenty wounded, and the French about the same number, including six who were taken prisoner.[38] The fighting, however, occurred at close quarters, producing wounds that a British surgeon's mate thought were unusually gruesome.[39] Captain

---

[37] Cyril Falls, *The Art of War: From the Age of Napoleon to the Present Day* (New York, 1961), p. 11.
[38] Fyers, "Loss and Recapture of St. John's," p. 198; Perry, *Recollections*, p. 35.
[39] Stephen Brumwell, *Redcoats: The British Soldier and War in the Americas, 1755-1763* (Cambridge, 2002), p. 250.

Macdonell and Lieutenant-Colonel Bellecombe were both wounded, and an officer of the 60th Foot was killed. Bellecombe's injury was significant because it caused panic among his men, who in spite of their superior numbers abandoned their position and fled down the hill to Fort William. Parity in the casualty lists belied the tactical implications, for the British were now, in David Perry's words, "masters of the hill." As such, Fort William was at their mercy, or at least would be as soon as the unstoppable Amherst made his next move. That, however, would have to wait, for in addition to the fog, which made it impossible to see the fort from Signal Hill, it began to rain heavily, not to stop until midnight of the following day.

To the French, the pause was a godsend. Ever the opportunist, Ternay called a council of war which recommended making a run for it under cover of the fog. During the afternoon British troops who had advanced to Gibbet Hill could hear noises in the harbour, and a concerned officer sent word to Amherst in Quidi Vidi that the enemy were "very busy with their ships, as if they were going out." In a rare misstep, Amherst failed to relay the intelligence to Colvill, although with the fog as thick it was, any man rowing out to the squadron would have risked getting lost. The French had indeed decided to leave on the sixteenth, probably before sun-up, for who could say how long the fog might last? But early on the evening of the fifteenth, before the infantry had boarded the ships, Ternay took advantage of a sudden west wind and immediately weighed anchor, after which his five ships (the original four, plus the *Comtesse de Grammont*) passed the unhitched Narrows boom and nosed unseen into the void. Early the next morning Colvill's lookout spied the topmasts of some vessels just as they dipped below the horizon. Their identity was confirmed that afternoon when the admiral received word from Amherst that the enemy squadron had escaped. There would be no retribution for Sutton and the Whiteboys, who were among the ones that got away.

As for the men left behind in Fort William, no one appreciated their plight better than Amherst, who wrote in his journal that it would be "impossible for the enemy to live in the Fort when once our batteries are up." Concerned, however, that the French might destroy the fort and its guns, Amherst took time on the sixteenth to address a letter to "the Officer Commanding in St. John's"—he did not yet know d'Haussonville's name—in which he threatened to put him and his men to the sword if they damaged the fort before he could take it. D'Haussonville naively but gamely replied over his signature: "I wait for your Troops and your Cannon; and nothing shall determine me to surrender the Fort unless you shall have totally destroyed it, and that

I shall have no more powder to fire." Thus rebuffed, the British proceeded on the seventeenth to cut a road from Quidi Vidi across the neck of the Signal Hill Peninsula to an area below and northwest of Gibbet Hill, about 450 metres from the fort and giving total command of it. There they established batteries for one eight-inch, six Royal, and seven coehorn mortars, all of which, with their ammunition, were brought from Quidi Vidi as soon as the road was made. The batteries opened fire around midnight and kept at it until about two hours after sunrise on the eighteenth. David Perry recounted that the mortar shells "caused much screaming and hallooing in their ranks, and did great execution."[40] The French lobbed a few shells of their own from Fort William, managing to kill two of Amherst's men, but that was the extent of their resistance.

D'Haussonville's bravado aside, the result was a foregone conclusion. On the morning of the eighteenth a French officer holding a flag of truce climbed to the now quiet British line and delivered a message from d'Haussonville asking what terms Amherst was prepared to give. In an answer conveyed by one of his officers, Amherst stated that the only terms would be surrender as prisoners of war. D'Haussonville in turn promised to relinquish the fort if his

Fig. 16: The Bombardment of Fort William. Artistic rendition by Sid Butt. Source: Sid Butt/Parks Canada. Once the British gained Signal Hill, and with it command of Fort William, the French position was hopeless.

---

[40] Perry, *Recollections*, p. 37. The actual number of French casualties has never been determined.

counterpart would consent to various articles of capitulation, those being, principally, that the troops would surrender as prisoners of war, the officers would keep their arms, and ships would be provided to take them back to France. In an act of generosity that reflected both the times—victory, not annihilation, was the objective—and Amherst's personal respect for the young count, the British commander agreed.[41]

DÉNOUEMENT AND THE TREATY OF PARIS

The recapture of St. John's was the last campaign of the Seven Years' War in North America, and the Battle of Signal Hill was its decisive action. The British subsequently made a related gain on the other side of the ocean which took some of the sting out of Ternay's disappearing act. On 22 September the Royal Navy squadron off Brest captured the two vessels that were headed for St. John's with provisions and reinforcements of ninety-three men. Two days later 709 French prisoners of war left St. John's for Brest aboard the transports *James* and *Fanny*, the former having borne Amherst from New York just over a month ago.[42] Maxwell's and Macdonell's companies appear to have sailed for New York on the twenty-fourth, while the troops from Louisbourg and Halifax departed on 26 September and 1 October respectively. Finally, on the second, Amherst bade farewell to Colvill and shoved off for New York aboard HMS *Enterprise*, which had recently put into St. John's from Havana, whose Spanish garrison had surrendered on 14 August. At a modest cost of twelve killed and thirty-eight wounded, the British had achieved their goal of recapturing St. John's, demonstrating once again "the unprecedented degree of cooperation between sailors and redcoats" that characterized the British war effort.[43] The victory was marred, however, by the escape of Ternay's squadron, whose ships must have come agonizingly close to Colvill's as they crept across St. John's Bay in the murk. Colvill, who was lucky not to have lost Ternay when he swung down to Cape Broyle to meet Amherst, had managed to lose him for good. Although he lamely denounced Ternay for making "a shamefull Flight," the real shame was Colvill's, who now joined the exclusive group of British naval officers who had come up short against the French in Newfoundland.

---

[41] Peter Wilson, "Warfare in the Old Regime 1648-1789," in Jeremy Black (ed.), *European Warfare 1453-1815* (New York, 1999), p. 89.
[42] This figure is based on the number who surrendered at Fort William on the eighteenth. See Webster, *Recapture of St. John's*, p. 14.
[43] Brumwell, *Redcoats*, p. 42.

As for the fearless Ternay, Lady Luck would smile on him a bit longer. Spotted by two Royal Navy vessels as his squadron neared the coast of France, he outraced them and took refuge in the Spanish port of Corunna, even capturing a British privateer along the way. He finally reached Brest in January 1763 and declared his mission a success. In terms of his original orders, he was largely right. He had destroyed over 400 miscellaneous vessels in Newfoundland and had shut down the fisheries along most of the old English Shore in 1762. He had shown inexperience by disobeying orders and trying to hold St. John's, but he made up for it in daring. It was one thing to take St. John's in the dead of winter when the Royal Navy was absent, but no French commander, not even Iberville, had held it through most of a summer. As well, Choiseul was determined to rebuild the navy, and Ternay had not only saved his squadron but had added the *Comtesse de Grammont*, the privateer, and the unidentified vessel that took Courval to France. Ternay would rise to rear admiral before dying of fever in 1780 in Newport, Rhode Island.[44]

D'Haussonville, who reached France before the end of October, complained about Ternay's abrupt departure from St. John's, but got nowhere.[45] Far from being the mission's main strength, the French infantry had performed miserably, for which d'Haussonville must take the blame. He claimed to have been so impressed by the British and Provincial light infantry on Signal Hill—a battle the French could easily have won—that he vowed to convert four of his own battalions to light infantry as soon as he got back to France. Actually, the French army was already being reorganized to include smaller and more flexible divisions and to make greater use of light troops, trends motivated as much by events in Europe as in North America.[46] Mobility was the new trend, albeit too new for d'Haussonville.

Even though the short-lived occupation of St. John's was a rare bright spot for France in the last full year of the war, it is impossible to draw a connection between the occupation and the terms of the Treaty of Paris (1763) except to say that both reflected France's determination to cling to the North American fisheries. The treaty is best remembered for establishing British sovereignty over France's former North American holdings east of the Mississippi River. Her

---

[44] On Newport, see Lee Kennett, *The French Forces in America, 1780-1783* (Westport, CT, 1977) and "L'expédition Rochambeau-Ternay: un success diplomatique," *Revue historique des armées*, Vol. 3, No. 4 (1976), pp. 87-105.

[45] *DCB* (Toronto, 1979), Vol. 4, "Arsac de Ternay, Charles-Henri-Louis d'."

[46] T. C. W. Blanning, *The French Revolutionary Wars: 1787-1802* (New York, 1996), pp. 17-18. For the contrary argument that light infantry were a North American invention, see Brumwell, *Redcoats*, pp. 228-36.

Caribbean colonies were also diminished, although the return of Guadeloupe and Martinique and the retention of Saint-Domingue meant that French sugar production would not suffer. Ever since the surrender of Montreal, France had been resigned to the loss of New France; once resigned, she was not devastated to see it go. Choiseul himself believed that the fisheries were more important than Canada and Louisiana combined, and Voltaire issued a more famous dismissal, declaring that the Seven Years' War was about "a few acres of snow somewhere around Canada."[47] In light of such pronouncements, it is surprising that so many Canadian historians have overlooked events in Newfoundland, believing instead that the war, along with France's North American empire, ended with the deaths of Wolfe and Montcalm on the Plains of Abraham in 1759. They have failed to appreciate the extent to which empire was about trade, specifically seaborne commerce and all that sustained it, including the fisheries.[48] Not only was the fur trade of New France less important than the Newfoundland fisheries and the Caribbean sugar and slave trades, but it lacked their synergies: French Caribbean slaves were consumers of saltfish; French citizens were consumers of saltfish and slave-produced sugar; and shipping united all three enterprises and reinforced their value to the navy and the nation.[49]

The treaty gave France a reduced version of what Choiseul had sought in 1761, but the broad outline was there, and with it the means of recovery both for the fisheries and for its symbiotic twin, the navy. While the treaty placed Labrador under the jurisdiction of the governor of Newfoundland, it confirmed French rights on the Newfoundland coast between Cape Bonavista and Point Riche, and French fishermen were allowed to resume fishing in the Gulf of St. Lawrence, albeit without coastal access (except where the Newfoundland treaty shore faced the gulf).[50] France lost Île Royale and its other island possessions in the gulf (principally Île St.-Jean, soon to be known as Prince Edward Island), but acquired the

[47] Dull, *The French Navy and the Seven Years' War*, p. 199.
[48] Bob Harris, "War, Empire, and the 'National Interest' in Mid-Eighteenth Century Britain," in Julie Flavell and Stephen Conway (eds.), *Britain and America Go to War: The Impact of War and Warfare in Anglo-America, 1754-1815* (Gainesville FL, 2004), pp. 13-40.
[49] On sugar and slavery, see Robert Louis Stein, *The French Sugar Business in the Eighteenth Century* (Baton Rouge, 1988). On the consumption of saltfish by French Caribbean slaves, see Gabriel Debien, "La Nourriture des Esclaves sur les Plantations des Antilles Françaises aux XVIIè et XVIIIè Siècles," *Caribbean Studies*, Vol. 4, No. 2 (1964), pp. 3-27.
[50] Labrador was placed under Quebec's jurisdiction in 1774 but reverted to Newfoundland's in 1809.

archipelago of St. Pierre and Miquelon as a shelter (*abri*) and base for the French bank fleet, on condition that they could not be fortified and that any buildings erected on them would have to be fishery-related. Given that France had just been whipped, Choiseul's diplomacy, aided by a more pliable British government, had enabled France to salvage something more than mere pride. The treaty had laid the foundation for the postwar revival of its North American fisheries and, by extension, the navy, thereby ensuring the continuation of Newfoundland's role in Anglo-French rivalry.

THE KEY OF THE HARBOUR

"Northern Heights – Which originally was taken up as a Garrison to retreat to… gives us the Key of the Harbour, that no Enemy could possibly lay in it, and has all the lower Batteries, in such command, that it would be impossible for an Enemy to remain in them were they to gain possession." Lieutenant-Colonel Thomas Skinner, 1797

THE INCREDIBLE EXPANDING DEFENCE NETWORK

Although Choiseul soon managed to restore the navy to its pre-war strength, Louis XV dismissed him in 1770 when his hawkish position on the Falkland Islands dispute threatened to plunge France into a war it could not afford.[1] The navy's recovery was reflected in the flourishing state of the French fisheries in and around Newfoundland, which by 1774 employed over 15,000 men.[2] Since the fisheries typically supplied one-third of the manpower of the wartime navy, this was a resource of great strategic value.[3] Unfortunately for France the good news cut both ways. By 1771 the British migratory fleet to Newfoundland consisted of 369 vessels—244 of them bankers—and 6,000 men.[4] The passenger traffic was also considerable, fluctuating between 5,800 and 7,500 people annually in the 1770s.[5] Most of these were bye-boat keepers, whose fares had become a pillar of the migratory fishery's economic viability; the rest were mainly servants going out to work for residents, of whom there were still only some 7,000. For the British, too, the Newfoundland fisheries remained an economic powerhouse and nursery of seamen, but the relative parity between residents and migrants was an ominous development.

Despite a stagnant resident population for the island as a whole, St. John's was thriving, especially as a supply centre, and with 1,389 permanent residents in 1774 it was also increasing its share of the Newfoundland total.[6] As for the town's physical appearance, flakes and stages now jostled for space with wharves and stores crammed with

---

[1] Olwen Hufton, *Europe: Privilege and Protest 1730-1789* (Oxford, 2000), pp. 91-92.
[2] Matthews, "West of England-Newfoundland Fishery," p. 396, n. 3. French saltfish production in 1774 was 386,215 quintals.
[3] Dull, *The French Navy and the Seven Years' War*, pp. 248-49.
[4] Matthews, "West of England-Newfoundland Fishery," pp. 414-15.
[5] Handcock, *Origins of English Settlement*, pp. 84-85.
[6] Macpherson, "Demographic History of St. John's," p. 9. On St. John's as a supply centre, see Head, *Eighteenth Century Newfoundland*, pp. 150-53.

fishery supplies for residents and with saltfish awaiting transport to market. Visitors unfamiliar with the fisheries were unimpressed, among them English naturalist Joseph Banks, who in 1766 wrote that "For dirt & filth of all Kinds St Johns may in my opinion Reign unrivald... Every thing here smells of fish...."[7] However, the same fish that offended Banks's delicate nose was gold to merchants and fishermen and a foundation of naval strength to the British nation. The continuing importance of St. John's was reflected in military developments after 1763, although for a while it looked as though it might not have a military future at all. The problem was that people in authority were reluctant to spend another shilling on a place that seemed indefensible, a reputation that the events of 1762 had done nothing to dispel.

In 1766 the Secretary of State for the Southern Department, the Duke of Richmond, ordered Captain Hugh Debbieg of the Royal Engineers to proceed to Newfoundland to "examine such Harbours as may be found most likely to answer the object of a place where British vessels fishing on that coast may, in case of a sudden Attack, safely retreat to, and be protected from an Enemy's Ships of War."[8] Richmond's instructions, which specified that "the protection of the inhabitants settled on the Island is neither practicable nor desirable," reflected the influence of Captain Hugh Palliser, who as Governor of Newfoundland from 1764 to 1768 tried to turn back the clock by reducing the resident population and reserving the fisheries for the migratory fleet. Although in a sense Palliser was only doing his patriotic duty, he has rightly been skewered for attempting to undo settlement, for which the time had passed.

Thorough to a fault, Debbieg did not submit his report until 1769, when contrary to all expectations he recommended keeping the garrison right where it was.[9] None of the other harbours that he looked at possessed the "great natural strength" of St. John's, he said, and all were flawed in one way or another. Having accompanied William Amherst to St. John's in 1762, Debbieg understood the challenges it posed to invaders, especially the narrowness of the harbour entrance, which could easily be secured by a boom and some well placed batteries. This left the old complaints of the town's vulnerability to landings elsewhere along the coast, and of Fort

---

[7] A. M. Lysaght (ed.), *Joseph Banks in Newfoundland and Labrador, 1766: His Diary, Manuscripts and Collections* (Berkeley, 1971), p. 147.
[8] TNA:PRO, C. O. 194, Vol. 27, fols. 241-44, Richmond to Debbieg, 28 June 1766.
[9] TNA:PRO, C. O. 194, Vol. 29, fols. 36-44, "The Report of Captn. Hugh Debbieg," 18 Oct. 1769.

William's susceptibility to fire from nearby hills. Debbieg could see no reason to reject St. John's on the first count, since every other harbour he examined was equally approachable from the landward. As for what could be done about it, here he was strangely weak. Quidi Vidi, he suggested, could be eliminated as a landing site by permanently closing the gut with rubble, after which the nearest landing place would be at least eight miles (12.9 kilometres) away, by which he must have meant Torbay. In order to reach St. John's from there an enemy would have to cut roads through "a country covered with thick Woods, full of Swamps, Mountains, and many other impediments... Labours that require much time, many hands, and are enough to discourage the most hardy Veterans." This was an odd conclusion from a man who had been present in 1762, when the terrain between Torbay and Quidi Vidi had stopped nobody. He was more plausible about Fort William's major weakness, which Amherst had exploited for all it was worth. To counter it, he recommended building a new fort, still on the north side of the harbour, but on an elevated position well to the west of Fort William and beyond the range of guns that an enemy might place on Signal Hill. Because of the more central location of the proposed work, along with its greater height—ninety-one metres above sea level, versus Fort William's thirty-two metres—it would not only be largely impervious to fire from enemy vessels, but would also command the entire harbour.

Borrowing from the French, Debbieg also advised that a redoubt or tower should be built at South Head "to give the most early and immediate protection to vessels that may fly to the Harbour for shelter from an Enemy." Significantly, he rejected the "favourite National Idea" that British naval superiority alone was sufficient for the defence of Newfoundland, observing that once the French had taken St. John's in 1762, "the whole Fishery was deserted." The lesson he took from this was that "whilst the Enemy is in possession of a Port in Newfoundland, Great Britain can have no Fishery there." Even if the naval force in Newfoundland were to be tripled, he argued, it would make no difference, since "a Land force must be kept there also, great enough to drive away the Enemy."

Debbieg's report saved the St. John's garrison and guided construction for the next decade. His original plans were altered along the way, but of his principal recommendations, only the infilling of Quidi Vidi Gut was abandoned outright.[10] A small work for two guns

---

[10] TNA:PRO, C. O. 194, Vol. 30, fols. 55-56, "Claims of the Inhabitants of Quiddi Viddi Cove for their Indemnification in case of its Demolition, with Certificates etc." [1771]

called North Battery was fully operational at Chain Rock Point by 1769,[11] and in 1771 work began on the South Head tower, which was completed in 1777 and christened Amherst's Tower, after either William Amherst or his older brother Sir Jeffery.[12] Construction of the new town fort began in earnest in 1775 and was finished in 1780, although things were far enough along for it to be occupied in 1779.[13] It was called Fort Townshend, after George Townshend, Master-General of the Board of Ordnance, the army branch responsible for building and maintaining military facilities at home and in the colonies. As a sign of its preferred status, the new fort included a governor's residence for use during those few months when the governor was actually in Newfoundland. It replaced Fort William as the main post, although the old fort continued with a reduced manpower complement. To connect the two the aptly named Military Road was cut through The Barrens, a deforested zone on high ground to the rear of the main residential area, which still clung barnacle-like to the north side of the harbour.

Fort Townshend's emergence coincided with conflict between Britain and a new foe. After the Seven Years' War Britain imposed a series of duties on colonial imports in order to defray its war debt and

Fig. 17: Amherst's Tower, 1786, from Log book of HMS Pegasus. Source: Library and Archives Canada. Completed in 1777, Amherst's Tower (far right) eventually became known as Fort Amherst. It would be the most seaward of the harbour's defences until the Second World War.

[11] TNA:PRO, C. O. 194, Vol. 28, fol. 97, 'Survey of Brass and Iron Ordnance and their Carriages at St. John's, Newfoundland" July 1769.
[12] TNA:PRO, C. O. 194, Vol. 33, fols. 138-39, Montagu to Germain, 27 Nov. 1777.
[13] DCB, Vol. 4, "Shuldham, Molyneux"; TNA:PRO, C. O. 194, Vol. 34, fols. 73-74, Pringle to Edwards, 12 Sept. 1779, and Vol. 35, fols. 40-41, Report of the State of the Fortifications St. Johns [sic] Newfoundland 1st August 1780."

to offset the spiralling cost of administering and defending the empire. Those duties triggered organized opposition in the American Colonies, whose people felt it was unfair to be taxed while they went unrepresented in Parliament. As the British reaction grew more heavy-handed, protest gave way to revolt (American Revolutionary War, 1775-83).[14] For Britain an already difficult situation became even more daunting when France entered the fray in February 1778, motivated by a desire to undo some of the damage of the previous war and thereby to make the global balance of power more favourable to its interests.[15] In a related objective—related because of its connection to naval power—France also hoped to improve its diminished position in the northwest Atlantic fisheries. It was risky business, but France would have the advantage of fighting without the usual distraction of battles in continental Europe, while the Royal Navy would have to contend on two fronts—Europe and North America.

Vue de la Rade de L'isle de St. Pierre proche de Terre neuve

Fig. 18: "Vue de la Rade de L'isle de St. Pierre proche de Terre neuve" (View of the roadstead of the island of St. Pierre near Newfoundland), by Jean-Dominique Cassini, ca. 1768. Source: Library and Archives Canada. After the conquest of New France, St. Pierre played a major role in the French fisheries in and around Newfoundland.

---

[14] Larry Sawers, "The Navigation Acts Revisited," *Economic History Review*, Vol. 45 (1992), pp.262-84.
[15] Jonathan R. Dull, *The French Navy and American Independence: A Study of Arms and Diplomacy, 1774-1787* (Princeton, 1975), p. 37; Orville T. Murphy, "The Comte de Vergennes, the Newfoundland Fisheries, and the Peace Negotiations of 1783: A Reconsideration," *Canadian Historical Review*, Vol. 46, No. 1 (March 1965), p. 33; Dallas D. Irvine, "The Newfoundland Fishery: A French Objective in the American War of Independence," *Canadian Historical Review*, Vol. 13, No. 3 (Sept. 1932), pp. 268-84.

For obvious reasons France sent no fishing vessels to Newfoundland between 1778 and the end of the war, and in September 1778 the 1,400 inhabitants of St. Pierre and Miquelon, some of them former Acadian deportees, were rounded up and shipped to France.[16] French entry into the war also had an adverse impact on the British bank fishery, already much reduced because of American privateering. This was now compounded by the Royal Navy's enforcement of a general press in order to satisfy its increased appetite for sailors.[17] The press also caused labour problems for Newfoundland residents, whose lot was further aggravated by the loss of trade with New England, which had grown steadily during the course of the century. This brought high food prices and, in some places, outright famine. Nonetheless, the migratory fishery was by far the bigger loser, and residents would outnumber migrants by a three-to-one ratio by war's end.[18]

Until 1782 American privateering was a problem in Newfoundland waters, which New England's fishermen, whalers, and especially traders had come to know intimately. The Royal Navy's Newfoundland squadron provided convoy escorts to the fishing fleet at the beginning and end of the season, and left small warships in St. John's and Placentia (and occasionally elsewhere) for extra security in winter.[19] But because the navy could not be everywhere, and because its primary mission was to look for privateers on the transatlantic trade lanes south of the island, privateers were virtually free to attack fishing vessels and coastal communities as far north as Labrador.[20] Although such targets were less profitable than merchantmen, the threat to them generated widespread defensive activity. The slumbering Placentia garrison, slated for abandonment and containing a mere eleven men in 1776, was increased to sixty by 1779.[21] Two-man artillery detachments were established in St. Mary's, Trepassey, Renews, Ferryland, Bay Bulls, Torbay, and Trinity, and firearms were distributed to residents in these places.[22] From 1778 onward the people of St. John's expected to see

---

[16] Marc Dérible, "Saint-Pierre et Miquelon: 'Origines et originalités'," *Les Cahiers* (Société Historique Acadienne), Vol. 32, No. 4 (décembre 2001), pp 213-15.

[17] Olaf Uwe Janzen, "The Royal Navy and the Defence of Newfoundland during the American Revolution," *Acadiensis*, Vol. 14, No. 1 (Autumn 1984), p. 31.

[18] Head, *Eighteenth Century Newfoundland*, p. 196.

[19] Janzen, "Newfoundland and British Maritime Strategy," p. 184.

[20] Charles Wendell Townsend (ed.), *Captain Cartwright and His Labrador Journal* (London, 1911), pp. 240-47; Prowse, *History of Newfoundland*, p. 350.

[21] TNA:PRO, C. O. 194, Vol. 34, fol. 78, "General Return of His Majesty's Troops in Garrison in the Island of Newfoundland," 5 Nov. 1779; Janzen, "Newfoundland and British Maritime Strategy," p. 127.

[22] TNA:PRO, C. O. 194, Vol. 34, fols. 71-73, Edwards to Germain, 12 Sept. 1779; and, in the same volume, fol. 78, "General Return of His Majesty's Troops in Garrison in the Island of Newfoundland," 5 Nov. 1779.

a French squadron just about every time the fog lifted, which was often. But no other community boasted anything like Fort Townshend, which with an armament of thirty-one guns and eight mortars was genuinely imposing, at least on the face of it. In addition to being safe from guns on Signal Hill, it commanded both the harbour and the landward approaches from the westward, from which an enemy landing at Bay Bulls would have to come. This was apparently unforeseen by Debbieg, who did not mention it in his report.

Fort Townshend's advantages were mainly theoretical. From a practical perspective, the defence of St. John's was guided by the need to secure The Narrows and to discourage enemy landings along the coast, to which the new fort contributed nothing. If not for its barracks, which at one point housed over 400 men, it would not have had a day-to-day role.[23] By 1779 the battery at the mid-way point of the south side of The Narrows was a solid work for nine guns. It also had a name,

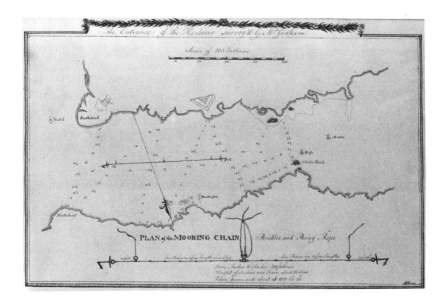

Fig. 19: "The Entrance of the Harbour survey'd by Mr. Graham," 1786, from Log book of HMS Pegasus. Source: Library and Archives Canada/C-00254. The mooring chain was an adaptation to the challenges of entering The Narrows during the age of sail. Frederick's Battery, which is unnamed on this plan, now complements Amherst's Tower (at South Head) on the south side of The Narrows. On the north side Chain Rock Battery has temporarily disappeared.

---

[23] TNA:PRO, C. O. 194, Vol. 35, fol. 39, "General Return of His Majesty's Troops in the Island of Newfoundland," 1 Aug. 1780.

Frederick's Battery, after Captain Thomas Lenox Frederick of HMS *Spy*, which overwintered in St. John's and Placentia during the war.[24] The former North Battery had now become, for the first time, Chain Rock Battery, and still mounted only two guns. This left the heavy hitting to Amherst's Tower, which with nine 24-pounders and four 18-pounders was up to the task. (The 24-pounders had an extreme range of about 2,200 metres, but were most effective within 1,800 metres). Chief Engineer Captain Robert Pringle proudly declared that all three Narrows works were in "a perfect State of Defence."[25] In late 1780 a log boom and connecting chain made The Narrows even more formidable, the ringbolts for the chain being fixed on Chain Rock and in front of Frederick's Battery.[26]

Memories of 1762 loomed large in the defence network's growth beyond the confines of the harbour and The Narrows. The Torbay and Bay Bulls artillery detachments were meant not only to repel privateers, but also to hamper enemy landings and to give as much notice as possible to St. John's that company was coming. Cox's Marsh Battery was built along the road from Torbay to St. John's, and Hay's Battery (after Lieutenant-Colonel David Hay of the Royal Artillery) on the road from Bay Bulls. Quidi Vidi and Signal Hill, both of which had been central to the British recapture of St. John's, also received attention. In the summer of 1780, with invasion fears at fever pitch, a council of war re-examined the idea of filling in Quidi Vidi Gut but concluded that "an Enemy could make no use of that Harbour till in Possession of the High Grounds about the Signal Hill and the Grove."[27] Still, engineer Pringle was ordered to prepare "three or Four Boats ... loaded with Stones" to be sunk in the gut if an enemy landing were imminent. The council felt that Quidi Vidi's best hope lay in two recently completed two-gun batteries on either side of Cuckold's Head, the seaward extremity of the Signal Hill Peninsula. One of these commanded Quidi Vidi Gut, and the other Cuckold's Cove, both potential landing sites.[28] It is worth noting that these works, like

---

[24] TNA:PRO, C. O. 194, Vol. 33, fol. 69, "Present State of Fort William...," 20 Oct. 1776; Vol. 34, fols. 3-5, Pringle to Germain, 22 Nov. 1777; and Vol. 35, fols. 147-48, "Report of the Fortifications of the Harbour of St. Johns [sic] Newfoundland...," 10 Sept. 1782; Janzen, "Newfoundland and British Maritime Strategy," pp. 218-19.
[25] TNA:PRO, C. O. 194, Vol. 34, fols. 73-74, Pringle to Edwards, 12 Sept. 1779.
[26] TNA:PRO, C. O. 194, Vol. 35, fol. 39, "General Return of His Majesty's Troops in the Island of Newfoundland," 1 Aug. 1780, and fols. 71-74, Edwards to Germain, 15 Nov. 1780.
[27] TNA:PRO, C. O. 194, Vol. 35, fols. 42-46, "Proceedings of a Council of War, held at Fort William," 1 Aug. 1780.
[28] TNA:PRO, C. O. 194, Vol. 35, fols. 40-41, "General Return of His Majesty's Troops in the Island of Newfoundland," 1 Aug. 1780.

Amherst's Tower, were on or near sites that the French had used in 1762.

At peak strength during the Revolutionary War the St. John's garrison reached 735 men, including 339 from the Newfoundland Regiment of Foot, a local infantry corps raised and commanded by Robert Pringle and quartered in the old barracks at Fort William, which as a result got a new lease on life.[29] Although St. John's had never been so primed to meet an enemy, peace brought the usual reductions, including disbandment of the Newfoundland Regiment; by 1784 only eighty-five regulars of the 37th Regiment and forty-nine artillerymen remained.[30] Every other military post on the island except Placentia was abandoned, and its half a dozen artillerymen were left to wonder what to do with so much time and so little money.

The fishery clauses of the Treaty of Versailles (1783) reflected the inescapable fact that Britain had suffered defeat. Prior to the war, France had complained about British settlers pushing north of Cape Bonavista into territory that it believed was exclusively its own, to which British diplomats had replied with the novel argument that the fisheries north of the cape were concurrent ones and therefore open to both countries. While silent on the access issue, the treaty acknowledged the northward spread of British settlement by changing the shore's eastern terminus from Cape Bonavista to Cape St. John, seemingly a victory for Britain, but not really, since France retained the all-important Petit Nord. As clearer evidence of France's improved position, the treaty also shifted the shore's western terminus from Point Riche to Cape Ray, giving French fishermen access to the entire west coast. Significantly, the total length of coastline now available to French fishermen was longer than what it had been under Utrecht. The treaty also contained a British declaration that St. Pierre and Miquelon were "ceded for the purpose of serving as a real shelter to the French fishermen," which France interpreted as an endorsement of its right to settle there. As for the newly minted United States of America, its negotiators secured for their fishermen the liberty to fish in the inshore waters of the whole of British North America, Newfoundland included.

---

[29] TNA:PRO, C. O. 194, Vol. 35, fol. 125, "General Return of His Majesty's Troops in the Island of Newfoundland," 28 Sept. 1781; G. W. L. Nicholson, *The Fighting Newfound-lander: A History of the Royal Newfoundland Regiment* (St. John's, 1964), pp. 17-23.
[30] TNA:PRO, C. O. 194, Vol. 35, fol. 255, "State of the Company Commanded by Major W. Archer Huddleston's Battr. Of Artillery and detachment of 37th Regimt. Commanded by Captn. Northand Nichols St Johns [sic] Newfoundland," 13 Nov. 1784.

FORT IMPREGNABLE

Favourable treaty terms did not translate into prosperity for French and American fishermen. Their diplomats had done a wonderful job, but someone forgot to tell the cod, which deserted the French treaty shore in 1787 and took their sweet time coming back.[31] That was not the worst of it, for the cost of fighting the war had brought France to the brink of bankruptcy. Postwar inflation and high taxes were compounded by poor harvests, creating a stew of social and political unrest that erupted into outright revolution in 1789. The ensuing years of domestic and international turmoil effectively removed France from the Newfoundland fisheries until 1815. Meanwhile, the New England fisheries had been drastically curtailed during the Revolutionary War, and although privateering had picked up some of the economic slack, the fishery infrastructure was in shambles when the war ended.[32] Rebuilding was slowed by loss of access to the British Caribbean saltfish market, which had always been more important for New England than for Newfoundland.[33] It was a solid decade before American fishermen got back up to speed.

With two of its major competitors all but gone from the marketplace, Newfoundland gladly picked up the slack. The resident population swelled to 10,000 by 1793, of whom 3,190 lived in St. John's.[34] In straight numerical terms the British migratory fishery also flourished, attaining a postwar zenith in 1788 when 389 ships and 4,306 men went to Newfoundland.[35] That year's output of nearly 950,000 quintals of saltfish was more than markets could bear, and prices began to decline; as they did, migratory activity slid back to an average of 260 ships a year until 1793. [36] On the face of it this was still impressive, but the numbers concealed one of the great paradoxes of Newfoundland history, because the migratory fishery was actually dying. All of the so-called bank vessels—that is, two-thirds of the total—now brought

---

[31] Matthews, "West of England-Newfoundland Fishery," pp. 499-500.

[32] Raymond McFarland, *A History of the New England Fisheries* (New York, 1911), p. 130. Contrary to McFarland's long-standing claim, the New England fisheries did not stop during the war, although they were greatly constricted. See Christopher P. Magra, "The New England Cod Fishing Industry and Maritime Dimensions of the American Revolution" (Unpublished PhD thesis, University of Pittsburgh, 2006), pp. 224-40.

[33] John J. McCusker and Russell R. Menard, *The Economy of British America, 1607-1789* (Chapel Hill, NC, 1985), p. 108; James E. Candow, "Salt Fish and Slavery in the British Caribbean," in Starkey and Candow (eds.), *The North Atlantic Fisheries*, pp. 165-94.

[34] Handcock, *Origins of English Settlement*, p. 96; Macpherson, "Demographic History of St. John's," p. 10.

[35] Shannon Ryan, "Fishery to Colony: A Newfoundland Watershed, 1793-1815," *Acadiensis*, Vol. 12, No. 2 (Spring 1983), p. 35.

[36] Head, *Eighteenth Century Newfoundland*, p. 204.

supplies to sell to residents when they came out in the spring, and many carried fish to market when they left at the end of the season.[37] Fishing, then, was only one activity among many that made operations viable, and its relative importance was waning. In addition, the market glut of 1789 forced many bye-boatmen into bankruptcy, further undermining the banking activity that their fares had subsidized.[38]

A new paradigm was beginning to emerge from the haze of demographic growth and changes in the organization and conduct of the island's fisheries. The resident population was attaining a critical mass that would enable migratory interests to abandon production altogether—as many already had—in favour of the supply and carrying trades, leaving local arrangements to resident merchants.[39] These trends would come to a head during the French Revolutionary and Napoleonic Wars (1792-1815), the ponderous title that historians apply to the multiple wars between France and rival European powers that wanted no part of republicanism or of Napoleonic expansion, and whose monarchs preferred to keep their heads. Alliances on both sides shifted with great fluidity, and supporters in one contest were as likely as not to be enemies in the next. But from the moment that France declared war on Britain in February 1793, hostility between the two was unwavering; except for a single pause between March 1802 and May 1803, the old foes went at it for a generation. Much of the world, Newfoundland included, would be unrecognizable when the dust settled.

Just as in 1778, St. Pierre and Miquelon were first to bear the brunt of hostilities. The small garrison at St. Pierre, site of the only good harbour in the archipelago, surrendered in May 1793 to a joint army-navy expedition from Halifax and St. John's.[40] Some five hundred residents were removed to Halifax, as were Governor Antoine-Nicolas Dandasne-Danseville and his soldiers, and another one thousand inhabitants stayed put under the watchful eye of a British garrison pending a final decision on their fate. The following summer the St. Pierre residents and most of the Halifax detainees were deported to the Channel Island of Guernsey, and the British garrison was transferred to Cape Breton.[41] The seizure of the French islands had a

---

[37] Matthews, "West of England-Newfoundland Fishery," pp. 528-29.
[38] Handcock, *Origins of English Settlement*, pp. 82-84.
[39] Matthews, "West of England-Newfoundland Fishery," pp.487-93.
[40] Dérible, "Saint-Pierre et Miquelon," p. 217; J. Mackay Hitsman, "Capture of Saint-Pierre-et-Miquelon, 1793," *Canadian Army Journal*, Vol. 13, No. 3 (July 1959), pp. 77-81; T. Watson Smith, "Halifax and the Capture of St. Pierre in 1793," *Collections of the Nova Scotia Historical Society*, Vol. 14 (1909), pp. 80-105.
[41] J. Mackay Hitsman, *Safeguarding Canada 1763-1871* (Toronto, 1968), p. 63.

direct impact on the St. John's garrison, since three of its five infantry companies took part in the action.[42] To fill the void caused by their absence, Chief Engineer Captain Thomas Skinner organized a local force known as the Royal Newfoundland Volunteers. In 1795 he went one better by raising the Royal Newfoundland Regiment of Fencible Infantry. Like fencible regiments in neighbouring Nova Scotia and New Brunswick, this was a legitimate British Army regiment in every respect except that it was intended for service in its colony of origin only.[43] That condition, however, would prove to be malleable.

It was fine that Skinner, like Captain Robert Pringle before him, could make time to recruit for the British Army, but as chief engineer his primary responsibilities were the construction and maintenance of fortifications and other military property, matters that always came into focus during wartime. Grandson of Lieutenant-General William Skinner, the former chief engineer of Great Britain, Skinner was thirty-one years old when he arrived in St. John's from Gibraltar in 1790.[44] He came with prior knowledge of his posting, since his colleagues in Gibraltar included Robert Pringle, after whom he named one of his sons, indicating that they were close friends. In some ways their Newfoundland careers were strangely parallel, for each man played a formative role in the history of the Royal Newfoundland Regiment, and each altered the physical layout of the St. John's defence system. But while Pringle was associated with Fort Townshend and Amherst's Tower, and with the creation of defences in outlying areas, Skinner's name was about to become synonymous with Signal Hill.

Prior to Skinner's time the only defences on the Signal Hill Peninsula (that is, besides the temporary ones built by the French and the British in 1762) were Quidi Vidi and Cuckold's Cove batteries and the various works that had come and gone at Chain Rock Point. While not a defence *per se*, the signal mast, which from at least 1762 was accompanied by a signalman's hut or some other shelter, was part of the defence system. The only other man-made feature on the hill was the gibbet, where bodies of executed criminals were suspended by ropes or chains as a warning that criminal acts would not go unpunished. Gibbeting, which was also a form of public entertainment, was legal in Britain until 1834, the year in which it was

---

[42] Nicholson, *The Fighting Newfoundlander*, p. 23.
[43] See, for example, George F. G. Stanley, "The New Brunswick Fencibles," *Canadian Defence Quarterly*, Vol. 16 (1938-39), pp. 39-53.
[44] David A. Webber, *Skinner's Fencibles: The Royal Newfoundland Regiment 1795-1802* (St. John's, 1964), p. 6; *DCB* (Toronto, 1983), Vol. 5, "Skinner, Thomas."

also last used in Newfoundland.[45] The earliest mention of a gibbet in Newfoundland comes from St. John's in 1754, when three men and a woman convicted of murdering magistrate William Keen were sentenced to be executed and hung in chains.[46] It was a remarkable end for Keen, but then, the Boston native had led a remarkable life, one that included incarceration in Plaisance in 1709. The Signal Hill gibbet appears to have been built around 1760 when the town's original gibbet was dismantled to make way for, of all things, a new Anglican church. This timing dovetails with mention of Gibbet Hill in William Amherst's account of the recapture of St. John's in 1762; as with Signal Hill, Amherst can lay claim to the first recorded use of the name "Gibbet Hill."

If there was little on the Signal Hill Peninsula when Thomas Skinner arrived, the same could not be said when he left. Change was almost imperceptible at first, beginning in 1791 with construction of a guardhouse at the entrance to the summit, a puzzling thing given that, other than the signal mast, there was nothing on the summit that needed guarding.[47] Even the two batteries at Cuckold's Head were well to the north and more easily accessible from Quidi Vidi. But something was afoot, because Quidi Vidi and Cuckold's Cove batteries, along with Chain Rock Battery, all three of which had gone to ruin by 1790, were rebuilt in 1791.[48] In hindsight the guardhouse can be seen as the first step in a master plan that took a while not only to be fully thought out, but also to be couched in such a way that the Board of Ordnance would commit to the expense. Although no copies of Skinner's proposal have survived, the available evidence suggests that it was submitted to the Board in 1794 and approved sometime that year or early the next, because in 1795 work began with a vengeance.[49]

The projects that garnered early attention are noteworthy for what they reveal of Skinner's priorities. One of the first was a two-story blockhouse on the highest point of the summit in the area now known as Ladies' Lookout, a modern corruption of the hill's early name.[50]

---

[45] In Harbour Grace, not St. John's. See The Rooms Provincial Archives Division (hereafter TRPAD), GN 2.2, Incoming Correspondence, Office of the Colonial Secretary fonds, Danson et al. to Crowdy, 30 April 1834.

[46] Tom Hooper, "The St. John's Gibbet," in "Miscellaneous Historical Reports on Sites in the Atlantic Provinces," *Manuscript Report No. 107* (Ottawa, 1960-70), pp. 156-67.

[47] David A. Webber (comp.), *Documents relating to St. John's, Newfoundland and to Signal Hill National Historic Park [copied from Public Record Office: Record Books of the Royal Engineers]* (Ottawa, 1964), Orders, Fort Townshend, 5 Oct. 1791.

[48] Webber, *Documents*, "Estimate of the Expence [sic] of Repairs Necessary to be done to the Barracks, Fortifications, etc. ... for the Year 1791."

[49] Philip Tocque, *Newfoundland: as it was and as it is in 1877* (Toronto, 1878), pp. 23-24.

[50] TNA:PRO, C. O. 194, Vol. 41, fols. 120-22, "State of the Fortifications, Barracks etc. at St. Johns [sic] in the Island of Newfoundland," 15 Oct. 1795.

In addition to being a defence work—six guns were mounted in its upper level in 1796—the blockhouse also became the new signal station, with the Royal Artillery supplying the signalmen. Although no signal code has been found for this period, it is almost certain to have indicated the type, nationality, and number of ships that had been sighted passing or nearing the port.[51] British warships approaching St. John's could also signal in advance that they were friendly by firing two guns in succession, which the artillerymen at Amherst's Tower were obliged to acknowledge in kind.[52]

Other work in 1795 included the erection of frames for an officers' barracks of wooden construction nestled into the relatively sheltered, southeastern face of Ladies' Lookout. Putting it there was no accident, for Signal Hill is subject to gale-force winds, and any location that might mitigate their impact was going to be exploited to the hilt. (Because of its signalling role, the blockhouse had to be as visible as possible and was therefore totally exposed.) Frames for the barracks were assembled in town and carried to the summit, probably by hand, as there was still no route fit for carts. When Wallace's Battery (after Governor Sir James Wallace) was erected on Gibbet Hill during the same 1795 construction season, the path from town was so crude that the battery's guns had to be hoisted up the cliff face by ropes.[53] In addition to marking the disappearance of the gibbet, the establishment of Wallace's Battery was a sign that The Narrows were going to become even stronger. The battery also commanded the landward approach to Signal Hill from town, a crucial role that hinted at the main reason for Skinner's interest in Signal Hill in the first place.

Construction activity in 1796 left no doubt as to Skinner's intentions. The Narrows defences were stiffened by the addition of Queen's Battery, a major work for nine heavy guns, which technically was not completed until 1797.[54] At an elevation of 110 metres, it dangled on the edge of a cliff directly above Chain Rock Battery. Even more impressive was Duke of York's Battery, perched on the southern extremity of the summit at an elevation of 152 metres. Like Queen's Battery, it would not be entirely finished until the following year, when it mounted eight guns, two mortars, and three or four carronades.

[51] I have extrapolated this from the signal code of 1780, for which see TRPAD, GN2/1/a, Outgoing correspondence, Office of the Colonial Secretary fonds, Edwards to Commandant of Amherst's Tower, 15 July 1780.
[52] Murray, *Journal of Aaron Thomas*, p. 49.
[53] Tocque, *Newfoundland*, pp. 23-24.
[54] TNA:PRO, C. O. 194, Vol. 39, fols. 62-63, "State of the Fortifications, Barracks and other Buildings at St John's in the Island of Newfoundland," 24 Oct. 1795.

While it offered commanding views to the seaward and of the eastern half of The Narrows, cannon balls fired from this height plunged so steeply that accuracy was out of the question, meaning that it was not a Narrows battery *per se*. Its main role was to anchor the southern end of the summit. By fall the barracks that had been started in 1795 was almost finished, and, more importantly, a passable road had been cut from town all the way to the summit.[55] While hardly the final piece of the puzzle, the road left no doubt as to Skinner's goal. The summit was to be a citadel, or stronghold, to which men in the town forts could retreat and take refuge "in case of a very superior Enemy attacking this place."[56] This function was embodied in its nickname, Fort Impregnable.[57] Those guards would have something to guard after all.

THE LAST WALTZ

With all the construction on Signal Hill and the usual waterfront hustle and bustle, 1796 had been shaping up to be a memorable year even before a French squadron appeared off The Narrows in September. All summer long the air was filled with the sounds of officers barking orders and of workers driving nails, pulling saws, hacking stones, and yelling curses when a limb or a finger accidentally got mangled or banged. Colour was added by the predominantly blue and white uniforms of seventy-four Royal Artillerymen, and by the red coats of the five hundred or so men of the Royal Newfoundland Regiment. Time would show that there were evil-doers among the latter, but for now saint and sinner alike could take pride in defending against an enemy who had not been seen in more than thirty years, and who if all went well would avoid Newfoundland in the present conflict, just as he had in the last. But the biggest story—that is, until September—was the fire, and not an urban fire, of which there had already been a memorable example in 1779, a foretaste of a curse that would plague St. John's for much of its existence. This one was a forest fire that broke out north of town around 20 August and burned uncontrollably for three weeks. Whenever the wind blew from that direction there was so much smoke that breathing became difficult, and embers borne by the wind threatened to ignite the tinder-dry town.[58] Nerves had been on edge for so long that when, on the first of

---

55 Tocque, *Newfoundland*, p. 26.
56 Webber, *Documents*, Skinner to Waldegrave, 15 Oct. 1797.
57 Webber, *Documents*, "Return of Provisions remaining at Fort Impregnable," 18 Sept. 1797.
58 "Reminiscences of the Year 1796," by "An Eye Witness," in *Royal Gazette and Newfoundland Advertiser* (St. John's), 20 Nov. 1832, p. 2.

September, a signal indicating an enemy fleet was hoisted at the blockhouse, skepticism gave way to relief, for here at last was something bound to take people's minds off the interminable fire.

If they had known who was in charge of the French squadron, they might have preferred their chances against the flames. Thirty-eight-year-old Rear-Admiral Joseph de Richery was an accomplished veteran who had joined the navy as a cabin boy at age nine and worked his way up to captain in 1793.[59] Although he had served primarily in the Pacific and Indian oceans, he saw action in the Caribbean during the American Revolutionary War and was with the French fleet that won the Battle of the Chesapeake Capes—the defeated British fleet was commanded by Rear-Admiral

Fig. 20: Rear-Admiral Joseph de Richery, by Antoine Maurin. Source: Library and Archives Canada/Biographie maritime, ou, Notices historiques sur la vie et les campagnes des marins célèbres français et étrangers/AMICUS 5151773/Page 332. His raid against Newfoundland and Labrador in 1796 was the last hostile action by French forces against British subjects in North America. In St. John's it reinforced the military significance of Signal Hill and The Narrows.

Sir Thomas Graves, former governor of Newfoundland—which prevented the relief of Cornwallis's besieged army in Yorktown.[60] Of noble blood, Richery was dismissed in 1794 as part of the revolutionary purge that cost France so much of its naval leadership.[61] But he was soon reinstated and promoted to rear-admiral, in which capacity he led a squadron from Toulon in September 1795, ostensibly bound for Saint-Domingue, Newfoundland, and the Azores.[62] However, after happening upon and capturing thirty British merchantmen off Cape St. Vincent, he changed course and put into Cadiz to sell his prizes. For

---

[59] The best biographical sketch of Richery is Joseph François Gabriel Hennequin, *Biographie maritime ou notices historiques....* (Paris, 1836), Tome 2, "Richery (Joseph de)." See also François-Xavier Feller, *Biographie universelle ou dictionnaire historique....* (Paris, 1849), Tome 7, "Richery (Joseph de)"; and Louis-Gabriel Michaud, *Biographie universelle ancienne et moderne....* (Paris, 1843), 45 tomes, Tome 35, "Richery (Joseph de)."

[60] Richery was on the *Hector.* On the Battle of the Chesapeake Capes, see Charles Lee Lewis, *Admiral de Grasse and American Independence* (New York, 1980 [originally published 1945]), pp. 156-70.

[61] On this subject, see William S. Cormack, *Revolution and Political Conflict in the French Navy 1789-1794* (Cambridge, 1995).

[62] E. H. Jenkins, *A History of the French Navy: From its Beginnings to the Present Day* (London, 1973), p. 221.

various reasons, including his role in negotiations for a new alliance between France and Spain, he did not leave until 4 August 1796, by which time his original mission had been scaled back to a single objective: to attack fishing establishments in Newfoundland and Labrador.

Richery's squadron of seven battleships and three frigates reached the Grand Bank on 28 August and immediately started burning and sinking every British vessel they could find. Richery then turned his attention to what promised to be a more difficult but more lucrative target—St. John's. If the wind had not been blowing out of The Narrows on the first of September, he might have sailed right in; instead, he was forced to mark time in St. John's Bay. While he did, Governor Wallace seized the advantage and declared martial law. Every able-bodied male from the richest merchant to the lowliest flake worker—some 3,000 men in all—abandoned their duties and made their way to The Barrens to be enrolled, armed, and given their orders. Although some were assigned to the forts and batteries, most were about to spend the night on top of Signal Hill.

When the sun rose behind Richery's squadron on the morning of the second, the summit presented an entirely new aspect to the French sailors. An unbroken line of canvas tents snaked all the way from Duke of York's Battery northward to Cuckold's Head, a scene replayed in miniature on the south side around Amherst's Tower. A boom had been drawn across The Narrows, with three fire ships arrayed behind it, and behind them were Wallace's small squadron of one ship of the line, two frigates, and a sloop, which by themselves would have been no match for Richery. The French seemed taken aback and spent the day pondering their options, or so the defenders deduced from the flurry of signals that were hoisted and lowered from the yards, and from the number of boats that went scurrying to and from the flagship. One more day the French spent in similar activity, broken only by a brief feint toward Amherst's Tower that caused its defenders some anxious moments. Then, on the morning of the fourth, the squadron abruptly departed, only to put into Bay Bulls around midday, where officers enquired after the condition of the road to St. John's and the size of the garrison. Supposedly upon being told that it numbered 5,000 men, they abandoned all thoughts of moving against it. Instead, Richery dispatched a division of two battleships and a frigate under Zacharie-Jacques-Théodore Allemand to the Labrador coast, while he and the remaining ships left for the southward on the eighth, although not before burning Bay Bulls—no French campaign was complete without it—and nearby Witless Bay. Richery made his way to St. Pierre, where he destroyed boats and other property associated with the British fishery that had sprung up there since 1793. He returned to France in early November, just in time for December's disastrous Irish invasion attempt. Allemand, who also reached home in November, would have done more damage than he did on the Labrador coast had not most of the British fishing vessels left before he got there, but he still torched the fishing premises in Chateau Bay and captured a convoy laden with furs. In addition to relieving the British Newfoundland fisheries of an estimated one hundred vessels, Richery and Allemand sent a shipload of prisoners (probably from Bay Bulls and St. Pierre) to Halifax, and carried another 300 or so back to France.[63]

Two months shy of a century after Iberville, the last hostile action by French forces against British subjects in North America was over. Although distant in time, the two campaigns had related results. Iberville had caused the establishment of the St. John's garrison; Richery, by removing any possible doubt as to ongoing French interest in the Newfoundland fisheries, ensured its continuation. Richery's expedition was also fraught with implications for the defence of St. John's, confirming the importance of The Narrows and reinforcing Skinner's citadel concept, which suddenly looked visionary. Initially it was also good for Fort William, whose Narrows Battery was reactivated during the standoff with Richery, and which was likely to be secure so long as Signal Hill was in friendly hands. But it was bad news for Fort Townshend, which had been remote from all the activity. Worse still, the three hundred men who had been posted to the fort on the first of September had drunk the wells dry in half an hour, meaning that it could never withstand a siege, and if that were the case, what good was it? The lesson was not lost on Sir James Wallace, who in one of his last letters as governor urged the Home Secretary, the Duke of Portland, to complete the plans for Signal Hill, which unlike the hapless fort was "well supplied with wood and water."[64] In 1797 the new governor, Vice-Admiral William Waldegrave, echoed Wallace's support for the hill and added another black mark against Fort Townshend: because it possessed so many wooden buildings, "a single Royal [mortar] might set on fire the whole in less than a quarter of an hour."[65] Faced with so much backing for Signal Hill and so little for Fort Townshend, and not even convinced of the need for the Fort William Narrows Battery, the Board of Ordnance decided by April 1799 "to establish the Principal

---

[63] William James, *The Naval History of Great Britain....* (London, 1859), 6 vols, Vol. 1, p. 409.
[64] TNA:PRO, C. O. 194, Vol. 39, fols. 66-67, Wallace to Portland, 2 Feb. 1797.
[65] Webber, *Documents*, Waldegrave to Skinner, 5 Aug. 1797.

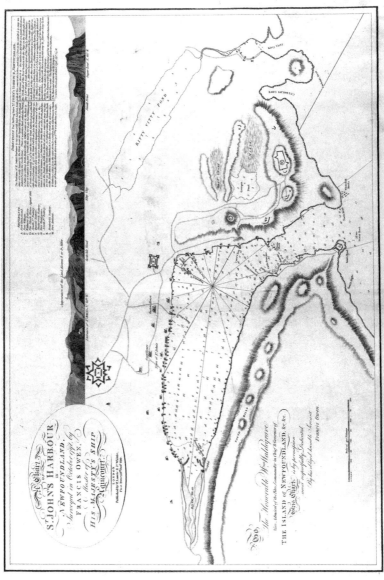

Fig. 21: "A Chart of St. John's Harbour in Newfoundland, Surveyed in October 1798, by Francis Owen, Master of His Majesty's Ship Agincourt." Source: Courtesy of the Centre for Newfoundland Studies, Memorial University Libraries. Owen's chart shows the position of Signal Hill relative to Fort Townshend (A) and Fort William (B). On the Signal Hill Peninsula can be seen Wallace's Battery (C), the blockhouse (D), Duke of York's Battery (E), Queen's Battery (F), Chain Rock Battery (G), Waldegrave Battery (H), North Point Battery (I), and Carronade Battery (K).

Post for the defence of the Harbour of St. John's upon Signal Hill and no longer to repair Forts Townshend and William."[66]

BETWEEN A ROCK AND A HARD PLACE

Like the French and American negotiators at Versailles, no one bothered to check with Mother Nature about what would succeed on Signal Hill, and that, as it turned out, would be a good deal less than any engineer could imagine. Still, Thomas Skinner was almost as stubborn as the hill he had decided to tackle, and this, together with the impetus provided by the French threat, seems to have accounted for much of the early progress. There was no slacking in 1797, when great energy went into finishing projects begun the previous year, including Queen's and Duke of York's batteries.[67] Because the latter was separate from the rest of the summit works, Skinner designed a wooden stockade that stretched along the western face of the summit to Ladies' Lookout. He regarded this as a temporary feature to be scrapped whenever he could afford to replace it with a proper masonry wall. At the opposite end of the summit, overlooking Cuckold's Cove, was North Point Battery, which would have been a detached work except that Skinner connected it to the summit by another stockade, this one extending from the northwest corner of Ladies' Lookout.[68] The creation of North Point Battery spelled the end of Cuckold's Cove Battery, which was never heard from again. New to the scene was Carronade Battery, built on a rise north of George's Pond and commanding the landward approaches both from Quidi Vidi and from town.

The hectic pace continued in 1798 when work commenced on a stone powder magazine between Duke of York's Battery and Ladies' Lookout.[69] The magazine was essential to the fulfillment of Signal Hill's role as a citadel, since no fortification could withstand a siege without a powder supply for its guns. Nor could there be a citadel without quarters for the garrison, but as yet the only barracks on Signal Hill were for officers, a sign of where the army's priorities always lay. There was some space for the men in the guardhouses at the various batteries, but this was seen as a stopgap until proper barracks could be

---

[66] Webber, *Documents*, Crew to Mackenzie, 12 April 1799.

[67] TNA:PRO, C. O. 194, Vol. 39, fols. 253-55, "State of the Fortifications and Buildings, at St. John's, in the Island of Newfoundland," 20 Oct. 1797.

[68] TNA:PRO, C. O. 194, Vol. 39, fols. 253-55, "State of the Fortifications and Buildings, at St. John's, in the Island of Newfoundland," 20 Oct. 1797.

[69] TNA:PRO, C. O. 194, Vol.40, fols. 204-06, "State of the Fortifications and Buildings at St [sic] John's in the Island of Newfoundland," 19 Oct. 1798.

built.[70] To compound matters, a fire at Fort William in March destroyed the officers' barracks and a portion of the soldiers' barracks there.[71] It was with some urgency, then, that construction began that same summer on a new barracks for seventy-two men near the southeastern face of Ladies' Lookout. Before it was finished the following year, orders were issued for a second with the same capacity and in the same vicinity, which was completed in 1800.[72] Skinner also added yet another Narrows defence during the 1798 season. Situated beneath Wallace's Battery at an elevation of 41 metres, it was named Waldegrave (or Waldegrave's) Battery, possibly as a sop to the governor, with whom Skinner waged a running feud over command issues.[73] Waldegrave Battery was at least one too many for The Narrows, and no others would be built there. (On the summit, the saturation point came in

A View of the Entrance of St. John's Newfoundland.

Fig. 22: "A View of the Entrance of St. John's Newfoundland," by the Reverend J. Hall, 1802. Source: Courtesy of the Centre for Newfoundland Studies, Memorial University Libraries. Waldegrave Battery is at the far left.

---

[70] TNA:PRO, War Office 55 (hereafter W. O. 55) (Ordnance Office: Miscellanea), Vol. 857, fols. 289-90, "Memoranda taken from Mr. Martins [sic] Report of the State of the Barracks at St. John's in the Island of Newfoundland March 1799," enclosure in Crewe to Morse, 18 March 1799.

[71] Webber, *Skinner's Fencibles*, pp. 50-51.

[72] TNA:PRO, W. O. 55, Vol. 857, fols. 289-90, "Memoranda taken from Mr. Martins [sic] Report of the State of the Barracks at St. John's in the Island of Newfoundland March 1799," enclosure in Crewe to Morse, 18 March 1799; TNA:PRO, C. O. 194, Vol. 42, "State of the Fortifications and Buildings at St[sic] John's Newfoundland," 20 Oct. 1800.

[73] *DCB*, Vol. 5, "Skinner, Thomas."

1802 with the appearance of two circular batteries that faced toward St. John's, in keeping with the citadel concept.)[74]

The pace slowed noticeably after 1800, with human factors as much to blame as natural ones. Although it might appear to be unconnected, a mutiny in the ranks of the Royal Newfoundland Regiment cast a pall over the whole garrison. The mutiny's roots lay in the United Irish Rising (or Irish Rebellion) of 1798, a failed attempt to overthrow English rule in Ireland. Thanks to vigorous wartime traffic in goods and labour between Newfoundland and southern Ireland, the United Irish movement made its way to St. John's, where more than two-thirds of the residents were Irish or of Irish descent.[75] Recruited from among this population, the Royal Newfoundland Regiment was bound to contain United Irish sympathizers, although the Royal Artillery, which was raised elsewhere, also had its share of dissidents. The mutineers' exact motives were never known, but it was widely believed that they intended to kill the regiment's officers along with the town's merchants.[76] That goal seems to have been inspired by the mutineers' hatred of Brigadier-General John Skerrett, a martinet who had succeeded Skinner as commanding officer in 1799, prior to which he had fought against the United Irishmen in Ireland.[77] On the night of 24 April 1800 a Sergeant Kelly and twelve rank and file of the Royal Newfoundland Regiment deserted from Signal Hill, made their way to the rear of Fort Townshend, and rendezvoused with six men of the Royal Artillery. There ought to have been more than that, but the duty officer on Signal Hill, a Captain Tremblett, realized that men were missing and sounded the alarm before the rest could join. Also, Thomas Skinner had been entertaining in his quarters at Fort William, and the comings and goings of his guests made it impossible for sympathizers at that post to get away without being noticed.

Sixteen mutineers were eventually captured, but three, including Sergeant Kelly, got away. Of the captives, five were executed at Fort Townshend (presumably by order of a Regimental Court Martial) and eleven were sent in irons to Halifax to be tried by a General Court Martial. These were sentenced to death by firing squad, but His Royal Highness the Duke of Kent, Commander-in-Chief in North America,

---

[74] TNA:PRO, C. O. 194, Vol. 43, fols. 103-04, "State of the Fortifications at Saint John's Newfoundland," 9 Sept. 1802.
[75] John Mannion, "Transatlantic Disaffection: Wexford and Newfoundland, 1798-1800," *Journal of the Wexford Historical Society*, Vol. 17 (1998-99), p. 32. See also Webber, *Skinner's Fencibles*, pp. 62-68; and Cyril J. Byrne, "The United Irish Rising of 1798 and the Fencibles' Mutiny in St. John's, 1800," *An Nasc*, Vol. 11 (Fall 1998), pp. 15-24.
[76] Nicholson, *The Fighting Newfoundlander*, p. 43.
[77] *DCB*, Vol. 5, "Skerrett, John."

commuted eight of the sentences to life imprisonment. The executions of the other three, which took place on 7 July, were witnessed by men of the Royal Newfoundland Regiment, who had been transferred to Nova Scotia on the duke's orders. They were replaced in St. John's by the 66th Regiment, whose men did not carry the taint of disloyalty. This particular incarnation of the Royal Newfoundland Regiment was disbanded on 31 July 1802, during the lull after the Peace of Amiens (27 March 1802).

After the mutiny Thomas Skinner's name appears much less frequently in the historical record, something that cannot be entirely explained by Skerrett's appointment as commanding officer. Ordered to return to England in 1802, Skinner had not yet reported as of June 1803.[78] The reasons are unknown, but his failure to do so left Skerrett and the Board in the lurch, because it was now too late in the year to name a replacement. This derailed the 1803 construction season, and things went from bad to worse in 1804 when, again for reasons unknown, the new Royal Engineer failed to show. Somewhere along the way the wind had gone out of Thomas Skinner's sails, and it is difficult not to conclude that the mutiny was to blame. The Royal Newfoundland Regiment was his creation, and no father can be expected to feel the same toward his children after they contemplate patricide.

It was not all Skinner's fault. A shortage of carpenters and building materials delayed the completion (until 1806) of a substantial new officers' barracks between the powder magazine and Ladies' Lookout, which was supposed to have been built in 1800 to replace the 1796 officers' barracks.[79] The dearth of skilled labour remained a problem until detachments of the Royal Military Artificers, a corps of tradesmen officered by the Royal Engineers, arrived from England over the course of 1807 and 1808.[80] Even then, however, the engineer establishment needed regular troops to do the grunt work, and this required the cooperation of the officer commanding the troops, who was not inclined to be helpful while the garrison was under-manned.

As the arrival of the artificers proved, there was always a chance that human factors could be overcome. Natural forces were another matter. Because parts of the summit, especially Ladies' Lookout, sloped a bit

---

[78] TNA:PRO, C. O. 194, Vol. 43, fols. 117-18, Skerrett to Gambier (extract), 5 Dec. 1802; and Vol. 43, fol. 305, Morse to Hadden, 11 June 1803.
[79] TNA:PRO, C. O. 194, Vol. 42, "State of the Fortifications and Buildings at St [sic] John's Newfoundland," 20 Oct. 1800; and Vol. 45, fols. 168-69, "Report upon the State of the Fortifications at St [sic] Johns [sic] Newfoundland," 4 Oct. 1806.
[80] T. W. J. Connolly, *History of the Corps of Royal Sappers and Miners* (London, 1855), 2 vols., Vol. 1, p. 158; TNA:PRO, W. O. 55/858, fols. 50-51, Ross to Morse, 2 Aug. 1808.

too gently to the landward, the Board ordered that its western face should be given a uniform vertical height of at least 10.4 metres along its entire length.[81] The scarping (as the process was known) proved easier to conceive than to execute, for the rock was inordinately hard and would bedevil the engineers for years.[82] Then there was the wind, which made even routine jobs difficult, and which, once a building was up, tested it almost daily. Its power was on full display in 1804 when the smaller of the two soldiers' barracks simply blew down, the first of many buildings on Signal Hill to suffer the fate.[83] Even if the rock might eventually be tamed, the wind never would.

As the work stalled, people began to question Skinner's vision. In 1802 there were twenty batteries and 114 cannons in St. John's, distributed over a wide area and needing constant attention.[84] This made it difficult for troops to perform even routine garrison duties, and things grew worse when, after the Peace of Amiens, the 66th Regiment was withdrawn, leaving the garrison with a paltry sixty-three men of the Royal Artillery.[85] An irate Skerrett complained to the Board:

Fig. 23: View of the Summit, ca. 1805. Artistic rendition by Ron Pelley. Source: Sandra Pelley/Parks Canada. In addition to depicting soldiers of the Nova Scotia Regiment of Fencible Infantry, this image shows the stockade and (left to right) the blockhouse, the guardhouse, and one of the circular batteries.

---

[81] TNA:PRO, W. O. 55, Vol. 858, fols. 16-18, Twiss and Nepean to Morse, 29 April 1807.
[82] TNA:PRO, W. O. 55, Vol. 857, fols. 506-08, "State of the Fortifications and Ordnance Buildings at St [sic] Johns [sic] Newfoundland," 24 Oct. 1803.
[83] Webber, *Documents*, Gower to Chatham, 19 Nov. 1804.
[84] TNA:PRO, C. O. 194, Vol. 43, fols. 117-18, Skerrett to Gambier [extract], 5 Dec. 1802.
[85] TNA:PRO, C. O. 194, Vol. 43, fols. 153-54, Gambier to Hobart, 21 May 1803.

"There has certainly too much money been burried [sic] in Fortifications here, and… an intelligent Engineer would demolish every thing that is useless—our Force being so very small we could not protect them, or keep possession of them."[86] Unwilling to wait, Skerrett began to recruit a new Royal Newfoundland Regiment of Fencible Infantry, which numbered 564 men by July 1805, when, however, the entire unit was transferred to Nova Scotia in exchange for 399 men of the Nova Scotia Regiment of Fencible Infantry.[87] Skerrett and Governor Erasmus Gower agreed that it would take "at least two thousand men" for the defences to be properly manned and to do justice to the commercial importance of St. John's, through which, according to Gower, two-thirds of Newfoundland's imports now passed.[88] Their hankering for more bodies was also motivated by a desire to put some of them in Bay Bulls and Torbay to prevent enemy landings, a historic vulnerability that had gotten lost in Skinner's infatuation with the hill. New Commanding Royal Engineer Captain George Ross picked up on this theme and was even more adamant about it, advising the Board that the harbour and The Narrows were so well guarded "and its entrance requiring so many favourable circumstances of weather, that an enemy can scarcely be supposed rash enough to dare the attempt," from which he concluded that the enemy would have no choice but to land elsewhere.[89] Accordingly, he felt that batteries for Bay Bulls and Torbay should be the new priorities.

Disappointingly for the critics, Skinner had spun his web all too well. Board members mulled over the complaints and found no reason to change course, deciding that even if an enemy captured the town from the landward, he would be unable to bring ships into the harbour or to occupy the town so long as Signal Hill and The Narrows remained in British hands.[90] As if to reinforce the point (but also to prevent civilian encroachments), in October 1807 Governor John Holloway granted the greater part (130 hectares) of the Signal Hill Peninsula to the Master-General of the Board of Ordnance and forbade the erection of private buildings within its limits.[91] This, however, was about the extent of what happened on Signal Hill for awhile. Forts

---

[86] TNA:PRO, W. O. 55, Vol. 857, fols. 381-85, Skerrett to Crewe, 2 May 1803.
[87] TNA:PRO, C. O. 194, Vol. 44, fols. 119-23, Gower to Cambden, 18 July 1805.
[88] TNA:PRO, C. O. 194, Vol. 44, fols. 119-23, Gower to Cambden, 18 July 1805.
[89] TNA:PRO, C. O. 194, Vol. 44, fols. 146-57, "Report upon the defences of St. Johns [sic] Newfoundland," 13 July 1805.
[90] TNA:PRO, W. O. 55, Vol. 858, fols. 16-18, Twiss and Nepean to Morse, 29 April 1807.
[91] *Royal Gazette and Newfoundland Advertiser*, 5 Nov. 1807, p. 4, enclosure in TNA:PRO, W. O. 44 (Ordnance Office: In-Letters), Vol. 153, fol. 127.

William and Townshend, which had been retained for their barracks and storage facilities but whose defences had gone to ruin, suddenly began receiving attention.[92] Conversely, several of the works on the peninsula, notably Quidi Vidi Pass and Queen's batteries, were getting run down; the summit stockade, never intended as anything more than a stopgap, was decaying; and salt air was rusting out the bores of the iron guns.[93] With things in such a state, in 1808 the Board appointed a committee of engineers to re-evaluate the citadel project and to recommend a new scheme for its completion.[94]

The committee's report was long on generalities and short on details, which it nonchalantly allowed would be worked out later by "the officer on the spot."[95] Nonetheless, it proposed a scheme more elaborate than anything envisioned by Thomas Skinner, and he was a starry-eyed dreamer. The committee's chief recommendation was for a new configuration (or "line," in military parlance) to embrace the summit works, something that would entail even more scarping than what had already been planned. The line itself was to be a grand affair containing a new masonry wall topped by a masonry parapet. After giving the committee's report more consideration than it deserved, the Board decided to entrust the job to an experienced officer, whose first order of business would be the preparation of detailed plans and estimates to bring the committee's conceptual musings into the real world.

Remaining in St. John's until his successor (Elias Walker Durnford) arrived in the summer of 1809, Ross deferred as much of the work as possible, informing the Board in his final report that "the line of new works pointed out by the Committee of Engineers at home, has only been marked upon the ground—but not commenced on by the Miners—Those have principally, therefore, been engaged in excavating flats on the east side of the hill to receive the necessary buildings for the post—and in repairing roads."[96] Elsewhere the only major development was reconstruction of the sea wall at Amherst Battery (formerly Amherst's Tower), the first step in a badly needed overhaul of the position. Ross, who would die in 1813 during the siege

---

[92] Webber, *Documents*, "Report upon the State of the Fortifications at St. John's, Newfoundland," 4 Oct. 1806.

[93] TNA:PRO, W. O. 55, Vol. 858, fols. 4-5, Payne to Principal Officers of His Majesty's Ordnance, 20 July 1806.

[94] TNA:PRO, C. O. 194, Vol. 47, fols. 84-86, "Report upon the State of the fortifications at St. John's Newfoundland," 21 Oct. 1808.

[95] TNA:PRO, W. O. 55, Vol. 857, fols. 524-27, Board of Ordnance to Morse, 15 March 1808.

[96] TNA:PRO, C. O. 194, Vol. 47, fols. 84-86, "Report upon the State of the fortifications at St. John's Newfoundland," 21 Oct. 1808.

of San Sebastian, would be remembered in St. John's. At his suggestion, eighteen men of the Royal Military Artificers (masons, miners, carpenters, blacksmiths, and the like) who arrived in 1808, many with families in tow, erected a dozen huts as "temporary" living quarters in the valley between the summit and North Head, which was thereafter known as Ross's Valley.[97] The decline to the valley was so steep that it had once been deemed a natural defence against attack from that direction; now an enemy could take the same path that the artificers trod on their way to work.

Thirty-five-year-old Captain (soon to be Lieutenant-Colonel) Elias Walker Durnford was a man in a hurry. His early career had been marred by capture and imprisonment in Guadeloupe and France, and he gave every impression afterward of wanting to make up the lost time.[98] A new awareness of time was also very much in the air, for the Industrial Revolution had brought a modern emphasis on clock time as a means of imposing discipline on factory workers, whose lives had traditionally been attuned to the seasons, the tides, or some other of earth's natural rhythms.[99] Whatever the source, time was an obsession for Durnford, as demonstrated by his efforts to persuade the Board to send him a clock "to regulate the working Hours" on Signal Hill.[100] In a sign of chaos to come, the Board shipped the clock but refused to approve Durnford's estimate for a building to house it. Five years later an exasperated Board demanded its return.[101]

The messiness with the clock was also evident elsewhere. The committee of engineers had explicitly stated that the local man must work out the details of the summit's redevelopment, but Durnford had the mistaken impression that a comprehensive plan would be coming from London. Until he got that, he felt it would be "imprudent" to do anything on the summit besides continuing to scarp the northwest face, the only job for which he claimed to have received specific instructions. Thus he expended his energies elsewhere in 1809: Fort Townshend, where he repaired the powder magazine and erected a new building for the Royal Artillery; Fort William, where the big priority was a new kitchen for Skerrett's replacement, Major-General

---

[97] Connolly, *History of the Corps of Royal Sappers and Miners*, Vol. 1, p. 158; Webber, *Documents*, "Barracks Signal Hill," 20 Sept. 1811.
[98] Mary Durnford (ed.), *Family Recollections of Lieut. General Elias Walker Durnford, a Colonel Commandant of the Corps of Royal Engineers* (Montreal, 1863), p. 41. Durnford was imprisoned from October 1794 to July 1796.
[99] E. P. Thompson, "Time, Work-Discipline, and Industrial Capitalism," *Past and Present*, Vol. 38, No. 1 (1967), pp. 56-97.
[100] TNA:PRO, W. O. 55, Vol. 858, fols. 72-74, Durnford to Morse, 11 Sept. 1809.
[101] TNA:PRO, W. O. 44, Vol. 153, fol. 17, Hogan to Crew, 9 July 1814.

Francis Moore; and Amherst Battery, which he improved so much that within two years people had taken to calling it Fort Amherst.[102]

That fall Durnford did what he ought to have done sooner: he wrote a detailed proposal that caught the gist of the committee's report while putting some meat on its rickety bones. Mailed before the end of the year, the proposal failed to elicit a response from the Board during the whole of 1810. Durnford, who had only begun to be stubborn, kept up the scarping, grumbling, however, that "the rock in its nature is hard and its Strata [is] so remarkably cross and confused."[103] The sappers increasingly resorted to gunpowder in their war against Nature, and in so doing made their work more dangerous. One day as Durnford was walking toward the summit accompanied by his son, a charge exploded and ejected a sapper's lifeless body above the telltale cloud of smoke and dust.[104] Durnford saw no point in tackling the summit batteries, "as they must be demolished in order to carry into effect, either the Committee's Line of Defence, or those I had the honor to recommend myself last year...." The upside was that many of the detached works—that is, works outside the summit—including

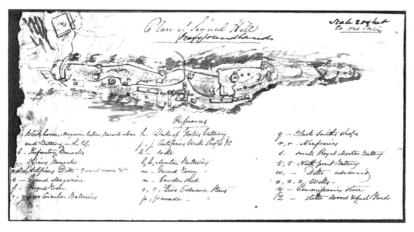

Fig. 24: "Plan of Signal Hill, Newfoundland," ca. 1811. Source: Courtesy of the Centre for Newfoundland Studies, Memorial University Libraries. The recently completed artificers' workshops appear in the top left of this plan, which was probably drawn by Elias Walker Durnford.

---

[102] TNA:PRO, C. O. 194, Vol. 48, "Report upon the State of the Fortifications at St. Johns [sic] Newfoundland," 19 Oct. 1809; *Royal Gazette and Newfoundland Advertiser*, 24 Oct. 1811, p. 1.

[103] TNA:PRO, C. O. 194, Vol. 49, fols. 106-11, "A Report on the present State of the Fortifications at St. Johns [sic] Newfoundland," 16 Oct. 1810.

[104] Durnford, *Family Recollections*, p. 67.

Queen's, Waldegrave, and Quidi Vidi batteries, got some much-needed attention. And so it went again in 1811, by which time a complex of artificers' workshops and related buildings had taken shape in the relatively flat area between the summit and Queen's Battery, which was about the most hospitable ground on the peninsula. Other than the scarping, the only sign that the summit project was still alive was a prodigious amount of building stone that had been stockpiled on the south side of The Narrows, 180 tonnes of it imported from a Cape Breton quarry and another seventy tonnes from the ruins of Louisbourg.[105]

Changing tack again, Durnford submitted a modified scheme to the Board in the fall of 1811 proposing to do away altogether with the summit batteries and to replace them with a martello tower on Ladies' Lookout, the tower to be complemented by casemated barracks and storehouses within the new defensive line. Inspired by a circular stone tower at Mortella Point, Corsica—misspelled "martello" in contemporary British dispatches and called such ever since—martello towers had become the darlings of the Royal Engineers, who built 103 of them in southeast England between 1805 and 1812 and exported the concept to the farthest reaches of the empire.[106] Durnford intended not merely to bring St. John's into the martello tower family but to place it at the head, for the tower he had in mind would be the biggest in the world if it were built. He had heard nothing, however, by late July of 1812, when word reached St. John's that the United States had declared war against Britain.

The War of 1812 had several causes: the Royal Navy's seizure of American vessels carrying trade goods to France; the Royal Navy's impressment, on the high seas, of real and alleged British nationals serving in the United States Navy and merchant marine; and American resentment of British support for North American First Nations who were hindering the westward spread of white settlement.[107] With the Royal Navy reigning supreme on the east coast from its bases in Halifax and Bermuda, most of the fighting in British North America was confined to Upper and Lower Canada (as Ontario and Quebec were then known), with assistance from the Newfoundland, New Brunswick, and Nova Scotia fencible regiments, and volunteers from Prince Edward Island. Although American privateers captured twenty

---

[105] TNA:PRO, C. O. 194, Vol. 50, fols. 382-87, "A Report on the present State of the Fortifications of St. Johns [sic] Newfoundland," 16 Oct. 1811.
[106] The standard text is W. H. Clements, *Towers of Strength: Martello Towers Worldwide* (Barnsley, 2000).
[107] Donald R. Hickey, *The War of 1812: A Forgotten Conflict* (Chicago, 1989), pp. 5-28.

Newfoundland fishing vessels in 1813, the reinforcement of the Royal Navy's Newfoundland station ended the problem for the rest of the war.[108] That knowledge, however, lay in the future. In St. John's the war's outbreak sparked rumours that a French fleet was on its way to North America.[109] Based on Newfoundland's prior experiences, French designs, whether real or imagined, were sure to get attention, and they immediately got that of Major-General Moore and Governor Sir John Duckworth, who pressured Durnford into reviving both the Fort Townshend Grand Sea Battery and the Fort William Narrows Battery.[110] This directly contravened the Board's long-standing directions, to which Duckworth in particular had been opposed from the start. Durnford also hurried the reconstruction of Chain Rock and Frederick's batteries, which he had started the previous year, and in the process dipped into the stone reserved for the citadel project. Not that the latter was dead, for by mid-October Durnford had received orders to submit detailed financial estimates based on his proposal of the previous year.

Sensing a breakthrough, Durnford allowed himself to hope for definitive orders in 1813. Although those orders were actually issued in triplicate in London, enemy vessels captured both the May and June transatlantic mail packets, and the third copy must have been retained for filing, because no other papers bearing on the subject ever found their way into Durnford's hands.[111] Fate had thus conspired with Nature and bureaucratic inertia to impede the project's completion. As usual, bad tidings for Signal Hill meant good things elsewhere, and by the end of 1813 the Narrows batteries were all in top shape.[112] The three 32-pounders at Chain Rock Battery constituted its strongest armament to date; with an effective range of about 1,800 metres, these guns would have had a murderous effect on an enemy ship in The Narrows. Bowing to pressure from Moore and Duckworth's successor, Sir Richard Keats, Durnford also addressed another familiar concern by placing a couple of two-gun field batteries along the road between St. John's and Petty Harbour, over which an enemy advancing from Bay Bulls would have to pass. This had been preceded by a "Signal House and staff" at Red Head, 6.4 kilometres north of St. John's, an outward

---

[108] Glenn Keough, "Economic Factors and Privateering at Newfoundland during the War of 1812" (Unpublished MA Thesis, University of New Brunswick, 1995), pp. 88-89.
[109] TNA:PRO, W. O. 55, Vol. 859, Moore and Duckworth to Durnford, 27 July 1812.
[110] TNA:PRO, C. O. 194, Vol. 52, fols. 110-12, "A Report on the present State of the Fortifications at St. John's," 12 Oct. 1812.
[111] TNA:PRO, W. O. 44, Vol. 152, fols. 117-19, Mann to Crew, 2 April 1814.
[112] TNA:PRO, C. O. 194,Vol. 54, fols. 176-78, "A Report on the State of the Fortifications at St. Johns [sic] Newfoundland," 15 Oct. 1813.

extension of the signalling system which, however, does not seem to have survived the war.[113] Everything old was becoming new again, including at Fort William, where a substantial new barracks for officers and three hundred men was well under way by mid-October, to be completed the following year. This was not a good omen for the citadel, which as Elias Durnford knew full well was a signature project that could make his professional reputation. Frustrated by the endless delays and tired of serving too many masters, he sought permission to return to England to sort out once and for all the priorities for St. John's.

Durnford's request was ignored, but the dam finally seemed to break in 1814 when he got orders to begin the martello tower. By then, however, he faced an obstacle that all but brought the project back to square one. For several years he had had at his disposal a small army of skilled workmen recruited for the summit development, among them thirty-two masons and stonecutters who had come out from Ireland in 1810. But by 1814 the Irishmen had been laid off because of inactivity, leaving only a single company of the Royal Sappers and Miners (formerly the Royal Military Artificers), whose ranks were not only depleted, but also "deficient in the quality of the workmen most particularly requisite for prosecuting such works Viz. Carpenters and Masons."[114] Nor could he employ civilian workers to make up the difference, because high wartime wages in St. John's made that option too expensive. He was paralyzed again.

Although Durnford levelled the blockhouse in 1815 to make way for the tower, the Board reversed itself and withheld funding so that the surveyor-general could give the project, already studied to death, another look. In the meantime Durnford erected a new blockhouse between the powder magazine and Duke of York's Battery, in the process shifting the signalling function from the highest point on the north side of The Narrows—and thus its most logical site—to an elevation six metres lower. This permanently altered the cultural landscape of Signal Hill and St. John's, for all subsequent blockhouses and signal stations would be built on or near the site that Durnford chose. He also saw to a long overdue rebuilding of the stockade, even though this feature, which from the beginning was seen as a short-term substitute for masonry walls, was unlikely to withstand any kind of artillery bombardment, thereby making a mockery of the whole citadel concept.

---

[113] Webber, *Documents*, Durnford to Duckworth and Moore, 7 Sept. 1812.
[114] Webber, *Documents*, Signal Hill General, 30 Sept. 1814.

The martello tower was still in limbo in May 1816 when Durnford left for Quebec, where by overseeing construction of its citadel he found the professional fame that eluded him in St. John's. His successor, Lieutenant-Colonel Richard Vicars, received detailed plans for the tower and even laid the foundation in hopes of finishing the job in 1817. By then, however, the tower had become a casualty of the postwar spending cuts that affected the entire British Army. Not long after, on 6 February 1818, Thomas Skinner passed away in France, trailing his dream into the grave.

A Mighty Fondness for Flags

"One of the prevailing signs of the place, at least in St. John's, is a mighty fondness for flags...." Sir Richard Henry Bonnycastle, *Newfoundland in 1842: A Sequel to "The Canadas in 1841"* (London, 1842)

CHANGING OF THE GUARD

The war years were ones of profound change in Europe and North America. The Industrial Revolution spread rapidly in Britain, which by 1815 was the world's most industrialized nation. During the course of this transition, many West Country merchants turned their backs on Newfoundland in order to invest in manufacturing, and many fishermen abandoned their boats to take jobs in factories. Other merchants continued the trend, now greatly accelerated, of withdrawing from fishing in order to focus on the supply trade, leaving the fishing to residents.[1] These developments, together with the usual wartime factors of impressment and threats to shipping, virtually destroyed the migratory fishery. Although it would slightly recover after 1815, it died out in the 1840s, not to be resurrected until British factory freezer trawlers, as if making up for lost time, began to pillage the Grand Banks in the 1950s.

The contrast between Britain and France was pronounced. Defeated in war and behind in industrial development, France faced a long and difficult recovery. The Newfoundland fisheries had a role in that recovery, since they continued to be seen as a building block for the navy.[2] Fuelled by a generous bounty system, the French fisheries roared back to life; by 1830 there were over 10,000 fishermen on the treaty shore and another 2,000 on the Grand Banks.[3] Settlement resumed in St. Pierre and Miquelon, which became integral to the migratory fishery as a place for drying and transhipping fish, and for obtaining bait. Much of the bait came from Newfoundlanders who

---

[1] John Mannion, Gordon Handcock, and Alan Macpherson, "The Newfoundland Fishery, 18th Century," in R. Cole Harris (ed.) *Historical Atlas of Canada: Volume I: From the Beginning to 1800* (Toronto, 1987), Plate 25.
[2] Arthur Girault, *The Colonial Tariff Policy of France* (Oxford, 1916), p. 52; Frederic F. Thompson, *The French Shore Problem in Newfoundland: An Imperial Study* (Toronto, 1961), pp. 18-30.
[3] Peter Neary, "The French and American Shore Questions as Factors in Newfoundland History," in James K. Hiller and Peter Neary (eds.), *Newfoundland in the Nineteenth and Twentieth Centuries: Essays in Interpretation* (Toronto, 1980), p. 113.

Fig. 25: French Fishing Station, Cap Rouge, Newfoundland, ca. 1860. Source: Library and Archives Canada/NL21827. Opposition to French fishing rights in coastal Newfoundland was a cornerstone of early Newfoundland nationalism.

lived on the south coast, and for whom the French islands became a welcome and profitable gateway for contraband Caribbean rum.[4] Under these various stimuli St. Pierre's population nearly tripled between 1820 and 1848 (from 800 to 2,130).[5]

In Newfoundland itself the wartime struggles of the British migratory fishery and the prolonged suspension of the French fisheries had triggered an unprecedented economic and demographic boom. The resident population stood at roughly 20,000 by 1815, of whom half (10,018) lived in St. John's, a dirty, rowdy, congested town where the fisheries, while still the largest employer, had been surpassed in overall economic importance by fishery-based commerce.[6] Buoyed by near-monopoly conditions in markets because of the wartime absence of French and American competition, Newfoundland exported 1,182,661 quintals of saltfish in 1815, a record that would

---

[4] For a popular account of this rum trade in a later period, see J. P. Andrieux, *Rum-runners: The Smugglers from St. Pierre and Miquelon and the Burin Peninsula from Prohibition to Present Day* (St. John's, 2009).

[5] Harold A. Innis, *The Cod Fisheries: The History of an International Economy* (Toronto, 1954), p. 378.

[6] Handcock, *Origins of English Settlement*, pp. 96-98; Macpherson, "Demographic History of St. John's," p. 10.

stand until 1856.[7] The rise of the seal hunt and the Labrador fishery ensured further economic growth in the postwar era. The waning demographic importance of St. John's—in 1836 its 14,946 residents accounted for twenty percent of the total population of 73,705—was offset by the iron grip of the city's merchants, for St. John's, London, and Liverpool had replaced the West Country as the fulcrum of Newfoundland's economic life.

These developments made further opposition to settlement redundant. In 1817 the governor became a year-round resident, and in 1824 Newfoundland gained colonial status, signifying rule by governor and appointed council. Eight years later it won representative government—that is, government that included an elected assembly— which neighbouring Nova Scotia had enjoyed since 1758. Newfoundlanders took to politics like ducks to water, and in tough economic times their assemblymen could be counted on to blame the French, whether they had anything to do with it or not. Cutting through class, ethnic, and religious differences, Francophobia became the cornerstone of an emerging Newfoundland national identity, which by definition required something on which large numbers of people could find common political ground.[8] There was nothing unique about this, as fear and loathing of the "Other" were hallmarks of national identities everywhere, including Britain, where Francophobia also fit the bill.[9] When, in 1857, Britain concluded a draft convention with France that would have reserved parts of the treaty shore exclusively for French fishermen, the Newfoundland government objected so strongly that the British abandoned the deal. Colonial Secretary Henry Labouchere's assurance to Governor Sir Charles Darling that "the consent of the community of Newfoundland is regarded by Her Majesty's Government as the essential preliminary to any modification of their territorial or maritime rights" became the local Magna Carta.[10] Nonetheless, French treaty rights persisted,

---

[7] Shannon Ryan, *Fish Out of Water: The Newfoundland Saltfish Trade 1814-1914* (St. John's, 1986), pp. 258-59.

[8] Neary, "The French and American Shore Questions," pp. 117-18. It almost goes without saying that Francophobia was not universal. It was strongest in St. John's and weakest in those parts of the island where the French presence brought social and economic advantages. My treatment of national identity stems from Benedict Anderson's definition of a nation as "an imagined political community—and imagined as both inherently limited and sovereign." See his *Imagined Communities: Reflections on the Origin and Spread of Nationalism* (New York, 1996 [revised edition]), p. 6.

[9] Anderson, *Imagined Communities*, p. 141; Linda Colley, *Britons: Forging the Nation 1707-1837* (New Haven, CT, 1992); François Crouzet, "The Second Hundred Years War: Some Reflections," *French History*, Vol. 10, No. 4 (Dec. 1996), p. 448.

[10] Cited in Gertrude Gunn, *The Political History of Newfoundland 1832-1864* (Toronto, 1966), pp. 145-46.

complicating economic and demographic growth in the region, and preventing Newfoundlanders from becoming masters of their own house.

Despite the transfer of the remnants of the Placentia garrison to St. John's in 1811, the demise of the British migratory fishery undermined Newfoundland's historic role as a training ground for the Royal Navy, and thus adversely affected its strategic value. Halifax and Bermuda, both of which had been bases for naval operations against the United States during the War of 1812, overshadowed it as regional strategic factors.[11] The new reality was driven home in 1824 when the Royal Navy decided to discontinue its Newfoundland station and to place the island under the command of the senior naval officer of the North America and West Indies station, who spent summers in Halifax and winters in Bermuda.[12] Thereafter the navy's presence in Newfoundland consisted of the one or two warships that were sent

Fig. 26: "View of the Entrance of St. John's Harbour, Newfoundland. From Fort Townshend," by P. C. Le Geyt, 1823. Source: © National Maritime Museum, Greenwich, London. This charming lithograph is evocative of many things. As shown by the laundry on Fort Townshend's dilapidated fence, military preparedness is not one of them.

---

[11] C. P. Stacey, "Halifax as an International Strategic Factor, 1749-1949," *Canadian Historical Association: Annual Reports*, Vol. 28, No. 1 (1949), p. 50.
[12] *Flag Officers and Senior Naval Officers Responsible for the Halifax Station 1755-1959* (Ottawa, 1959), p. 58. Despite the restructuring, the local Naval Office continued to function until 5 January 1826. See TRPAD, "Abstract of the Net Revenue and Expenditure, of the Island of Newfoundland for the Year 1825" (Blue Book), p. 65.

each summer from Halifax to patrol the treaty shore, a mostly routine affair broken by the occasional side trip to St. John's for some heavy socializing, which oddly enough tended to coincide with the city's annual regatta. Long an afterthought to the navy where Newfoundland was concerned, the British Army was cast in a new role as the colony's main imperial force. But the St. John's garrison was part of the Nova Scotia command, and local officials were subservient to the Lieutenant-General or Major-General Commanding in Halifax. Also, the postwar years were a time of stagnation in the army, and this was compounded in Newfoundland's case by the fact that veterans' regiments, comprised of older men and cast-offs from regiments of the line, made up the bulk of the garrison. The lapsing of the Newfoundland station and the secondary status of the St. John's garrison reflected the island's diminished role in imperial eyes.

ONCE MORE WITH FEELING

The expression *Pax Britannica* was coined near the end of the nineteenth century to describe the period after 1815 when the Royal Navy ruled the waves and the British empire became the largest and most powerful the world had ever known.[13] Mighty Britain nonetheless had to tread carefully in its dealings with the United States, where the War of 1812 fostered self-confidence and a desire to expand both the nation's influence and its territorial limits.[14] Newfoundlanders directly felt the effects, for one of the war's legacies was an agreement (the Convention of 1818) recognizing the liberty of American fishermen to catch and dry fish on the coast of Labrador and on Newfoundland's west and southwest coasts. Although American exploitation of herring stocks in Newfoundland waters would not begin in earnest until after mid-century, by 1820 there were an estimated 530 American fishing vessels with crews of 5,830 men in the Gulf of St. Lawrence and along the Labrador coast.[15] The fisheries therefore had the potential to put Newfoundland in the middle of any future tensions between Britain and the United States, and these were not long in coming.

In 1823 talk of a possible joint effort by France and Spain to reassert Spanish control over its former Latin American colonies set off alarm bells in London and Washington. That December, President

[13] Kennedy, *Rise and Fall of British Naval Mastery*, chapter 6.
[14] Hickey, *The War of 1812*, pp. 303-09.
[15] G. Brown Goode and J. W. Collins, "The Labrador and Gulf of St. Lawrence Cod Fisheries," in G. Brown Goode *et al.* (eds.), *The Fisheries and Fishery Industries of the United States* (Washington, 1887), Section V, Vol. I, p. 133.

James Monroe announced that the United States would regard any European recolonization of the Americas as a hostile act. By essentially declaring Europe and the Americas to be separate spheres of influence, the Monroe Doctrine (as it later came to be known) added to Britain's initial concerns about France and Spain, and raised new fears about British North America's ability to counter an American attack. A concerned Duke of Wellington, now Master-General of the Board of Ordnance, appointed a commission under Waterloo veteran Major-General Sir James Carmichael Smyth to review British North America's defences. Submitted in September 1825, the Carmichael Smyth report proposed extensive new works for Halifax, Montreal, Kingston, and the Niagara frontier; road development in New Brunswick (to facilitate the transportation of troops to the Canadas during winter, when ice made the Gulf of St. Lawrence impassable); and completion of the Ottawa and Rideau canals.[16] Since the commissioners did not have time to visit Newfoundland, Wellington subsequently ordered the Commanding Royal Engineer in Halifax, Lieutenant-Colonel Gustavus Nicolls, to proceed to St. John's, study the ground, and recommend a new defence system. And so the stage was set for another Royal Engineer to fall in love with Signal Hill.

Submitted in 1827, the Nicolls report contained an overview of where things currently stood and also gave direction for the future.[17] Although Wallace's Battery had virtually gone to seed (only a wooden barracks remained), the rest of the Narrows defences and Quidi Vidi Battery were all in reasonable shape thanks to their renewal in the recent wars. Nicolls confessed to some initial reservations about the effectiveness of Queen's Battery as a Narrows defence because of its height, but a demonstration with howitzers and case shot persuaded him that it would be effective against enemy ships in The Narrows, and he also felt it might come in handy against an enemy on the south side. He was less optimistic about the town forts. At Fort William "the Mounds shewing where the Ramparts have been, and the excavations of the Ditches, are the only remains of the Defences...." Nonetheless, the north barracks (presumably the one erected in 1813-14) was in "pretty good order," housing forty-eight men of the Royal Newfoundland Veteran Companies. Although the old south barracks

---

[16] Kenneth Bourne, *Britain and the Balance of Power in North America 1815-1908* (London, 1967), pp. 38-39; Hitsman, *Safeguarding Canada*, pp. 120-23.

[17] LAC, R3607-0-6-E (Gustavus Nicolls Papers), F23, Vol. 2, "Report to the Most Noble the Marquis of Anglesey ... Relative to the State of the Fortifications and Public Buildings at St. John's Newfoundland, and upon the System of Defense on that Station," 25 Aug. 1827.

had been condemned, it continued to be occupied by a handful of veterans and civilian artificers. Fort Townshend had fallen so far that Nicolls barely mentioned it except to note that its two barracks were still occupied, the best one by the Royal Artillery, and the other, which was rat-infested, by veterans and artificers.

The presence of so many personnel in the town forts spoke to the general abandonment of Signal Hill as a military position. Nicolls found the artificers' complex vacant but in decent shape, as were an adjoining armoury and armourer's shop that had previously been part of the artificers' complex, but which had been converted to armoury purposes in either 1814 or 1815.[18] On the summit the officers' and soldiers' barracks were "in pretty good condition" despite their wooden construction, and had been appropriated as hospitals for the veterans. All that remained of the once elaborate defences were the blockhouse and eight scattered mortars, seven of them on wooden platforms that had rotted away. Nicolls's assessment of the stockade— "entirely gone in some parts, and the remainder decaying fast"—was an apt characterization of the summit as a whole.

Fig. 27: "The Town and Harbour of St. John's," 1831. Source: Library and Archives Canada/Credit: William Eagar/C-003371. The armoury/artificers' complex occupies the centre foreground, with Queen's Battery to its immediate left, overlooking The Narrows.

---

[18] TNA:PRO, W. O. 44, Vol. 209, fols. 5-6, Respective Officers to Byham, 20 Sept. 1832.

Although Signal Hill had fallen on hard times, Nicolls proceeded to make it the focal point of his grandiose scheme for the future defence of St. John's. It was grandiose because he recommended the erection of seven martello towers on the Signal Hill Peninsula, one at each end of the summit, which was to be enclosed by an *enceinte* (masonry wall), and five more in a roughly semi-circular line extending across the neck of the peninsula from Quidi Vidi Lake to Waldegrave Battery. As before, the intention was to render Signal Hill a citadel. Completion of the towers and other essential components, such as casemated barracks on the summit, would spell the end of Forts William and Townshend, which Nicolls advised should be phased out and their men and resources concentrated on Signal Hill as soon as the new facilities were completed there. He also urged the abandonment of Fort Amherst and Frederick's Battery on grounds that they were likely to fall easily to a land force coming from the south. To replace them, a new fort or an additional martello tower could be erected on North Head, covering not only The Narrows, but also part of Freshwater Bay, currently a blind spot from Fort Amherst. (This was a moot point, since if Freshwater Bay had been suitable for landing purposes—and it was not—it would have been used long ago.)[19]

Aware that the cost to implement his scheme (£102,500) was steep, Nicolls identified at least one way to contain expenses: stone for the project could be quarried on Signal Hill. Regardless of how hard the stone was—and Nicolls was under no illusions on the point—it would be cheaper than paying cartage fees to bring stone from the town's main quarry, then located near Fort Amherst. The Gibbet Hill quarry would prove to be one of Nicolls's many legacies.

Four years would pass between the submission of Nicolls's report and a decision on its recommendations. The main stumbling block was the commencement of work in 1827 on a massive new governor's residence—and, at a cost of nearly £40,000, a massively expensive one—on The Barrens between Forts William and Townshend. This was, incidentally, the first major building to incorporate stone from the Gibbet Hill quarry. Because Government House took so long to finish, it ate up the lion's share of money allotted to Newfoundland for military purposes in the period.[20] Eager to please Governor Sir Thomas Cochrane, the engineers let even routine maintenance slide, with predictable results. Some buildings, among them Queen's Battery

---

[19] I am grateful to Don Parsons for this insight.
[20] King, "History of the Rocks and Scenery in and near Signal Hill National Historic Park," p. 7.

barracks, were so neglected that they had to be torn down, and matters were compounded on Signal Hill by a remorseless Nature. In July 1831 a bolt of lightning shivered the signal mast at the blockhouse, split the ceiling of the corporal's room below the deck, and "stunned the Corporal & his wife."[21]

In December 1831, with Cochrane finally settling into Government House, the Board of Ordnance was able to pronounce on the Nicolls report. It ordered the immediate evacuation of the dilapidated south barracks at Fort William and the transfer of its occupants to Signal Hill and Fort Townshend.[22] This was to be merely a respite for Fort Townshend, because the Board simultaneously approved Nicolls's recommendation to concentrate everything on the hill "as the present Military Works and Buildings become unserviceable." The Board had thus embraced a gradual approach in order to spread out the cost. Concentration became the order of the day and found its first devotee in the person of Commanding Royal Engineer Lieutenant-Colonel John Oldfield, who rode roughshod over civilian concerns that the removal of the troops to Signal Hill would reduce their availability to fight fires and maintain civil order, roles in which the community had come to rely heavily on military personnel.

Alas for Oldfield and his successors, the task of making Signal Hill a citadel would prove as Sisyphean as it had for Skinner and the rest, although as usual with the Royal Engineers it was not for lack of trying. A masonry barracks was built at Queen's Battery during 1832 and 1833 as part of an overhaul that included new guns and platforms. By March 1833 the two veterans' hospitals on the summit had been converted back into officers' and soldiers' barracks.[23] Owing to the presence among the veterans of greater numbers of married men than army regulations normally allowed, room had to be found not only for 337 men (as of June 1832), but also for 91 women and 220 children. Signal Hill could not yet accommodate that many bodies, and until it could the town forts would still have a role to play. Moreover, the summit facilities were old, with the officers' barracks dating from 1806 and the soldiers' from 1799 or 1800. Oldfield therefore decided to replace them with a new masonry barracks for officers and men, on which work began in 1836. Local circumstances dictated an immediate resolution of the barracks problem, even though Nicolls had identified the two

---

[21] TNA:PRO, W. O. 55, Vol. 868, fols. 387-88, Oldfield to Bryce, 4 July 1831; and fols. 406-07, Oldfield to Bryce, 1 Aug. 1831.

[22] TNA:PRO, W. O. 55, Vol. 868, fols. 328-29, Byham to Bryce, 16 Dec. 1831.

[23] TNA:PRO, W. O. 55, Vol. 870, fols.257-63, Oldfield to Pilkington, 15 March 1833.

summit martello towers as the priorities. It is noteworthy, too, that Oldfield decided against casemated barracks because they were too expensive. Concentration was proceeding, but not exactly as planned.

With Signal Hill now the focus, other elements of the defence network were discarded or neglected. In 1834 the Board ordered the removal of the guns from Frederick's Battery and gave the colonial government temporary use of its barracks for a cholera hospital.[24] Expenses at nearby Fort Amherst were limited to the upkeep of the lighthouse and the fog gun. As the defences of the town forts became more decrepit, civilian buildings sprouted like mushrooms in their vicinity. Houses became so numerous around Fort William that they partially obscured the view to The Narrows. Even more tellingly, a large parcel of Ordnance Department land adjacent to Fort Townshend was set aside for a new Roman Catholic church, on which work began in 1839.

The fate of the concentration scheme was foretold by that of a two-story masonry commissariat store that was erected in 1835 along with a masonry canteen (or military pub). Both buildings were near the wooden soldiers' barracks at the southeast face of Ladies' Lookout,

Fig. 28: Buildings at the Southeast Face of Ladies' Lookout, ca. 1841. Artistic rendition by Larry Mahoney. Source: Larry Mahoney/Parks Canada. Left to right: Commissariat store, canteen, soldiers' barracks. The commissariat store and the canteen were among the first buildings to be erected as a result of plans to concentrate the St. John's garrison on Signal Hill. The failure of the commissariat store—here showing signs of neglect after being abandoned—foretold that of the concentration scheme as a whole.

---

[24] TNA:PRO, C. O. 194, Vol. 90, fols. 30-33, "Report upon the present State of the Fortifications in this Island," 31 Dec. 1834.

Fig. 29: Signal Hill Barracks, 1841. Artistic rendition by Sid Butt. Source: Sid Butt/Parks Canada. The recently completed masonry barracks appears to the right of the wooden barracks for officers.

generally a sheltered area. However, the commissariat store was the most easterly structure ever built on the summit, and thus was completely exposed to easterly winds off the ocean.[25] Whether because of this or faulty construction, or a combination of the two, it leaked badly and was never occupied, and slowly went to ruin. The Commissariat Department, meanwhile, stayed right where it was in town. Much would therefore depend on successful completion of the masonry barracks, a two-storey structure measuring 56.7 metres long and comprising two separate ranges, one a cavernous affair for eleven officers, the other even larger but meant for 192 men, or roughly two-thirds of the garrison, women and children excepted.[26] Although the barracks was nominally finished by November 1840, it is not clear if the officers' range was ever occupied, and in 1841 new Commanding Royal Engineer Lieutenant-Colonel Sir Richard Henry Bonnycastle proposed to convert it into additional rooms for enlisted men.[27] The

[25] TNA:PRO, W. O. 55, Vol. 875, fols. 566-68, Bonnycastle to Inspector General of Fortifications, 18 Sept. 1840.
[26] TNA:PRO, C. O. 194, Vol. 109, fols. 362-65, "Report upon the present state of the Fortifications in this Island," 26 Nov. 1840.
[27] TNA:PRO, W. O. 55, Vol. 876, fols. 535-40, Bonnycastle to Inspector General of Fortifications, 26 June 1841.

barracks, which rested precariously on the eastern edge of the summit above Ross's Valley, was impossibly cold and damp, and high winds lifted slate shingles off the roof and forced smoke back down the chimneys and into the rooms. Bonnycastle used every trick in the book to make the place liveable, but the gains were slight, and in the summer of 1841 he began to consider converting the barracks into storage space, with a view to erecting separate officers' and soldiers' barracks farther down the hill in the less exposed George's Valley.[28] Work on the summit could then focus on the two martello towers, the *enceinte*, a new guardhouse and provost establishment (that is, a military prison), and a new North Point Battery.

Bonnycastle, who had won fame and knighthood for his roles as builder and defender of Fort Henry in Kingston, Upper Canada during and after the 1837 rebellion, evidently hoped to leave his mark on Newfoundland. Signal Hill, however, was about to deal him the most abject defeat of any engineer who tried to master it. The *coup de grâce* for the new barracks—and ultimately for the concentration scheme itself—came in January 1842 when fifteen soldiers were hospitalized because their rooms were cold as ice, and when the baby of a Royal Artillery gunner suffocated in its mother's arms because the smoke was so dense.[29] These events erased any lingering doubts as to the wisdom of making people live in the building, and Governor Sir John Harvey, in his capacity as Major-General Commanding for Newfoundland, mercifully ordered the removal of the troops and their families. Some ended up in the barracks at Fort William, while the rest moved back into the wooden soldiers' barracks beneath Ladies' Lookout, ironically one of the buildings whose shortcomings had prompted construction of the masonry barracks in the first place.

The Civilian Invasion

Bonnycastle put on a brave face and spoke of "the new Concentration system at George's Pond," where he hoped to have enough barracks within three years to accommodate the entire garrison.[30] But first he had to complete a previously approved garrison hospital on elevated ground south of George's Pond. Eager to return to the real business of erecting barracks, he took the unusual step of employing the workers through the winter months. Despite

---

[28] TNA:PRO, W. O. 55, Vol. 877, fols. 626-40, Bonnycastle to Inspector General of Fortifications, 21 June 1841.
[29] *Newfoundlander* (St. John's), 20 Jan. 1842, p. 3.
[30] TNA:PRO, W. O. 55, Vol. 877, fols. 604-09, Bonnycastle to Inspector General of Fortifications, 24 Sept. 1842.

encountering rock of "an Iron hardness" in the excavation phase of the project, the men finished the hospital before the spring of 1843, an impressive accomplishment given that it was of masonry construction, stood two stories tall, and measured 42.7 metres long by 12.2 metres wide. Bonnycastle's boast that it was "the best stone building in the Colony" was premature, because it proved to be every bit as smoky as the summit barracks.[31] It was just as well that he left Newfoundland for good that summer, because while his successor, Lieutenant-Colonel Alexander Watt Robe, concluded that raising the height of the chimneys would alleviate the smokiness, he also felt that the building would still be unfit for patients.[32] Accordingly, Robe sought the Board's permission to convert it into a barracks. The Board complied, and by January 1846 the deed was done.[33] As with the failed commissariat store, events on Signal Hill had implications elsewhere in the city. After it became clear that Bonnycastle's hospital would instead be a barracks, a new garrison hospital was built on Forest Road, near the west end of Quidi Vidi Lake.

The events of January 1842 had soured Sir John Harvey on the concentration scheme, and in 1845 he won the influential support of the Earl of Cathcart, who examined the city's defences while en route to Montreal to begin duties as Commander of the Forces, British North America.[34] The following spring, in what appeared to be a setup, Harvey proposed to Robe and the local army and artillery commanders that heavy guns ought to be placed in the dormant harbour batteries of Forts William and Townshend, and that consideration should be given to rearming Fort Amherst and Frederick's Battery.[35] Robe dutifully sent the governor's letter to the Board with a note indicating that he and his colleagues "entirely concur in his views."[36] This suggests, incidentally, that the concentration scheme may already have been abandoned, even though the first official word that it had comes from December 1847.[37] Of the priorities that Bonnycastle had

---

[31] TNA:PRO, W. O. 55, Vol. 878, fols. 383-86, Bonnycastle to Inspector General of Fortifications, 22 March 1843.

[32] TNA:PRO, W. O. 55, Vol. 879, fols. 528-29, Robe to Inspector General of Fortifications, 9 May 1845.

[33] TNA:PRO, W. O. 55, Vol. 880, fols. 795-96, Robe to Inspector General of Fortifications, 17 Jan. 1846.

[34] TNA:PRO, C. O. 194, Vol. 122, fols. 260-66, Cathcart to Harvey, 9 June 1845.

[35] TNA:PRO, W. O. 55, Vol. 881, fols. 773-74, Memorandum for the Respective Officers, 25 March 1846, by Governor Harvey.

[36] TNA:PRO, W. O. 55, Vol. 881, fols. 771-72, Respective Officers to Secretary, Board of Ordnance, 27 March 1846.

[37] TNA:PRO, W. O. 55, Vol. 881, fols. 767-70, Byham to Inspector General of Fortifications, 3 Dec. 1847.

identified in the summer of 1841, only the guardhouse was ever completed.[38] Unlike Bonnycastle, Robe had no wish to put barracks near George's Pond, and the conversion of the hospital into a barracks gave him the excuse he needed to ignore the rest of Bonnycastle's scheme.[39] But more than anything else, it was the increasing use of Signal Hill for civilian purposes that spoke, if not to the end of the concentration scheme, then at least to its irrelevance.

Civilian encroachments on military property were nothing new, but the more St. John's grew—in 1845 its population was 20,941—the greater the pressure became. At the most obvious level, as shown by the granting of land for the Roman Catholic church, the pressure was physical. Signal Hill was able to resist while the concentration scheme held sway, but it became fair game when cracks appeared. Two early ones came in 1846 when the Board of Ordnance approved the use of George's Pond as the city water supply and simultaneously allowed the Newfoundland Ice Company to harvest ice from the pond.[40] With the opening of the Windsor Lake water system in 1862, the George's Pond water supply, which began operations in 1849, became an auxiliary source, although it continued to service some institutions until 1892.[41]

After the city jail was consumed in the Great Fire of 9 June 1846, the Board allowed the colony to use the former masonry barracks on the summit as a jail.[42] Purely coincidentally, Robe had applied to the Board in July 1845 for permission to convert half of this same structure into a military prison.[43] The Board gave the okay the following spring, and as work was well advanced when the fire struck, the accommodation of displaced prisoners and staff proceeded smoothly. The arrangement, which was meant to be temporary, would last until 1859, when the Signal Hill jail was finally replaced by a new colonial penitentiary. Unfortunately for the prisoners, the Great Gale of 19

---

[38] TNA:PRO. W. O. 55, Vol. 877, fols. 604-09, Bonnycastle to Inspector General of Fortifications, 24 Sept. 1842.

[39] TNA:PRO, W. O. 55, Vol. 879, fols. 526-27, Robe to Inspector General of Fortifications, 25 April 1845.

[40] TNA:PRO, W. O. 55, Vol. 880, fols. 773-74, Byham to Inspector General of Fortifications, 25 Feb. 1846, and fol. 794, Byham to Inspector General of Fortifications, 27 Nov. 1846.

[41] James E. Candow, "The British Garrison's Contribution to Firefighting in St. John's, 1824-1862," *Newfoundland Quarterly*, Vol. 87, No. 3 (Summer/Fall 1992), pp. 30-31. Until 1892 George's Pond supplied water to the penitentiary and the General Hospital (formerly the garrison hospital). See *Times and General Commercial Gazette* (St. John's), 1 Oct. 1892, p. 3.

[42] Melvin Baker and James E. Candow, "Signal Hill Gaol 1846-1859," *Newfoundland Quarterly*, Vol. 85, No. 4 (July 1990), pp. 20-23.

[43] TNA:PRO, W. O. 55, Vol. 879, fols. 531-32, Robe to Inspector General of Fortifications, 22 July 1845.

signals—which the blockhouse relayed to the city—substantially increased the amount of notice that could be given of vessels approaching from the southward, where most of the port's traffic originated.[49] This gave merchants several more hours to organize docking facilities and to find crews to unload their ships, which in turn enabled them to get incoming goods onto store shelves as soon as possible, or else to put them aboard schooners for dispatching to outport clients. Since harbour pilots also took their cue from the blockhouse, the extension of the signalling service to Cape Spear improved the safety of human and commercial cargoes alike.

Merchants and pilots were not the system's only civilian users. Tugboat operators and customs and public health officials could tell from the signals if their services were needed, and post office employees kept a sharp eye out for the signal indicating the approach of the mail packet, as did ordinary citizens.[50] Actually, citizens monitored all the signals, a phenomenon first observed by seaman Aaron Thomas, who in 1794 wrote in revealing if ungrammatical prose that "as soon as a Signal is hoisted the Inhabitants looks at them from his door, then refers to a copy, which most Housekeepers provides themselves with, and he knows what is coming from the Northward or Southward, without asking any questions."[51] The attraction seems fairly obvious, for in a maritime community such as St. John's, signals constituted news. In that regard, one signal was bound to create more excitement than any other, and that was the signal announcing that a vessel had been spotted on its way back from the seal hunt. This indicated not only that loved ones were safe, but also, with any luck, that the vessel had gotten a "bumper crop," signifying that the next eleven months would be good ones for the sealers and their families.

The use of flags was not confined to the signalling service *per se*. Flags also adorned the mercantile premises, and schools and churches used them to summon their respective flocks. It was all too much for Sir Richard Bonnycastle, to whom the "mighty fondness for flags" conveyed a false impression that "the utmost state of active warfare existed"; even worse, overuse had made "a common hack" of the British ensign.[52] The old killjoy failed to understand that flags lent a welcome dose of colour to the city, which unlike today was a dreary-

[49] *Newfoundlander*, 9 May 1839, p. 3.
[50] Richard Henry Bonnycastle, *Newfoundland in 1842: A Sequel to "The Canadas in 1841"* (London, 1842), 2 vols., Vol. 2, p. 141; Donal M. Baird, *Under Tow: A Canadian History of Tugs and Towing* (St. Catharines, ON, 2003), p. 149.
[51] Murray (ed.), *Journal of Aaron Thomas*, p. 184.
[52] Bonnycastle, *Newfoundland in 1842*, Vol. 2, pp. 141-42.

looking place. Nor did he appreciate that they were a function and a legacy of its maritime orientation. Like smug people everywhere, Bonnycastle was a hypocrite, since it was he who ordered the erection of a flagpole on the grounds of Government House. At any rate, by the 1840s everyone knew that the signalling service was solely for the use of the civilian community. With occasional help from the Chamber of Commerce, the colony began to assume some of the costs of maintaining the blockhouse.[53] In 1859, when a new blockhouse was built, the colony acknowledged the obvious and footed the bill.[54]

Not all signals were visual. The earliest codes had incorporated cannon or musket fire to warn of an enemy approach, and audible signals were eventually added for timekeeping purposes. In 1781 the daily corporal of the guard at Fort William was required to ring a bell and to shout the hour at 9:00 a.m., 12:00 p.m., and 8:00 p.m.[55] That same year an evening gun was fired from Fort Townshend, upon which all men were expected to be inside the fort's walls; by 1813 a morning gun had been added to the fort's repertoire.[56] In a community that lacked a public clock until 1850, and in which most people could not afford personal timepieces, civilians came to rely on the "daily gun," as they did in Halifax and countless other garrison towns.[57]

The daily gun shifted around a bit before coming to rest on Signal Hill. It was first transferred to the hill—exactly where and when, we do not know—during the 1830s as part of the concentration scheme. After Governor Harvey's order of January 1842 to evacuate the masonry barracks, the commanding officer of artillery took the gun with him to Fort William, but when sensitive neighbouring residents complained about the noise, he moved it to Frederick's Battery.[58] On 25 January a notice appeared in the *Royal Gazette* advising that the gun would be fired from the battery "exactly at noon every day." This, the first reference to a noon firing, was also an indication that the morning

---

[53] TNA:PRO, W. O. 55, Vol. 887, fols. 396-97, Bridge to Salter, 15 Aug. 1855; PANL, GN2/2, Bridge and Tunbridge to Law, 22 Oct. 1856; TNA:PRO, War Office 30 (War Office, predecessors and associated departments, Miscellaneous papers) (hereafter W. O. 30), Vol. 86 (Commandant's Order Book, Royal Newfoundland Companies), fol. 113, Law to Kent, 25 Oct. 1856.
[54] TNA:PRO, C. O. 194, Vol. 156, fols. 262-65, Bannerman to Nelson, 20 Sept. 1859.
[55] TRPAD, MG 707, Lieutenant John Dun diary, 1780-81 [reproduction], 20 Feb. 1781.
[56] Webber, *Skinner's Fencibles*, p. 56 and p. 78; TNA:PRO, C. O. 194, Vol. 54, fols. 176-78, "A Report on the State of the Fortifications at St. Johns [sic] Newfoundland," 15 Oct. 1813.
[57] Malcolm M. Thomson, *The Beginning of the Long Dash: A History of Timekeeping in Canada* (Toronto, 1978), pp. 23-24.
[58] TNA: PRO, W. O. 55, Vol. 877, fols. 597-98, Bonnycastle to Fanshawe, 15 March 1842; Paul O'Neill, *The Oldest City: The Story of St. John's, Newfoundland* (Erin, ON, 1975), p. 675.

and evening firings had been temporarily dropped. Proponents of the noon gun had not reckoned on Sir Richard Bonnycastle's devotion to Signal Hill. Never one to beat around the bush, he went straight to Harvey, and in mid-March, with a mixture of pride and relief, was able to report that "the Gun is again fired from the Citadel."[59] We do not know precisely where the gun was based at this time, but Queen's Battery is a likely candidate; certainly, the gun was there by 1859.[60]

The other audible signals were the fire alarm and fog guns. Fire was the scourge of nineteenth-century British North America, and while the timber towns of Quebec and Saint John, New Brunswick suffered the most, St. John's experienced countless small-to-medium fires and three conflagrations. Naval officer William Glascock was only slightly exaggerating when he said of St. John's that "an annual fire was as regularly looked for as the coming of the frost."[61] Given the extent of Ordnance Department holdings in the city, the military had a vested interest in detecting and combatting fires, and military firefighters mentored their civilian counterparts.[62] The earliest reference to a fire alarm gun—technically, there were two—comes from 1843, when a garrison order described the signal as "2 guns fired quick, on the first discovery of the fire, from Signal Hill, and repeated."[63] As with the daily gun, the fire alarm gun was probably located at Queen's Battery; it is definitively known to have been there in 1857.[64] Fort William played a complementary role in fire detection: a regimental standing order of 18 January 1859 directed that guns in the fort were to repeat the original signal from Queen's Battery to confirm that it had been received.[65]

The fog gun was first used at Fort Amherst in 1811, although it does not seem to have become regular until around 1830.[66] Unlike the peripatetic daily gun, it would stay put for the rest of the century. Military personnel at the fort fired the gun hourly in foggy weather to warn mariners that they were nearing land and were therefore at risk. While the gun would have benefitted the occasional naval vessel that

---

[59] TNA:PRO, W. O. 55, Vol. 877, fols. 597-98, Bonnycastle to Fanshawe, 15 March 1842.
[60] *The Newfoundland Almanac, For the Year of Our Lord 1859....* (St. John's, 1858), p. 39.
[61] An Officer [William N. Glascock], *Naval Sketch-Book; Or, The Service Afloat and Ashore....* (London, 1831), 2 vols., Vol. 1, p. 131.
[62] See Candow, "The British Garrison's Contribution to Firefighting in St. John's, 1824-1862," pp. 25-32.
[63] *Royal Gazette and Newfoundland Advertiser*, 24 Oct. 1843, p. 3.
[64] *Journal of the House of Assembly ... 1857*, Appendix, p. 499.
[65] TRPAD, GB 7.1.A, Companies stationed at Newfoundland, 1847-1867 [reproduction], War Office collection, Regimental Standing Order of 18 Jan. 1859.
[66] Webber, *Documents*, Durnford to Moore, 5 May 1811; TRPAD, GN 2.2, Burke to Cochrane, 31 March 1830.

still called at St. John's, the service was expressly created "for the safety of the Trade."[67] In 1834 the colony began to reimburse the military for the cost of gunpowder and related materials.[68] This was six years earlier than it began covering blockhouse expenses, which suggests that the fog gun was thought to be more important than visual signalling. The Chamber of Commerce sometimes gave cash rewards to the fog gun's operators, as it did in 1854 because of their efforts "last spring in affording assistance to a boat & Crew when in danger off this Port."[69] Thus, in addition to firing the gun, the men also provided a rescue service.

Because of its role in marine safety, the fog gun, like the Cape Spear and Fort Amherst lighthouses, can be classified as an aid to navigation. For a less obvious reason—its role in calculating longitude—so can the daily gun.[70] To understand why this was so, some background is necessary. Longitude and latitude, both of which are required to fix a ship's position at sea, had been conceived by the ancient Greeks but could not be measured until much later. The Portuguese mastered latitude in the late fifteenth century when they learned that by measuring the height of a guide star (usually Polaris in the northern hemisphere) above the horizon, they could obtain a ship's position on an imaginary east-west line parallel to the equator. Because the equator was equidistant between the poles, it marked zero degrees latitude. The measurement of longitude, an imaginary north-south line between the poles, proved more elusive, partly because Nature did not oblige with a zero degree line (prime meridian), and partly because time was integral to its calculation. Longitude required not only knowledge of the local time at sea—usually solar noon, when the sun was at its apex, and thus easily determined—but also the simultaneous time at a fixed location, such as the port from which the ship had sailed. Because earth rotates 360 degrees roughly every twenty-four hours, each degree of longitude corresponds to four minutes of time. Thus, if a mariner could compare local time with the

[67] TRPAD, GN 2.2, Burke to Cochrane, 31 March 1830.
[68] TRPAD, GN 2.2, Respective Officers to Crowdy, 10 Nov. 1834.
[69] TNA:PRO, W. O. 30, Vol. 86, fol. 84, D'Alton to Grieve, 7 Oct. 1854.
[70] This consideration of longitude and timekeeping is based on Ian R. Bartky, *Selling the True Time: Nineteenth-Century Timekeeping in America* (Stanford, CA, 2000); Dava Sobel, *Longitude: The True Story of a Lone Genius Who Solved the Greatest Scientific Problem of His Time* (New York, 1995); J. E. D. Williams, *From Sails to Satellites: The Origin and Development of Navigational Science* (Oxford, 1992); David W. Waters, "Nautical Astronomy and the Problem of Longitude," in John G. Burke (ed.), *The Uses of Science in the Age of Newton* (Berkeley, 1983), pp. 143-69; and Derek Howse, *Greenwich time and the discovery of the longitude* (Oxford, 1980).

time at his home port, every hour of difference, for example, would equate to his ship having travelled fifteen degrees.

Although Christiaan Huygens' invention of the pendulum clock in 1656 ushered in the era of truly accurate timekeeping, the mechanism required a stable platform to operate correctly and thus was useless at sea. The challenge of building a seaworthy clock that could keep time to within an acceptable margin of error was not overcome until Englishman John Harrison invented the marine chronometer around 1760. Six years later, in a closely related development, the Greenwich Royal Observatory published *The Nautical Almanac and Astronomical Ephemeris, for the Year 1767*, which established Greenwich as the prime meridian of longitude for British vessels. Since chronometers were not infallible, mariners had to rate them frequently, especially before and after lengthy voyages. The most obvious way of doing this—by removing the chronometer from the ship and taking it to a watchmaker (or clockmaker)—was frowned upon, since the mechanism might be damaged in the process.[71] Viable options included renting a chronometer from a watchmaker, or else having him rate the chronometer aboard ship while it was in port.[72] Yet another was to check the chronometer against a time signal, which was free and avoided the cost and bother of involving a watchmaker at all. Privately-arranged time signals, including gun firings, began to be used in Britain in the 1820s. The first public signal was probably the Royal Observatory time ball, which in 1833 began dropping daily at 1 p.m. for the benefit of shipping in the Thames. The signal was given at one instead of at noon so that the astronomers could determine the time at noon if it were a clear day. Otherwise they continued to base the time on the most recent measurement.

In colonial garrison towns such as St. John's, mariners took to using the daily guns for navigational purposes. Because of the implications for marine safety, firing times now had to be as precise as possible. Therefore, from at least 1852, military officials in St. John's contracted with Irish-born watchmaker and jeweller James A. Whiteford to provide the correct time to the daily gun crew.[73] Whiteford owned the city's only astronomical clock, which if used with

---

[71] Rupert T. Gould, *The Marine Chronometer: Its History and Development* (Woodbridge, UK, 1989 [originally published 1922]), p. 358.

[72] Alexis McCrossen, "Time Balls: Marking Modern Times in Urban America," *Material History Review*, Vol. 52 (Fall 2000), p. 7.

[73] TRPAD, GN 2.2, Petition of J. A. Whiteford, 28 Oct. 1852; TRPAD, GN 2.22.A, Reports and petitions. Office of the Colonial Secretary fonds, Burt to Officer Commanding the Troops, 18 May 1870.

a transit instrument or meridian circle—as Whiteford's almost certainly was—would have produced a reliable measurement of local time.[74] The daily gun's use as an aid to navigation was an accidental development, but accidental or not, it was a boon to the maritime community.

WITHDRAWAL OF THE IMPERIAL GARRISON

Civilian encroachments may have been a nuisance for the St. John's garrison, but they were nothing compared with the pressures coming from Britain itself, which ultimately spelled the garrison's doom. By depriving Britain of thirteen of its North American colonies, the American Revolutionary War had weakened the whole colonial system. Smaller territories acquired during the French Revolutionary and Napoleonic Wars were no substitute for what had been lost, and the Industrial Revolution exposed the shortcomings of the remaining colonies as markets and suppliers of raw materials. As a result, British industrialists began to lobby for access to wealthier markets and cheaper resources outside the empire. Parliament's formal adoption of free trade during the 1840s placed the colonies on much the same competitive footing as foreign countries. Acknowledging the new reality, Britain yielded to colonial demands for responsible government—that is, government with a cabinet responsible to an elected assembly—which was achieved in British North America between 1848 and 1855, with Newfoundland dragging up the rear. Eager to reduce their tax burden, industrialists seized on the inconsistency of quasi-independent colonies relying on British troops for their protection, and argued that the colonies should defend themselves. Luckily for the industrialists, these developments coincided with a revival of tensions with France, replete with rumours of imminent invasion from across the Channel. Whether the ensuing panic was justifiable or not, it drew attention to the weak and scattered nature of the British Army—well over half of its 100,600 infantrymen in 1846 were overseas—and provoked a clamour to bring the men home.[75] That same year the British government announced that the colonial garrisons would be reduced, and that in some cases a share of

---

[74] It follows from this and subsequent evidence that Whiteford based his calculations on the time of the transit of a certain star across a meridian. A meridian is a "projection on the sky of the circle of longitude through the place on the Earth's surface where the [time] measurements are made." G. J. Withrow, *What is time?* (London, 1972), p. 79; TRPAD, GN 2.22.A, Memorial of J. A. Whiteford, 22 Dec. 1885.
[75] Peter Burroughs, "An Unreformed Army? 1815-1868," in David Chandler and Ian Beckett (eds.), *The Oxford Illustrated History of the British Army* (Oxford, 1994), p. 164.

their costs would be unloaded onto the colonies. In British North America the plan had to be implemented cautiously because the United States was in an expansionist mood. In 1845 it had challenged the joint (since 1818) British and American occupation of Oregon, and in 1846 it went to war against Mexico. With both issues having died down by 1851—and the boundaries of the United States having grown substantially in the interim—garrison reduction began in earnest. This was the beginning of the end for the British military utilization of Signal Hill, and for the Newfoundland garrison as a whole.

In 1852 all eighty-one men of the Royal Artillery (No. 4 Company, 3rd Battalion) stationed in St. John's were ordered home; three years later the Royal Newfoundland Companies were cut from three companies to two, leaving only 218 men to perform the usual army duties plus those previously handled by the Royal Artillery, port signalling included.[76] Owing to the demise of the concentration scheme, the bulk of the remaining men were housed in the decaying barracks at Forts William and Townshend.[77] On Signal Hill, George's Barracks, as the converted hospital was known, accommodated twenty-eight married men, non-commissioned officers, and their families.[78] Because the barracks was still relatively new, one might assume that its

Fig. 31: George's Barracks, ca. 1870. Source: Courtesy of the Rooms Corporation of Newfoundland and Labrador, Provincial Museum Division. Described in 1843 as "the best stone building in the Colony," it became St. George's Hospital after the British garrison withdrew from St. John's.

---

[76] TNA:PRO, W. O. 17 (Monthly Returns), Vols. 2280 (1852) and 2283 (1855).
[77] TNA:PRO, C. O. 194, Vol. 147, fols. 258-63, Law to Darling, 29 April 1856; TRPAD, GB 7.1.A, Law to Synge, 14 July 1858.
[78] TNA:PRO, W. O. 30, Vol. 86, fols. 89-90, Law to Respective Officers, 28 March 1855, and fol. 95, Law to Respective Officers, 18 July 1855 (not sent but kept for reference purposes).

occupants were better off, and perhaps they were, but evidence of orders prohibiting the men from burning "bogwood" in the grates suggests that the fuel ration was inadequate and that the rooms were therefore cold.[79] On the summit the hustle and bustle of earlier times had yielded to relative peace and quiet, all of the wooden buildings having been "condemned as totally unfit for permanent occupancy, & in part reserved merely as a refuge for the Troops in case of the Barracks at either of the other Posts being destroyed by accidental conflagration."[80] Convicted criminals continued to make their way to and from the Signal Hill jail, a sad parade to be sure, but a welcome diversion for the signalmen, who would also have enjoyed having workmen around during the replacement of the blockhouse in 1859. But then, this was the same year in which the prisoners were transferred to the new penitentiary. As the 1860s dawned there were few sounds to be heard on the summit other than the screech of the gulls, the boom of the daily gun, the murmur of the signalmen's voices, and the pervasive roar of the wind.

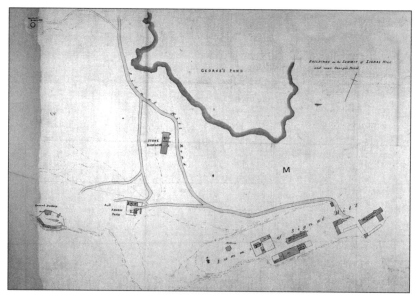

Fig. 32: "Buildings on the Summit of Signal Hill and near George's Pond," 1851. Source: The National Archives of the UK, Reference No. MR1/1772. With the end of the scheme to concentrate the garrison on Signal Hill, all of these buildings except the summit powder magazine were on their way to oblivion.

---

[79] TRPAD, GB 7.1.A, Quill to Acting Barrack Master, 5 October 1858.
[80] TNA:PRO, W. O. 30, Vol. 86, fol. 96, Law to Acting Colonial Secretary, 20 July 1855.

By now the defences might have had trouble against a horde of angry fishermen, let alone a hostile navy. On Signal Hill there was no citadel—and therefore no way of resisting a siege—and Wallace's Battery was a total ruin, killing any hopes for a martello tower. Nor were there any active defences on the south side of The Narrows. The fog gun was the sole armament at Fort Amherst, which in 1852 (the same year a new lighthouse was completed) had been transferred to the colony on the understanding that it would revert to the Ordnance Department if needed.[81] Frederick's Battery, which had been on borrowed time since 1834, had been abandoned outright after a fire destroyed its barracks in 1848.[82] The active defences nonetheless centred almost exclusively upon The Narrows, and well they might. For centuries the wind had bedevilled sailing vessels in The Narrows, slowing them down or stopping them in their tracks, and theoretically making them sitting ducks for the port's defenders. But navies were now beginning to build steam-powered warships that paid little heed to the wind and were able to penetrate tight spots like The Narrows at previously unheard-of speeds. From a defensive standpoint this favoured direct fire from low-lying batteries, which was strong and accurate, instead of plunging fire from elevated ones, which was weak and often wide of the mark. This likely explains why all three 32-pounder cannons in St. John's were now at Chain Rock Battery, supported by four 18-pounders at Waldegrave Battery and three 18-pounders and an old mortar in the Fort William Narrows Battery. In contrast, not a single cannon graced the ramparts of Fort Townshend, which staved off irrelevance because of its barracks and also because the commanding officer of the Royal Newfoundland Companies lived there, rendering it the regimental headquarters. At first glance it might seem puzzling that Queen's Battery, the most elevated position in The Narrows, possessed eight 24-pounders and two 8-inch howitzers, or more guns than any other work in the city. However, the battery's shortcomings against steamers were offset by its usefulness for firing the daily and fire alarm guns, and by its potential value against an enemy on the south side. Quidi Vidi Battery, with two 32-pounder carronades, was also an anomaly, although guns here would always offer some protection against an enemy trying to sneak in the back door.

---

[81] Power, *Fort Amherst*, pp. 54-55; TNA:PRO, W. O. 55, Vol. 1557(9), fols. 5-27, "Report on the Defences of Newfoundland," 13 Oct. 1859, and Vol. 886, fols. 778-79, Butler to Inspector General of Fortifications, 27 Sept. 1852.
[82] TNA:PRO, W. O. 55, Vol. 882, fol. 361, Byham to Inspector General of Fortifications, 31 May 1848.

If allowed to run its course, garrison reduction was going to lead to outright withdrawal, as it already had in Charlottetown, Prince Edward Island, and in Sydney, Windsor, and Annapolis Royal, Nova Scotia.[83] In 1861, however, two events reversed the tide, one of them unique to St. John's, the other common to all of British North America. The first was a riot on 13 May, in which men of the Royal Newfoundland Companies who had come to the aid of the civil power opened fire on a mob, killing three people and wounding several others. At the request of a panic-stricken Governor Sir Alexander Bannerman, reinforcements of eight officers and 214 men of the 62nd Regiment were rushed by steamer from Halifax, arriving in St. John's on 19 May and staying until 3 January of the following year. A second and much graver crisis arose out of the American Civil War (1861-65). During the 1850s the issue of whether slavery ought to be allowed in states that were being carved out of new territory, much of it acquired in the war with Mexico, underlined fundamental differences between North and South which in the end could be settled only through armed conflict. Although Britain had abolished slavery during the 1830s, its textile mills depended on Southern cotton, and among its upper classes there were those who scorned the democratizing tendencies of the United States, and hoped the war would destroy its republican institutions.[84] Official relations between the two countries took a turn for the worse on 8 November 1861 when Captain Charles Wilkes of USS *San Jacinto*, acting on his own initiative, intercepted the Royal Mail Packet *Trent* in the Old Bahama Channel and forcibly removed two Confederate emissaries on their way to Britain and France to drum up support for the Southern cause.[85] Wilkes became a hero at home and a villain abroad, where his rash behaviour spurred talk of war. But he had not done his country any favours by laying it open to the same charges of violating international law that the United States had levelled against Britain in the lead-up to the War of 1812. On Christmas Day President Abraham Lincoln ordered the release of the emissaries, by which time the British had realized that the last thing they needed was war with a major trading partner and industrial powerhouse. In the interim, however, fearing that the United States might invade British North America, the British government had sent

---

[83] Greg Marquis, *In Armageddon's Shadow: The Civil War and Canada's Maritime Provinces* (Montreal and Kingston, 1998), p. 14.
[84] James McPherson, *Battle Cry of Freedom: The Civil War Era* (New York, 1988), p. 551.
[85] Russell F. Weigley, *A Great Civil War: A Military and Political History, 1861-1865* (Bloomington and Indianapolis, 2000), pp. 77-81.

11,175 troops across the Atlantic Ocean to beef up the depleted garrisons.[86] Most were bound for the vulnerable border regions between the United States and the Canadas, but on 21 January 1862, 120 men of the Royal Artillery (8th Battery, 10th Brigade) arrived in St. John's via Halifax aboard the troopship *Magdalena*.

Any thoughts that garrison reduction was off the table were dispelled on 3 March 1862 when the British Parliament, alarmed by the enormous cost of sending the troops, passed a motion declaring that the self-governing colonies should be responsible for their own security and internal order.[87] This did not augur well for the long run, but in the short run it meant that Signal Hill and The Narrows were back in business. The most significant development occurred in 1863 when Fort Amherst was reacquired from the colony and outfitted with five gargantuan 68-pounder guns, each with an effective range of 2,000 metres.[88] This was a local manifestation of the global trend toward heavier guns to counter ironclad steamers, which although still in their infancy were transforming naval warfare and coast defence. Moreover, any steamer equipped with the new rifled artillery could fire on the city from outside The Narrows. Thus, in St. John's as elsewhere, inner harbour defences began to be secondary to defences that were closer to or actually on the coast, and therefore better able to engage the leviathans.

Fig. 33: "In the Narrows," ca. 1910. Source: The Rooms Provincial Archives Division, F 1-7/attributed to S. H. Parsons & Sons. Except for its guns, which were removed in 1870, Chain Rock Battery is little changed here from how it would have looked in the 1860s.

---

[86] Hitsman, *Safeguarding Canada*, p. 172.
[87] C. P. Stacey, *Canada and the British Army 1846-1871* (Toronto, 1963 [originally published in 1936], p. 129.
[88] TNA:PRO, C. O. 194, Vol. 170, fols. 37-39, Bannerman to Newcastle, 21 Feb. 1863.

Any ironclad, or for that matter any wooden sailing ship, that managed to get past Fort Amherst would still have to contend with some daunting firepower as it tried to gain the harbour. Queen's Battery was supposed to get six 32-pounders and two 68-pounders, although only the 32-pounders appear to have been installed.[89] (One of the 68-pounders found its way to Chain Rock Battery, complementing the three 32-pounders there.)[90] Notwithstanding the old concerns about plunging fire, Queen's Battery seems to have become more valuable than ever because it commanded Fort Amherst, which it could easily destroy if it were to fall into enemy hands.[91] Waldegrave Battery and the Fort William Narrows Battery were also strengthened, the former getting four 32-pounders and the latter three 32-pounders. The records make no mention of defences at Quidi Vidi Battery, but it is reasonable to suppose that it retained its two 32-pounder carronades. As usual, Fort Townshend was a non factor.

Although there was no more fanciful talk of a citadel, Signal Hill saw major activity for the first time since the early 1840s. In 1862 the summit powder magazine was enlarged to a capacity of 975 barrels in order to accommodate the increased amounts of gunpowder required by the newer and bigger guns.[92] In November of that same year George's Barracks became home to the men and families of the Royal Canadian Rifle Regiment, successors to the Royal Newfoundland Companies. The rest of the regiment was housed in Fort Townshend, while the Royal Artillerymen occupied Fort William and the small barracks at the detached batteries. Conditions at George's Barracks must have been grim for the married men and their families, because in 1864 they were moved into the former masonry soldiers' barracks, last occupied as a jail. However, the malfunctioning fireplaces that were the underlying cause of that barracks' abandonment in 1842 had never been fixed. Consequently, during the winter of 1864-65 the men and their families had to be relocated yet again, this time to the condemned wooden soldiers' barracks near Ladies' Lookout.[93] There they stayed until 11 October 1866, when they returned to the masonry

---

[89] TNA:PRO, C. O. 194, Vol. 167, fols. 337-38, War Office to Colonial Office, 14 Dec. 1861; and Vol. 199, fols. 20-31, "Report by Lieutenant Morgan, R. M., on the Batteries, Barracks, etc. at St. John's, Newfoundland," 1880.

[90] *Morning Chronicle* (St. John's), 3 Nov. 1870, p.2.

[91] TNA:PRO, C. O. 194, Vol. 199, fols. 20-31, "Report by Lieutenant Morgan, R. M., on the Batteries, Barracks, etc. at St. John's, Newfoundland," 1880.

[92] TNA:PRO, C. O. 194, Vol. 199, fols. 20-31, "Report by Lieutenant Morgan, R. M., on the Batteries, Barracks, etc. at St. John's, Newfoundland," 1880.

[93] LAC, RG8, C Series, Vol. 1766 (British Military Records: Newfoundland 1840-1877), pp. 68-69, Walker to Assistant Quarter Master General, 18 Oct. 1866.

barracks, someone having finally discovered that replacing the fireplaces with cooking stoves solved the smoke problem. Thereafter the wooden barracks served as a provost establishment, echoing the penal theme of the former civilian jail. Another condemned building on the summit, the wooden officers' barracks, was also brought back to life, this time as a regimental school, although it was briefly appropriated as a hospital in January 1867 when scarlet fever spread from the city to the hill.[94]

With so many people again on the summit, it occurred to someone in the Royal Engineer establishment—perhaps the same genius who recommended stoves for the masonry barracks—that it was a bad thing to have nearly a thousand barrels of gunpowder in an aging magazine so close to crowded barracks. This led to construction in 1867-68 of a new powder magazine and adjoining shifting room flush against the western face of Ladies' Lookout, where all the scarping had taken place back in the days when big men had entertained big ideas for Signal Hill.[95]

The garrison's retention reflected Britain's ongoing wariness of the United States.[96] However, the Prussian and Austrian invasion of Denmark in 1864 was a reminder of instability closer to home, and troop strength in British North America was reduced from 11,000 to 9,000 in its wake. During the American Civil War the British government had continued to urge the colonies to become more active in their own defence, and some success had been achieved in the formation of volunteer rifle companies, including in Newfoundland. When, in 1864, the British North American colonies began to discuss confederation (political union), British officials lent their full support, in part because defence costs could be shifted onto the new political entity.

Although it became clear soon after the war that the United States had no intention of unleashing its army against British North America, a new stumbling block appeared in the form of the Fenians, a radical Irish-American organization that proposed to invade British North America and to hold it as ransom for Irish independence. In the spring and summer of 1866 groups of Fenians gathered along the borders of

---

94 LAC, RG8, C Series, Vol. 1766, p. 88, Walker to Assistant Quarter Master General, 10 Jan. 1867.
95 TNA:PRO, C. O. 194, Vol. 199, fols. 20-31, "Report by Lieutenant Morgan, R. M., on the Batteries, Barracks, etc. at St. John's, Newfoundland," 1880; and Vol. 175, fols. 311-14, "Report of Committee convened for the purpose of reporting upon the Annual Estimate for Military Services," enclosure in Musgrave to Carnarvon, 13 Nov. 1866.
96 Hitsman, *Safeguarding Canada*, p. 183-86.

New Brunswick and the Canadas, and even launched a few unsuccessful raids. A Fenian navy being out of the question, Newfoundland was never at risk, although rumour had it that some Fenians were planning to sever the recently completed transatlantic telegraph cable near where it came ashore in Heart's Content, Trinity Bay.[97] The British took the Fenians seriously enough to send additional troops to mainland British North America, which paradoxically strengthened their resolve to withdraw the garrisons. Fortunately for the British, the Fenian raids increased awareness of the need for a home-grown British North American defence system, and thus were a factor in the confederation of Nova Scotia, New Brunswick, and the Canadas (thereafter known as Ontario and Quebec) as the Dominion of Canada on 1 July 1867. Unmoved by political arguments or, to them, a remote Fenian threat, Newfoundlanders rejected confederation in the 1869 general election.

Confederation, better relations with the United States, and mounting concern over Prussian military strength on the continent gave the British the resolve they needed to finish the job. In February 1870 they announced plans to withdraw all their North American garrisons except those at Halifax and Esquimault, which were to be retained because of their value to the Royal Navy. With the election violence of 1861 still fresh in their minds, Newfoundland's political leaders made a last-ditch attempt to convince the British that St. John's should also be exempted. They received ample encouragement from Governor Sir Stephen Hill, whose fear and contempt of Newfoundlanders, especially those of Irish-Catholic extraction, knew no bounds.[98] All pleas to retain the garrison, no matter what their source, fell on deaf ears, and on 8 November 1870 the last of the troops departed St. John's aboard HMS *Tamar*. Despite Hill's hysterical predictions, Newfoundland did not descend into anarchy. The Newfoundland Constabulary, formed in 1871 and patterned after the Royal Irish Constabulary, was more than capable of ensuring internal order. This left the Royal Navy, as always, to handle external threats.[99]

---

[97] TNA:PRO, C. O. 194, Vol. 175, fols. 320-22, Musgrave to Carnarvon, 10 Dec. 1866.
[98] On garrison withdrawal, see W. David MacWhirter, "A Political History of Newfoundland, 1865-1874 (Unpublished MA thesis, Memorial University of Newfoundland, 1963), pp. 65-78; and C. P. Stacey, "The Withdrawal of the Imperial Garrison from Newfoundland, 1870," *Canadian Historical Review*, Vol. 17, No. 2 (June 1936), pp. 147-58. For an example of Hill's attitude, see TNA:PRO, C. O. 194, Vol. 178, fols. 376-81, Hill to Granville, 20 Nov. 1869.
[99] Arthur Fox, *The Newfoundland Constabulary* (St. John's, 1971), pp. 42-51.

A BIG LOOKOUT

"There is a natural bent at spring time, in the minds of citizens, to give a big lookout on Sunday at Signal Hill, for the first sealer, if possible."
Evening Telegram, 15 April 1895

THE PEOPLE'S HILL

On 31 December 1870 Captain W. Phillpotts, the last Commanding Royal Engineer to walk the streets of St. John's, formally conveyed all local War Office property to the government of Newfoundland.[1] Residents and tourists wasted little time taking to Signal Hill to enjoy its views and bask in its natural surroundings. Given that mountains and hills were central to early tourism, the hill's appeal was practically a given. Indeed, as early as 1812 a Captain Courtenay had maintained a grotto there, which some anonymous poet lauded as "that happy spot" where "no cares annoy."[2] As military property, the hill received few visitors before 1870, although there were some.[3] The most famous was the Prince of Wales (the future King Edward VII), who toured the hill on horseback in July 1860. Only eighteen years old at the time, the prince's conclusion that "it was worth while [sic] to leave England for the sight that he there gazed upon" boded well for the hill's future as a tourist destination.[4]

By 1869 skaters were using Parson's Pond, which although inside the hill's Ordnance Department boundary was on its western fringe, remote from the active defences. It is also significant that Parson's Pond acquired its current designation, Deadman's Pond, after the garrison withdrew, since the very act of renaming it spoke to the hill's rebirth as a civilian entity.[5] By 1890 businessman Edgar Rennie Bowring of Bowring Brothers, Limited was taking guests up Signal Hill

---

[1] LAC, RG8, C Series, Vol. 1766, p. 299, Philpotts to Assistant Military Secretary, Halifax, 31 Dec. 1870.
[2] Cited in Pamela E. Coristine, "The Landscape of Home: The Role of Signal Hill in the Emergence of a Sense of Identity and Place in St. John's, Newfoundland" (Unpublished MA thesis, Memorial University of Newfoundland, 2002), p. 203.
[3] For one early tourist's impressions of the hill, see John Mullaly, "A Trip to Newfoundland," *Harper's New Monthly Magazine,* Vol. 12, No. 67 (Dec. 1855), p. 47.
[4] *Public Ledger* (St. John's), 31 July 1860, p. 2.
[5] The name Deadman's Pond probably stems from the accidental deaths of two female skaters and their would-be rescuer, who fell through the ice on 26 December 1869, less than a year before the garrison withdrew.

Fig. 34: Icebergs viewed from Queen's Battery, St. John's/R. E. Holloway, ca. 1910. Source: The Rooms Provincial Archives Division, E 7-19. After the withdrawal of the imperial garrison, Signal Hill became a destination for sightseers, tourists, and followers of the seal hunt.

Road in horse and carriage, a sign that the view had begun to work its magic on the upper crust.[6] Mass visitation, however, emerged in conjunction with the seal hunt, a source of immense national pride (and vast wealth for Bowring and his fellow merchants).[7] In 1842, when some sealing vessels got pinned in a northern ice field that carried them all the way back to St. John's, Sir Richard Bonnycastle wrote that "the anxious relatives of those on board mounted the signal-house, with their glasses endeavouring to ascertain their state."[8] Although this may have been an isolated case, the floodgates opened when the garrison left town. By the 1890s up to a thousand people would ascend the hill in March to witness the sealing fleet on its way out The Narrows, with thousands more thronging the waterfront.[9] Equally large crowds would visit the hill weeks later, especially on Sundays, to watch for the return of individual vessels. Since the

---

[6] *Evening Telegram* (St. John's), 4 March 1890, p. 4.
[7] This point is well made by Coristine in "The Landscape of Home," pp. 92-94. On the Newfoundland sealer as national symbol, see James K. Hiller, "Robert Bond and the Pink, White and Green: Newfoundland Nationalism in Perspective," *Acadiensis*, Vol. 36, No. 2 (Spring 2007), p. 124.
[8] Bonnycastle, *Newfoundland in 1842*, Vol. 2, p. 134.
[9] *Evening Telegram*, 15 April 1895, p. 4, and 26 March 1900, p. 4.

population of St. John's was around 29,000 in the 1890s, one thousand people represented 3.4 percent of the total; if a similar proportion of today's 183,500 residents converged on the hill, they would number over 6,200. This, then, was public participation on a broad scale.

All was not sweetness and light. The hill's dark side, represented in the past by the gibbet, the military hospitals, and the civilian and military jails, persisted after 1870. The same relative isolation that made the hill attractive to sightseers and nature lovers also made it ideal for the treatment of infectious diseases, which in the days before antibiotics generally meant quarantine. History and geography favoured the hill for such a role, and in 1871 George's Barracks was converted into a hospital. In a process similar to that which befell Parson's Pond, the building's name mutated during the military-civilian transition and became St. George's Hospital.[10] By 1874 it was officially deemed a quarantine hospital, enabling the former garrison hospital on Forest Road (to be known as the General Hospital) to handle routine medical and surgical cases. The heyday of St. George's Hospital occurred during a prolonged diphtheria epidemic in the late 1880s, which at one point was severe enough to force the closure of all city schools.[11] The epidemic brought women and children back to the hill in large numbers, women because the hospital was run by a matron and staffed by female nurses, with a city-based male doctor attending only as needed, and children because they were so vulnerable to the illness. In 1889 the hospital admitted 249 patients, twenty of whom experienced the suffocating death that diphtheria brings. St. George's Hospital came to an unexpected end during the Great Fire of 8-9 July 1892, which devastated St. John's and left 11,000 people homeless. The high winds that drove the fire carried flaming debris all the way up to Signal Hill, some of which landed on the hospital's roof and ignited it.

After the loss of St. George's Hospital, the former masonry barracks and prison atop the summit took over for hospital purposes. Since its construction in the late 1830s this building had always had two sections, one of which was now appropriated for people suffering from fever—code for smallpox—and the other for diphtheria patients, hence its name, the Diphtheria and Fever Hospital. It was used only sporadically, and its future looked questionable when a new fever wing was added to the General Hospital in 1906. In early 1910, however, it began to receive people infected with tuberculosis, which was the

---

[10] James E. Candow, "Signal Hill's Hospitals, 1870-1920," *Research Bulletin No. 121* (Ottawa, 1980).
[11] *Evening Telegram*, 29 May 1889, p. 4.

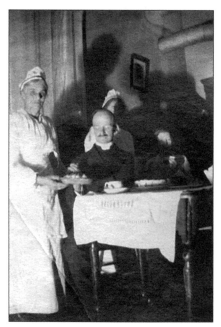

Fig. 35: Interior view of what is believed to be Signal Hill Hospital (formerly the Diphtheria and Fever Hospital), ca. 1910. Source: Carmen Wilson. Between 1910 and 1917 Signal Hill Hospital was the main tuberculosis hospital for the city of St. John's.

scourge of turn-of-the-century Newfoundland, accounting for twenty percent of all deaths annually.[12] In the absence of a vaccine, the prescribed treatment was exposure to fresh air, something the summit possessed in endless amounts. Later that same year a public health commission recommended that the building should be upgraded to receive more tuberculosis patients, and on this basis it quickly became the city's principal hospital for the disease. In keeping with the new role, it also got a new name: Signal Hill Hospital. Its heyday was brief, as it was superseded in 1917 by the St. John's Sanatorium, a new and much larger facility at Bowcock's Farm on Topsail Road. Signal Hill Hospital continued to receive fever patients until 18 December 1920, when it succumbed to a fire that was blamed on a defective chimney. There could not have been a more appropriate cause for the end of this monument to human suffering.

Signal Hill was host to one other hospital after 1870, although this one had no ties to the garrison. In the fall of 1892, when reports of cholera in European and American Atlantic ports began filtering into St. John's, public health officials took aggressive action to prevent the disease's appearance in a city still coming to grips with the ravages of the Great Fire, and in which the cholera epidemic of 1854—known locally as "the year of the cholera"—cast a long shadow. Those measures included construction of a quarantine facility known as the Marine Hospital, at the southern end of Ross's Valley.

---

[12] TRPAD, GN2.5, Special files, file 18-B, "Report of the Commission Appointed by the Government to Deal with and Report upon the Subject of Public Health in the Colony of Newfoundland, 1910."

Fig. 36: Ross's Valley Marine Hospital (far right), ca. 1905. Source: Archives and Special Collections, Queen Elizabeth II Library, Memorial University of Newfoundland. Built in anticipation of a cholera epidemic that never happened, it became known as Prowse's Folly, after the chairman of the Board of Health, Daniel Woodley Prowse.

Plans called for an inspector to board ships off The Narrows and to deny entry to foreign vessels with cholera on board. Newfoundland vessels would be allowed to enter, but only after anyone afflicted with cholera was landed near Chain Rock and conveyed to the Marine Hospital along a new road that hugged The Narrows. The scare passed without a single reported case of cholera, and other than receiving some smallpox patients in 1899 and 1903, the hospital went unused until it mysteriously burned down on 6 May 1911.[13] Galvanized by the accuracy of hindsight, a fickle public denounced the building as a white elephant. They also gave it a nickname, "Prowse's Folly," after Daniel Woodley Prowse—sportsman, historian, raconteur, district court judge, and chairman of the Board of Health.[14]

---

[13] O'Neill, *The Oldest City*, p. 301.
[14] George Story's affectionate portrayal of Prowse can be found in *DCB* (Toronto, 1998), Vol. 14, "Prowse, Daniel Woodley."

Fig. 37: Daniel Woodley Prowse [ca. 1900]. Source: The Rooms Provincial Archives Division, B 16-17. Author of the influential *A History of Newfoundland from the English, Colonial, and Foreign Records* (London, 1895), Prowse was a leading architect of Newfoundland nationalism. His career intersected with Signal Hill on two notable occasions.

Prowse countered that other than recommending that the road contract be given to railwayman W. D. Reid, he had "no more to do with it than the man in the moon."[15] This was slightly disingenuous, as Prowse had envisioned no mere road, but a scenic "marine drive" that would extend from The Battery—the aptly-named community that formed on the north side of The Narrows when the garrison withdrew—through Ross's Valley and Cuckold's Cove and all the way into Quidi Vidi, a fantastic idea that, happily for future generations, the government of the day ignored.[16] The chairman's defence fell on deaf ears, the folly tag

---

[15] James E. Candow, "Cabot Tower: The Prowse-Mariner Correspondence," *Research Bulletin No. 156* (Ottawa, 1981), p. 11.

[16] I am grateful to Bob Cuff for discussions on The Battery's origins.

stuck like glue, and many a laugh was had at his expense. It was a sound he would grow used to hearing where Signal Hill was concerned, but the last laugh would be his.

CABOT TOWER AND THE MAN IN THE MOON

Along with its emergence as a public space, Signal Hill continued in its everyday role as hub of the port signalling service. The signalman and his assistant, who as of November 1870 were colonial civil servants, resided on the hill, the former in an old artificers' workshop last used as the barrack master's house, and the latter in the Queen's Battery barracks. William Judge, signalman from 1870 to 1887, bridged the

Fig. 38: Former armoury/artificers' complex and blockhouse, ca. 1890. Source: Parks Canada. Left to right: Well house, former armoury, 1868 powder magazine, signalman's residence, blockhouse, noonday gun shed. Erected in 1859, this blockhouse would burn down in 1894.

military and civilian regimes, having spent five years and two months in the blockhouse during his army service.[17] The station continued to fly mercantile house flags and signals indicating the number and type of vessels that had been spotted, and the direction from which they were coming, as well as the International Code of Signals, adopted in 1857 to enable naval and merchant vessels of any nationality to communicate with one another or with shore-based stations.

---

[17] TRPAD, MG 633, St. John's Chamber of Commerce, William Judge to the Merchants of St. John's, 11 July 1870; GN2.22.A, Petition of William Judge, 16 Sept. 1887.

Fig. 39: Interim signal station, ca. 1895. Source: City of St. John's Archives. Built on the blockhouse ruins, the interim station would give way to Cabot Tower.

When the blockhouse caught fire and burned to the ground on 28 April 1894, a newspaper account of the equipment that Judge's successor Frank Scott and his assistant Michael Cantwell saved from the fire mentioned not only telescopes and signal flags, but also barometers, thermometers, and a telephone.[18] Somewhere along the way, the signalmen had become responsible for recording weather data, perhaps for shipowners, since the Newfoundland government had been recording weather data at the Colonial Building for its own purposes since 1857.[19] The blockhouse had had a telephone since at least 1885, when a harbour chart noted the existence of an "Unreliable" line between it and the Customs House.[20] If, as the chart suggests, this was the first telephone connection to the blockhouse, it amply reflected the overwhelming importance of customs' revenue to the Newfoundland Treasury. By 1889 the signalmen were using the

---

[18] *Evening Telegram*, 30 April 1894, p. 4.
[19] *The Newfoundland Almanack, for the Year of Our Lord 1861* (St. John's, 1860), p. 5.
[20] TRPAD, RG 58.1, British Admiralty Charts, Chart No. 298, "St. John's Harbour Surveyed by Commander G. Robinson, R. N., Harbour Master at St. John's. 1885."

telephone to request towage for disabled vessels, and we can safely assume that the leading mercantile firms were connected by then as well.[21] The telephone's presence begs the question of why flags were still being used at all. Adoption of the telephone was not instantaneous, and in Newfoundland as elsewhere the first users were businesses, governments, and the well-to-do. The vast majority of St. John's residents did not get telephones until after the First World War, and until then the signalling service retained its newsworthy function.[22] Tradition also carried great weight in St. John's, and for merchants the flags remained, as they always had been, an extremely visible form of advertising.

After the fire an interim station was erected atop the blockhouse ruins until a permanent replacement could be built. That replacement became the focus of efforts to mark the quatercentenary (400th anniversary) of John Cabot's alleged discovery of Newfoundland. As with the Marine Hospital, Judge Prowse was front and centre in the whole affair, which featured elements both comical and serious.[23] The gravity arose from the fact that Nova Scotia was simultaneously preparing to celebrate Cabot's alleged discovery of Nova Scotia, specifically Cape North on Cape Breton Island. Cape North's case had been given a scientific sheen by native son and Queen's Printer for Canada, Samuel Edward Dawson, whose article "The Voyages of the Cabots in 1497 and 1498" appeared in the *Proceedings and Transactions of the Royal Society of Canada* in 1894. The champion of Newfoundland's counter-claim was Judge Prowse himself, who in 1895 had argued Cape Bonavista's merits in his book *A History of Newfoundland from the English, Colonial, and Foreign Records*. In early 1897, when Edgar Bowring, now senior resident partner for Bowring Brothers, suggested to Prowse that the Cabot memorial ought to be a combined signal station and meteorological observatory atop Signal Hill, with telephone connections to the Cape Spear and Cape St. Francis lighthouses, and providing round-the-clock service to mariners, Prowse took the concept and ran with it. And when Daniel Prowse ran with something, even in this, his sixty-third year, he ran hard and he ran all the way.

---

[21] *Evening Telegram*, 17 Sept. 1889, p. 4.

[22] J. T. Meaney, "Communication in Newfoundland," in J. R. Smallwood (ed.), *The Book Of Newfoundland* (St. John's, 1937), Vol. 1, pp. 337-38.

[23] See James E. Candow, "Daniel Woodley Prowse and the Origin of Cabot Tower," *Research Bulletin No. 155* (Ottawa, 1981); Shane O'Dea, "Judge Prowse and Bishop Howley: Cabot Tower and the Construction of Nationalism," in Iona Bulgin (ed.), *Cabot and His World Symposium June 1997* (St. John's, 1999), pp. 171-79; Jirí Smrz, "Cabot 400: The 1897 St. John's Celebrations," *Newfoundland Studies*, Vol. 12, No. 1 (1996), pp. 16-31; Pope, *The Many Landfalls of John Cabot*, pp. 69-89.

The comical aspect of the Cabot celebrations derived from the high-handed manner in which Prowse took control of them, and from the backlash his actions provoked. As secretary of the original organizing committee that met privately in September 1896 to weigh the commemorative options, Prowse endured the slings and arrows of those who felt that the general public ought to have been involved. In November, when the process actually was thrown open to the public, he abruptly and unilaterally expanded its focus to include Queen Victoria's diamond jubilee, which as fate would have it coincided with the Cabot quatercentenary. Although this caused grumblings that the secretary had overstepped his bounds, it was a clever ploy that allowed the committee to seek financial assistance from Britain, and it reinforced the Anglo-centric focus of the celebrations.

Fresh criticism was not long in coming. This being Newfoundland, outport residents complained that the newly-created Diamond Jubilee and Cabot Celebration Committee was composed "wholly and solely" of St. John's men, and that taxpayers should not have to contribute to a St. John's monument.[24] Others invoked humanitarian concerns to question the appropriateness of government support for the initiative: the city was still getting over the Great Fire of 1892, the country was recovering from the bank crash of 1894, the fisheries were generally depressed, and alarming numbers of people were lining up at soup kitchens to get their daily bread. In that context, one commentator likened the erection of the signal tower/observatory to "the placing of a silk hat on the head of a man who had not a decent pair of boots to keep his feet warm."[25] Finally, there were those who felt that a signal tower/observatory would benefit only a few individuals—namely, merchants and shipowners—and that a new general hospital or public market would be more broadly useful.

Brickbats aside, Newfoundland contracted a severe case of Cabot fever in 1897. Michael Francis Howley, the Roman Catholic Bishop of St. John's, opened the Athenaeum lecture season with an address entitled "Cabot and Cabotage." Local bard Johnny Burke penned *The Cabot Songster*, and S. E. Garland's bookstore produced a calendar with illustrations of famous people and events from the period 1497-1896. The government issued a Cabot postage stamp series with a three-cent stamp depicting Cape Bonavista and its lighthouse above the words "Cape Bonavista The Landfall Of Cabot." Bishop Howley's brother,

---

[24] *Daily News* (St. John's), 16 Nov. 1896, p. 4.
[25] *Evening Telegram*, 5 March 1897, p. 4.

the museum curator and geological surveyor James Howley, challenged Judge Prowse to a public debate on the landfall, at which Howley was prepared to argue the case for Labrador. Quite out of character, Prowse declined. And the Mechanics' Hall sponsored a landfall billiards tournament for two teams, one designated Cape Bonavista, the other Cape Breton. Suspiciously, Cape Bonavista won by fifty-seven points.

No amount of frivolity, however, could mask the seriousness of the landfall debate. The Cabot celebrations took place in an era of rising Newfoundland nationalism, and as with contemporary nationalisms in Canada, Australia, New Zealand, and white South Africa, the British connection was paramount.[26] Daniel Prowse was a major architect of Newfoundland nationalism, maybe even *the* major architect, and John Cabot was his medium. Scaling the dizziest heights of hyperbole, Prowse alleged in his *History* that the Venetian navigator's "discovery" of Newfoundland was "one of the greatest events in history; it gave North America to the English by indefeasible right of discovery."[27] The judge was undeterred that Cabot's landfall was unknown and unknowable; that, geographically, Newfoundland was more French than English before 1713, hence the abundance of French in the names of the island's towns, bays, and offshore fishing banks; that French fishermen still plied their trade on the west and northeast coasts, as they had done for centuries; that parts of those same coasts were now home to Acadians and descendants of French fishermen who had deserted from their ships to become Newfoundlanders; and that St. Pierre and Miquelon, the last French terra firma in North America, could be seen from the Burin Peninsula on a clear day. Inconvenient details, especially ones acknowledging the French fact in Newfoundland's past and present, would not be allowed to sully nationalist mythology.[28] Cabot and Victoria were getting married beneath the Union Jack, Judge Prowse presiding.[29]

While Prowse advanced the nationalist cause, more prosaic types continued to snipe at the signal tower/observatory concept. Even though Edgar Bowring originated the idea, the public associated it

[26] On colonial nationalism, see John Eddy and Deryck Schreuder (eds.), *The Rise of Colonial Nationalism: Australia, New Zealand, Canada and South Africa first assert their nationalities, 1880-1914* (Sydney, 1988). In Newfoundland as elsewhere, the golden jubilee celebrations of 1887 were a dress rehearsal for 1897.
[27] Prowse, *History of Newfoundland*, p. 6.
[28] Denial of the French fact supports Benedict Anderson's claim that nationalisms exhibit "philosophical poverty and even incoherence." See his *Imagined Communities*, p. 5.
[29] Thank you, Frank Holden.

with Prowse, and it was he who bore the brunt of the hostility. This suited both men: Bowring because he avoided much of the adverse publicity, and Prowse because he loved the limelight. Inevitably, there were predictions that the memorial would become "a second Prowse's Folly."[30] To this the judge replied that an improved signalling service, far from being elitist, would benefit every fisherman who used the port of St. John's. And besides, he said, the business community was putting up half the money, leaving the Newfoundland government on the hook for only the other fifty percent. Still, the charges of elitism carried enough sting that damage control became necessary, and to that end Mrs. Edgar Bowring and the wives of several other businessmen, along with Prowse's wife Sarah, formed a women's Jubilee Committee to raise funds for the addition of a "Victoria wing" to the General Hospital.

In early April 1897, with harmony seemingly restored, E. D. Shea touched off a fresh round of anti-Prowse fireworks by unexpectedly resigning as chairman of the Diamond Jubilee and Cabot Celebration Committee. Although Shea cited "private reasons," it was widely believed that he had had all he could stand of Prowse's behaving as though the committee did not exist. Well known for his hunting expertise, Prowse was about to be snared in a trap of his own creation. He got his comeuppance at a committee meeting on the thirteenth, during which it was revealed that he had written an unauthorized letter to the Secretary of the United States Navy asking if a couple of warships could be spared to take part in the festivities. After the judge offered a pitiful defence, the committee relieved him of his minute-taking responsibilities and created separate funds for the Cabot and Victoria celebrations. The latter was meant to deter Prowse from soliciting funds from abroad in support of the diamond jubilee celebrations, to which some hair-splitters on the committee objected on grounds that these, unlike the Cabot celebrations, were an exclusively colonial concern. Clearly, Prowse was as much a victim of local jealousies as of his own enthusiasms.

Over the next few months the judge licked his wounds while the committee, now chaired by Edgar Bowring, made final arrangements. For the signal tower/observatory they chose a design by architect William Howe Greene based loosely on a lavish concept by Bishop Howley.[31] (Alone among contemporaries, Howley felt that the

---

[30] *Evening Telegram*, 24 Feb. 1897, p. 4.
[31] Edward G. Porter, "The Cabot Celebrations of 1897," *New England Magazine*, Vol. 17, No. 6 (Feb. 1898), pp. 653-71; "Cabot's Voyages: From a Lecture delivered by the Late Archbishop [Howley], January 11th, 1897," *Colonial Commerce*, Vol. 27, No. 2 (Jan. 1918), pp. 9-12.

Fig. 40: Edgar Bowring [1917]. Source: The Rooms Provincial Archives Division, A 23-125. Businessman and philanthropist extraordinaire, he was a driving force behind the construction of Cabot Tower.

observatory should be for astronomy as well as for meteorology.) A native of Liverpool, England and a member of the Royal Institute of British Architects, Greene was a grandson of Benjamin Bowring, the founder of the Bowring empire, and thus was Edgar Bowring's cousin. If there had been any doubt as to whose show this really was, Greene's selection removed it once and for all.

As the big week drew closer—22 June had been designated Jubilee Day, Cabot Day the twenty-fourth—plans hit a snag when Governor Sir Herbert Murray refused the committee's invitation to lay the cornerstone. Publicly Murray explained that the signal tower/observatory was contrary to Queen Victoria's wish that public works erected in her name during jubilee year should be humanitarian ones. Privately he confessed to Colonial Secretary Joseph Chamberlain that "it would be out of place for me to take part in a ceremony by which Her Majesty's fame was to be celebrated in conjunction with that of a foreign adventurer."[32] Such was the mind of the queen's representative in Newfoundland in 1897.

Jilted by Murray, the committee found a willing replacement in Bishop Howley. On 24 June he laid the cornerstone of the Cabot Memorial Tower and Observatory before some 5,000 spectators— nearly one in six people in the city—who gathered around an enormous platform that sagged with dignitaries, among them a beaming Judge Prowse. Beneath the cornerstone was placed a cache containing a set of the special Cabot postage stamp series and an abridged history of Newfoundland by one Daniel Woodley Prowse. In a further demonstration of the event's nationalistic significance, the

---

[32] TNA:PRO. C. O. 194, Vol. 237, fols. 486-88, Murray to Chamberlain, 29 June 1897.

Fig. 41: Laying Cabot Tower's cornerstone, 24 June 1897. Source: Provincial Resource Library, Newfoundland and Labrador Collection, C136. The moment captured here was the high-water mark of nineteenth-century Newfoundland nationalism.

interim signal station was wrapped in broad bands of pink, white, and green, the colours of the unofficial Newfoundland flag.[33]

The first speaker, the ubiquitous Edgar Bowring, went out of his way to explain that "no more suitable work of mercy could be erected than the signal station which had for its object the preservation of the lives of our hardy fishermen and mariners."[34] Almost as an afterthought he stated that the meteorological observatory would be added "when funds were available." This sounded ominous, but nobody seemed to notice or care at the time. Over the remainder of the ceremony it became clear that Prowse had been forgiven, with speaker after speaker singing his praises. The mood was best captured by the Reverend Canon Arthur H. Browne, who on behalf of the city's Anglicans extolled Prowse as "one of the most patriotic and loyal sons

---

[33] On Howley's role in promoting the pink, white, and green flag, see Carolyn Lambert, "Emblem of our Country: The Red, White, and Green Tricolour," *Newfoundland and Labrador Studies*, Vol. 23, No. 1 (Spring 2008), pp. 21-43.

[34] *Daily News*, 23 June 1897, p. 4.

Fig. 42: Construction of Cabot Tower, ca.1899. Source: City of St. John's Archives. Photograph No. 01-01-025. As the signal mast was stepped in bedrock, the tower had to be built around it. The interim station erected after the 1894 fire is on the left.

that ever Terra Nova had produced." The encomiums were music to the ears of Edgar Bowring, who after his opening remarks had taken a seat and merged with the platform notables. This time around, the judge and the man in the moon had everything to do with the building in question, and the man in the moon was Edgar Bowring.

History dictated that the cornerstone must be laid on 24 June 1897, but practicalities delayed the start of construction until August of the following year, when the contracts were finally sorted out. The primary contractor and builder was stonemason Samuel Garrett, while Henry J. Thomas was chosen to do the interior carpentry.[35] Although W. H. Greene's original plans were somewhat modified, the Cabot Memorial Tower that officially opened on 20 June 1900 was still the

---

[35] *Daily News*, 18 Jan. 1900, p. 4; *Evening Telegram*, 22 June 1900, p. 4.

Fig. 43: Cabot Tower, ca. 1900. Source: Archives and Special Collections, Queen Elizabeth II Library, Memorial University of Newfoundland. The rubble around the recently completed tower is evidence of stonemason Samuel Garrett's work.

most elaborate signal station the hill had ever known.[36] Except for its pudding-stone foundation and free-stone quoins and dentils, the Gothic Revival structure was made of Gibbet Hill sandstone and conglomerate, most or all of which Garrett recycled from the ruins of St. George's Hospital. The main section was two stories high, flat-roofed, and roughly square-shaped, two of the sides measuring 9.1 metres long, and the others proportional but broken in the southeast corner by a three-storey (15.2 metres high) octagonal turret. The sides and the turret were capped with parapets, giving the tower a military air. As protection against the wind, the three corners were buttressed

---

[36] *Daily News*, 18 Jan. 1900, p. 4; *Evening Telegram*, 6 July 1900, p. 4, and 18 July 1900, p. 4. See also Michael Harrington, "Buildings and Monuments," in Smallwood (ed.), *The Book of Newfoundland*, Vol. 1, p. 242.

and the base of the turret was flared. That turret, by the way, was the only feature that justified the building's designation as a tower. The *Oxford English Dictionary* defines turret as "A small or subordinate tower, usually one forming part of a larger structure." Curiously, Cabot Tower's turret is not especially subordinate, and while the adjoining square section is slightly larger in area, it is no castle. In comparison, the "other" Cabot Tower that was erected in Bristol, England during 1897-98 is a freestanding structure with a height of thirty-two metres, and thus undeniably a tower.

Beneath the building were a cellar and a coal furnace whose chimney ran up the turret's northeast angle. The first (or ground) floor was intended as the signalman's residence, and the second floor as the visitors' room. No fools, the signalman and his assistant chose to remain in their existing quarters, which were certainly more sheltered and probably roomier and warmer. The actual use that was made of these floors in the tower's early years is unknown. They were linked by a semi-winding staircase, while another staircase on the second floor gave access to the signal deck atop the roof of the main section, and to a room in the top of the turret. The latter held the flags, balls, telescope, and other tools of the signalman's trade, and thus was called the "look-out house," a usage that would in time be superseded by "signal room." Stepped in bedrock and measuring 21.9 metres long, the main signal mast passed directly through the centre of the building. The tower was connected by phone to the Cape Spear, Fort Amherst, and Cape St. Francis lighthouses, the first two of which maintained their ancillary roles in the port signalling service.[37] As Edgar Bowring had intimated, the observatory fell by the wayside, although the signalmen continued to record routine weather data and to relay temperatures and ice conditions to the newspapers.[38]

Despite being christened the Cabot Memorial Tower, the building gradually became known by its abbreviated form, Cabot Tower. Some people, however, found it hard to let go of the past. As late as 1932 the *Newfoundland Almanac* continued to advise that signals for the port of St. John's were hoisted at "the Block House, Signal Hill." Confusion over the name should not detract from the building's significance. First and foremost, the tower and the Venetian navigator after whom it was named were the pre-eminent symbols of late-Victorian Newfoundland nationalism. Also, by virtue of its function, its fort-like appearance, and

---

[37] *Evening Telegram*, 22 June 1900, p. 4.
[38] TRPAD, GN 18.19, Cabot Signal Station log book, 1 Oct. 1928 – 9 Dec. 1946, Department of Posts and Telegraphs fonds; *Evening Telegram*, 6 Feb. 1905, p. 2

the inclusion of stone from a former barracks and hospital, Cabot Tower was the embodiment of Signal Hill's military, communications, and medical traditions.

WHO STOPPED THE GUN?

On the eve of the British garrison's departure the Newfoundland government had purchased the fog and noonday guns, the daily gun service having lapsed in 1869 when the military cancelled the morning and evening firings.[39] After 1870, therefore, the signalmen's duties included firing the noonday gun, to which end the gun was moved from Queen's Battery to a position alongside the blockhouse (and later Cabot Tower), a logical choice given that two men now had to do the work formerly of many, and that powder for the gun was stored in the old summit magazine (soon to be known as the imperial magazine). The depth of civilian attachment to the gun was revealed by the outcry that greeted a government order to signalman Thomas Rose to suspend the gun's Sunday firing, effective Christmas Eve 1905. The seeds of that decision had been sown five years earlier when a letter-writer identified as "A. Nother Methodist" complained in the *Daily News* that the gun was disrupting the Lord's work, "as when it is fired, nearly all in our church who have watches, take them out to see how near right they are, and so lose the thread and effect of the sermon."[40] To prevent such wickedness, the disgruntled Methodist proposed that the gun be silenced on Sundays. Some influential person must have kept up the pressure behind the scenes, because when the Department of Marine and Fisheries suspended the Sunday firing, the official explanation was "that annoyance is caused in the churches."[41] The fiat was greeted with anger and ridicule, as well as a healthy dose of humour. St. John's was then in the grips of a temperance movement that had the support of all denominational leaders, not just the Methodists, and this seems to have fed the glee of critics for whom the religious justification was like a red cape to a raging bull. Demanding fair play, the *Daily News* wondered: "Why does the Minister of Marine who stops the Sunday gun, not enlist the services of that equally careful Sabbath serving official, the Minister of Justice, and prevent church bells ringing in the morning which keep men awake who wish to sleep comfortably in their beds?"[42]

---

[39] TNA:PRO, C. O. 194, Vol. 183, fols. 242-45, Hill to Kimberley, 12 June 1872; and Vol. 178, fol. 611, Under Secretary of State, War Office, to Under Secretary of State, Colonial Office, 5 July 1869.
[40] *Daily News*, 6 Sept. 1900, p. 4.
[41] *Evening Telegram*, 26 Dec. 1905, p. 3.
[42] *Daily News*, 28 Dec. 1905, p. 4.

The affair was immortalized in a rollicking poem that appeared in the 30 December issue of the *Trade Review*.[43]

Who Stopped the Gun.

"Now hasten forth reporter man,"
The editor did say,
"For some important news is out
About the town to-day.
Go down to Skipper Eli Dawe,
And ask of him, my son,
He knows,
I s'pose,
Who told Tom Rose
To stop the Sunday gun."

Then straight hied that reporter man
To Skipper Eli Dawe,
And sought the information
With considerable awe,
"I cannot tell," the skipper said,
"But ask E. C. Wat*son* —
He knows,
I s'pose,
Who told Tom Rose
To stop the Sunday gun."

E. C. received the pencil fiend
With bland and kindly smile,
And said "I'll get the news you want,
In just a little while,
I'll enquire of H. C. Morris
(He is now out for a run) —
He knows,
I s'pose,
Who told Tom Rose
To stop the Sunday gun."

---

[43] *Trade Review* (St. John's), 30 Dec. 1905, p. 4. I have simplified the poem's form but have retained its original spelling and punctuation, including the use of a period instead of a question mark after the title.

Ere long, the stalwart form of
Mr. Morris hove in sight,
He said "My dear reporter man,
Go call on Richard White.
For information of this sort
Good Richard takes the bun —
He knows,
I s'pose,
Who told Tom Rose
To stop the Sunday gun."

Good Richard in his kindly way,
Received the wandering scribe,
And said he always, always had
A liking for the tribe.
"But for such information,
Captain English is the one —
"He knows,
I s'pose,
Who told Tom Rose
To stop the Sunday gun."

The Captain calmly listened
To the scribbler's tale of woe,
And said he always told the papers
Anything he'd know.
"Try Mr. Wheatly, he's the man
Who'll ask no better fun —
He knows,
I s'pose,
Who told Tom Rose
To stop the Sunday gun."

To Mr. Wheatly's private den,
The wanderer led the way,
But lights were out, and doors were locked,
It was the close of day;
But round the vaulted corridor,
In echoing accents run —
"Who knows,
Who 'twose,
Who asked Tom Rose
To stop the Sunday gun."

The brave policeman on his beat,
Was shocked at dawn of day,
To find the body of a man,
Prone lifeless, by the way.
The spirit of the puzzled scribe
Had flown beyond the sun —
And now knows,
I s'pose,
Who asked Tom Rose
To stop the Sunday gun.

The poem was attributed to Wynn C. Brown, which was a pseudonym, and, like all good pseudonyms, a clever one. ("Wynn C." sounds like a play on "wince," a nod to the cringe-inducing logic for killing the gun.) The real author was King's Cove native Maurice A. Devine, who in addition to being owner and editor of the *Trade Review* was also a poet, songwriter, supervisor of debates in the Newfoundland legislature, and a leading Newfoundland example of that forgotten type, the platform entertainer. The poem's sly contents and the people named in it, including the fictional reporter who wore himself to death trying to identify the source of the fateful order, reflect the connected worlds of politics and journalism that Devine inhabited. Since signalman

Fig. 44: Maurice Devine. Source: Courtesy of the Centre for Newfoundland Studies, Memorial University Libraries, Encyclopedia of Newfoundland and Labrador, Vol. 1, p. 614. His satirical poem about the silencing of the noonday gun in December 1905 became the talk of the town.

Thomas Rose worked for the Department of Marine and Fisheries, the hapless reporter seeks the culprit within the maze of the departmental bureaucracy, starting with the minister, Eli Dawe, then working his way down through Ellis Cornish Watson (deputy minister), H. Charles Morris (accountant), Richard White (inspector of lighthouses), and Captain Edward English (St. John's harbour master), before setting out to find George Wheatley (Lloyd's surveyor), by which time, alas, the poor scribe has gone mad trying to assign responsibility to someone who wants no part of it.[44] Perhaps art was imitating life, as it is reasonable to suppose that Devine himself tried to find the order's origin and, having gotten stonewalled, wrote the poem to vent his frustrations.

Devine's lampoon of government decision making and evasion of responsibility struck a nerve with the public, and for months the refrain "He knows, I s'pose, who told Tom Rose" was on everyone's lips, easily fulfilling the prophecy of the *Daily News* that the poem would find "a prominent place in our local lyric literature."[45] It also provoked an avalanche of letters to the press criticizing the government's action, and inspired that surest sign of success— imitation—including a copycat poem that was not in the same league as the original.[46] A promotion for the Shamrock Club's masquerade and social on 24 January 1906 invited people to come and see "the Man from Signal Hill in gorgeous attire. He 'knows' who stopped the Sunday Gun."[47] This may have been a reference to Maurice Devine, who attended the event, delivered "a pleasing speech," and chaired the judges' committee.[48] (One of the revellers wore a dress with various sayings inscribed on it, including "Never mind who fired the Sunday gun, where's the solicitor?") As is their wont, advertisers climbed on the bandwagon and proceeded to beat the gag to death, hence this gem: "I spose you knows, where to get a special line of children's black and tan, laced and buttoned boots. Yes, we knows, we spose, at WHITEWAYS. Yes, you knows."[49] The poem's fame spread beyond the capital, and one tantalizing rumour had it that a ferry operator in Trinity East "knew for sure who told Tom Rose to stop the gun" and was prepared to name names unless he got a raise.[50] Perhaps the bribe was paid, because neither the outport ferryman nor anyone else ever divulged the source of the now thoroughly discredited order.

The matter eventually worked its way onto the floor of the Legislative Council, where on 21 March Daniel J. Greene asked "by whose order the firing of the noon-day gun on Sunday was discontinued, [and] if any instructions had been given as to its firing in the future [?]"[51] Answering for the government, Dr. George Skelton

---

[44] I am grateful to Melvin Baker for identifying Wheatley.
[45] *Daily News,* 10 Jan. 1906, p. 3.
[46] *Daily News,* 6 Jan. 1906, p. 4.
[47] *Daily News,* 19 Jan. 1906, p. 6.
[48] *Daily News,* 25 Jan. 1906, p. 1.
[49] *Daily News,* 14 Feb. 1906, p. 8.
[50] *Daily News,* 15 Jan. 1906, p. 4.
[51] *Daily News,* 20 March 1906, p.4.

claimed with a straight face that "no orders had been given for its discontinuance. A verbal order had been given by Marine and Fisheries Dept. to continue firing in the future as in the past; there was no correspondence on the subject."[52] That kind of glibness cried out for another Devine broadside, but the reply suggested that the Sunday firing had already been restored, or else was about to be, and so the storm abated. There was a coda of sorts when the gun fell silent on Thursday, 7 September 1906. As reported by the *Daily News*, "Mr. Rose says the fuse was bad, and he knows."[53]

TRANSATLANTIC CONNECTIONS
Esteemed though they were in Newfoundland and elsewhere, time guns and signal flags were not long for the world. The seeds of their demise had been sown in 1820 when Danish chemist and natural philosopher Hans Christian Oersted noticed that an electric current moving through a wire caused movement in an adjacent compass needle. Although knowledge of the relationship between electricity and magnetism was in early stages, there was enough progress over the next two decades to enable the nearly simultaneous invention of commercial electric telegraphy by William Cooke and Charles Wheatstone in Britain, and by Samuel Morse and Alfred Vail in the United States. In Morse's original recording telegraph, a modulated electric current (coded to the letters of the alphabet and the numbers zero through nine) passed through a wire and activated a magnet, causing movement in an attached marker that in turn made dots or dashes on a paper strip, which were decoded by an operator. The technology's paradigm-shifting nature can be gauged from Morse's tremulous first message of 24 May 1844: "What hath God wrought?" The words "telegraph" and "telegram" (that is, a telegraphic message) soon became synonymous with immediacy. Newspapers were among the technology's earliest users, and many—including, in 1879, the St. John's *Evening Telegram*—incorporated the words into their names, thereby seeking to assure readers that their news really was new.

Land-based telegraph lines spread rapidly throughout the world, and in 1851 the technology entered a new environment when the first successful submarine cable was laid across the English Channel. That achievement was eclipsed in 1866 by the laying of the first successful transatlantic cable, described as "the greatest engineering feat of the

[52] *Daily News*, 22 March 1906, p. 5.
[53] *Daily News*, 7 Sept. 1906, p. 6.

century."[54] The cable extended from Valentia Island, Ireland to Heart's Content, Newfoundland. By connecting with a pre-existing land line across Newfoundland and submarine cables across Cabot and Canso straits, then to land lines in Nova Scotia and beyond, messages that had once taken days by steamer or weeks by sail to pass between London and New York now took only minutes.[55] More transatlantic cables followed, as did cables under the rest of the world's oceans, the last of which, the Pacific, was conquered in 1902. By then the telephone, by which the human voice itself could be transmitted by wires, had emerged as a second formidable communication technology.

The telegraph—the prefix "electric" would soon disappear—and the telephone were radically different from all previous means of long-distance communication. For millennia the fastest option had been a messenger with access to fresh horses, a combination that under ideal terrain and weather conditions enabled a maximum coverage of roughly 150 kilometres a day.[56] There things stood until the 1790s, when the convergence of population growth and trade expansion, and the pressures of war and revolution, caused unprecedented demand among businesses, governments, and militaries for improved communications.[57] Although that demand caused naval signals to become more sophisticated, the biggest advances occurred on land, especially in France, where the need for rapid information was imperative for a revolutionary government fighting royalists inside its borders and foreign enemies beyond, while simultaneously remaking the nation's entire administrative framework. These forces begat Claude Chappe's mechanical semaphore system, in which operators stationed in a chain of relay towers sent coded signals based on a

---

[54] Ted Rowe, *Connecting the Continents: Heart's Content and the Atlantic Cable* (St. John's, 2009), p. 3.

[55] Owing to a break in the Cabot Strait cable, messages were carried across the strait by steamer during the system's first two weeks of operation. See D. R. Tarrant, *Atlantic Sentinel: Newfoundland's Role in Transatlantic Cable Communications* (St. John's, 1999), p. 67. Because of capacitance issues with the 1866 cable, the electric pulses corresponding to Morse code letters had to be well spaced in order to be legible. Accordingly, the original transmission speed was only six to eight words per minute. Speeds of forty words per minute were standard by the end of the century; at 400 words per minute, the Western Union cable laid between the Azores and Bay Roberts, Newfoundland in 1928 was the fastest of them all. Atlantic Cable website http://www.atlantic-cable.com/Cables/speed.htm, accessed on 27 Aug. 2009.

[56] James Burke, "Communication in the Middle Ages," in David Crowley and Paul Heyer (eds.), *Communication in History: Technology, Culture, Society* (White Plains, NY, 1995), p. 82.

[57] Headrick, *When Information Came of Age*, pp. 9-11.

system of movable wooden arms.[58] Inaugurated in 1794, it enabled news to travel from Lille to Paris (225 kilometres) in approximately twenty minutes. Inspired by Chappe's example, Britain adopted a less sophisticated shutter telegraph system in 1796, when amid fears of French invasion the Admiralty (the naval branch of the public service) established a link between London and the Portsmouth naval base.

Perhaps because operators used telescopes to read the signals, Chappe called his invention the *télégraphe*, merging the Greek *tele* (distant) and *grapheus* (writer), which entered the English language as the unadorned "telegraph." Ingenious though it was, Chappe's system had limitations. It relied on line of sight, could be used only in clear daytime weather, and could achieve a daily maximum of only six messages of twenty to thirty words apiece.[59] Nor did it incorporate any materials that were not already known, its most sophisticated component, the telescope, having been around since the early seventeenth century. The electric telegraph and the telephone, on the other hand, could be used day and night and in bad weather (provided the wires did not break), conveyed messages farther than the eye could see, and were exponentially faster. As a result, they became what Chappe's system could not: the basis of global communication, or, more properly, telecommunication.[60] These same qualities would also be true of the next great leap in communications history, in whose development Signal Hill and Guglielmo Marconi would play starring roles.

Guglielmo (pronounced "Gūl-yel-mō") Marconi was born on 25 April 1874 in Bologna, Italy, the second son of landowner Giuseppe Marconi and his Scotch-Irish wife, the former Annie Jameson, whose family made Jameson's Irish whiskey.[61] Despite his parents' wealth,

---

[58] Ken Beauchamp, *History of Telegraphy* (London, 2001), pp. 4-8; Headrick, *When Information Came of Age*, p. 195; Alexander J. Field, "French Optical Telegraphy, 1793-1855: Hardware, Software, Administration," *Technology and Culture*, Vol. 35, No. 2 (April 1994), p. 321, n. 20; Charles Foulkes, "Notes on the Development of Signals used for Military Purposes," *Journal of the Society for Army Historical Research*, Vol. 22 (1943), pp. 23-26.

[59] Peter J. Hugill, *Global Communications since 1844: Geopolitics and Technology* (Baltimore, 1999), p. 27.

[60] Headrick, *When Information Came of Age*, pp. 204-05; Anton A. Huurdeman, *The World-wide History of Telecommunications* (Hoboken, NJ, 2003), p. 88. Debate rages as to whether Chappe's system or the electric telegraph marked the true birth of telecommunications.

[61] Sungook Hong, *Wireless: From Marconi's Black-Box to the Audion* (Cambridge, MA, 2001); Gavin Weightman, *Signor Marconi's Magic Box: How an Amateur Inventor Defied Scientists and Began the Radio Revolution* (London, 2003); Stephan Dubreuil, *Come Quick, Danger: A History of Marine Radio in Canada* (Ottawa, 1998); Mary K. MacLeod, *Whisper in the Air: Marconi The Canada Years, 1902-1946* (Hantsport, NS, 1992); Degna Marconi, *My Father Marconi* (Toronto, 1982); Hugh G. J. Aitken, *Syntony and Spark — The Origins of Radio* (New York, 1976); W. P. Jolly, *Marconi* (New York, 1972); W. J. Baker, *A History of the Marconi Company* (London, 1970).

Marconi did not have a happy childhood. At home his father was hot-tempered and disapproving, and at school his classmates teased him because he was shy and spoke with an English accent.[62] The accent was a product of his closeness to his mother, the one person in whose eyes he could do no wrong. Outside of her love, he took comfort in solitary pleasures such as fishing, reading, playing piano, and tinkering with whatever he could put his hands on. An indifferent student, he nonetheless loved physics and was uncommonly curious. On one occasion, he took apart a sewing machine and reassembled it to turn a roasting spit. On another, he imitated Ben Franklin by flying a kite in a thunderstorm. When the kite was struck by lightning, the electrical charge travelled the length of its wire tether and rang a bell that the precocious boy had attached to the tail end.

Legend has it that in 1894 Marconi had an epiphany when he stumbled upon the subject of electromagnetic waves—that is, invisible waves with electric and magnetic components that propagate through space at the speed of light—while reading an obituary of German physicist Heinrich Hertz. It is more likely, however, that he had already learned about the waves from the obituary's author, physicist Augusto Righi, a family friend whose courses Marconi had audited at the University of Bologna. Prior to Hertz, electromagnetic waves existed only in the mathematical theories of the Scottish scientific genius James Clerk Maxwell, who in the 1860s unified existing knowledge of optics, magnetism, and electricity into a single electromagnetic theory. Hertz made Maxwell's abstractions real when, in 1887, he managed to generate and receive electromagnetic waves in his Karlsruhe laboratory.

Hertz's transmitter was powered by a battery that sent an electric current through a loop of copper wire that would have been closed except for a tiny air gap between the two ends, each capped by a small brass knob.[63] The current charged the knobs and caused sparks to jump across the gap, emitting electromagnetic waves in the process—hence "spark" or "spark-gap" transmitter. His receiver was also a loop of copper wire, but with one end pointed and the other sporting a brass knob. When the waves from the transmitter induced a current in the receiver, a spark appeared between its two ends, showing that a transmission had occurred. Hertz had actually created radio waves,

---

[62] Donald G. Schueler, "Inventor Marconi: brilliant, dapper, tough to live with," *Smithsonian Magazine*, Vol. 12, No. 12 (March 1982), p. 134.
[63] There is a surprising lack of consensus on Hertz's equipment. The description used here is based on Joseph Mulligan, "Heinrich Hertz and the Development of Physics," *Physics Today*, Vol. 42, No. 3 (March 1989), pp. 50-57.

which have the lowest frequencies and longest wavelengths in the electromagnetic spectrum.[64] Although he saw no practical use for them, he had in fact helped to lay one of the foundations of the modern world. Also, in the spark transmitter he had pioneered a technology that would dominate wireless transmission until the 1920s.

Inspired by the concept of electromagnetic waves, and driven to improve on Hertz's work, Marconi established a laboratory in the attic of his parents' country estate, Villa Grifone. Using a Righi-designed spark transmitter, he was so encouraged by the early results that he moved his equipment outdoors, where by grounding both the transmitter and the receiver and by adding an elevated antenna, he was able to send and receive waves over a distance of roughly two kilometres. This was impressive enough, but it might have earned him little more than bragging rights for distance had he not envisioned varying the transmission of the waves according to Morse code. It was this leap of the imagination that would give birth to the new communication system known as wireless, or radio.[65] From the outset Marconi saw that the system would have value for marine safety, because despite all that had been accomplished in telegraphy up to that time, a ship was still unreachable the moment it passed out of sight of shore or another vessel. It did not hurt that his humanitarian vision might also make him a fortune.

To achieve his dream, Marconi was going to need money, and lots of it. In February 1896, after the Italian government rejected his initial request for funding, he and his mother journeyed to London, where through Jameson connections he was able to raise the necessary capital (roughly 10 million dollars in today's Canadian currency) to buy patent rights and, the following year, to incorporate the Wireless Telegraph and Signal Company Limited (renamed Marconi's Wireless Telegraph Company Limited in 1900) and to assemble a research team. In December 1897, after a series of public demonstrations, he established a station on the Isle of Wight, from which he managed to communicate with ships thirty kilometres offshore. On 27 March 1899

---

[64] Wavelength is the distance between identical points on two consecutive cycles of a wave; frequency is the number of cycles per second, and is expressed as "hertz."

[65] The terms "wireless telegraphy" and the abbreviated "wireless" were initially used to describe the new technology. Although "radio"—because the waves radiated outward—was adopted in much of the world following the Berlin Radiotelegraphic Convention of 1906, "wireless" persisted in Britain and the dominions, Newfoundland included. In the late twentieth century "wireless" reasserted itself globally owing to the spread of mobile telephones and computers. See Lewis Coe, *Wireless Radio: A Brief History* (Jefferson, NC, 1996), p. 3. For consistency's sake I use "wireless" except when referring to broadcast radio or to that part of the electromagnetic spectrum occupied by radio waves.

he caused a sensation when he exchanged signals fifty-one kilometres across the English Channel. Since this was beyond the horizon, he realized that the waves were wrapping around the earth instead of shooting tangentially into space, but he had no idea why. Although theorized in 1902, it would be 1927 before scientists proved the existence the ionosphere, the uppermost layer of earth's atmosphere that reflects radio waves back to the surface.

Despite interest in Marconi's work by the Royal Navy and Lloyd's of London, public reaction tended to the sensational. Some thought wireless was the work of the devil; others, clearly untroubled by that possibility, thought it might be a means of reaching the dead. People took to calling the box in which Marconi toted his equipment a "magic box," or a "secret box." Marconi had a polarizing effect on the British scientific community, among whom his lack of academic qualifications was a major issue. Prejudice was also a factor. Echoing Governor Sir Herbert Murray's aspersions on John Cabot, one British scientist dismissed Marconi as "an Italian adventurer."[66] None of it seemed to bother Marconi, who was more concerned with his company's survival. Rival wireless systems were emerging on the continent, and greater distances than the English Channel would have to be spanned if his firm were to compete successfully against the telegraph companies, whose undersea cables linked most of the world. Moreover, wireless would have limited value even to ships at sea if distances could not be significantly increased. Marconi therefore decided to attempt something so outrageous that he dubbed it "the Big Thing." He would try to exchange messages across the Atlantic Ocean.

In October 1900 Marconi and his team, now strengthened by the addition of Britain's leading authority on electrical technology, John Ambrose Fleming, began work on a new station at Poldhu Cove, Cornwall. When completed, its other-worldly antenna system resembled a gigantic inverted cone. Twenty wooden masts, each sixty-one metres high, were arranged in a sixty-one-metre-diameter circle around the station, into which wires fed downward from the tops of the masts. The station housed a transmitter that was one hundred times more powerful than anything in existence at the time, batteries having been superseded by a Fleming-designed generator that produced enormous blue sparks accompanied by deafening sounds in which Marconi took a childlike joy. The following spring Marconi chose South Wellfleet, Massachusetts, 4,920 kilometres from Poldhu,

[66] Hong, *Wireless*, p. 38.

as the site for his North American station, which was to be an exact replica of Poldhu.

While outwardly impressive, in its reliance on spark technology Marconi's system was no different in principle from Hertz's. Logically enough at the time, Marconi assumed that signals would go farther the more he boosted the power, thereby generating waves of greater length (but lower frequency). Spark generation, however, had serious limitations: it was extremely wasteful of energy; transmission speeds were slow; signal strength waned as the sparks faded; and the pulse trains emanating from the sparks contained a "hash" of waves with different frequencies, causing considerable interference at the receiving end.[67] Some of these problems were insoluble with the technology of the day, but in 1900 the tireless Marconi devised a system that enabled transmitters and receivers to be tuned to the same frequency. Nonetheless, spark technology would not always admit of perfect tuning, and receivers at the time lacked the ability to amplify weak signals in order to make them more legible.

By the summer of 1901 transmissions from Poldhu were being detected 362 kilometres away, removing any lingering doubts that the waves might pass into space. But disaster struck on 17 September when a heavy gale reduced the antenna system to a jumble of fallen wires and masts. Rather than abandon the project, Marconi decided to erect a modest replacement system—a few fan-shaped wires suspended between just two masts—and to attempt a one-way transmission of a simple signal instead of a two-way exchange of messages. The signal would be sent not to South Wellfleet but to St. John's, Newfoundland, the nearest land mass in North America. Since St. John's was 3,425 kilometres from Poldhu, this would chop 1,495 kilometres off the distance to be spanned. The decision turned out to be wise in more ways than one, because on 26 November, as Marconi and his assistants George Kemp and Percy Paget were about to leave Liverpool for St. John's aboard SS *Sardinian*, they received word that the South Wellfleet antenna system had blown down, just like the wobbly Poldhu prototype.

The *Sardinian* reached St. John's on Friday, 6 December 1901. Perhaps to forestall potential embarrassment should the experiment fail, Marconi informed the press and officials of Prime Minister Sir Robert Bond's government that he had come to investigate the

---

[67] Aitken, *Syntony and Spark*, p. 73; Bartholomew Lee, "Marconi's Transatlantic Triumph—A Skip into History," *Antique Wireless Association Review*, Vol. 13 (2000), p. 83.

Fig. 45: Diphtheria and Fever Hospital, ca. 1901. Source: Library and Archives Canada, C 5980. The room that housed Marconi's receiver is denoted by the letter "X" above the window.

feasibility of a ship-to-shore wireless station and to attempt to make contact with ocean liners plying the shipping lanes south of Cape Race.[68] Marconi's fame was already so mesmerizing that no one thought to ask if any of those liners had wireless sets, to which the answer would doubtless have been "No." After scouting Cape Spear and Signal Hill, Marconi settled on the latter because, as he told the press, it had plenty of well water and was free of iron, which might interfere with reception. This may have been so, but the hill's nearness to St. John's would also have made for better logistics, and if Marconi had any sense of destiny, the name "Signal Hill" would have played to it for obvious reasons.

Recognizing an opportunity in the making, Sir Robert Bond was happy to give Marconi whatever he wanted, including permission to install his receiver in a ground-floor room of the Diphtheria and Fever Hospital. About as forlorn a place as could be found in St. John's, the hospital was a fitting home for Marconi's bare-bones equipment and irregular setup. Because the signal was expected to be weak, he opted to listen for it with a telephone earpiece instead of trusting to a Morse inker and tape. His wire antenna—he had brought several that were approximately 150 metres long—was attached to a pole at ground level

---

[68] *Evening Telegram*, 6 Dec. 1901, p. 4, and 9 Dec. 1901, p. 4.

and, depending on wind conditions, would be elevated by hydrogen balloon or kite. From the pole a second wire fed from the main antenna through a window into the hospital, where it connected with the receiver and earpiece. The antenna was grounded by metal plates buried in the earth (a scarce commodity on the summit) and covered with zinc sheets.[69] Ironically, Marconi's instructions for Poldhu to begin transmitting the prearranged signal—three dots, constituting the Morse letter "s"—had to be sent by transatlantic cable.

Soon after the transmission commenced on Wednesday the eleventh, a familiar part of Signal Hill's character—the wind—reared its head, tearing a balloon away from the antenna and bringing the day's efforts to a premature close. Next morning an even stronger gale carried off the first kite, but a second one stayed aloft long enough for Marconi to be able to hear through the static, at 12:30 p. m. Newfoundland time, the faint "click, click, click" of the prearranged signal. He then handed the receiver to Kemp, who also heard the signal before it faded away in the static. Signals were also detected at 1:10 p. m. and 2:20 p. m. that same day. Further efforts on the thirteenth were hampered by the wind and a driving mix of rain, hail, and snow, and although signals were detected, three more kites were lost. The wind was even worse on the fourteenth, making it impossible to elevate either kites or balloons. The resourceful Kemp and two local assistants then tried to attach an antenna to an iceberg in The Narrows, an act of desperation that convinced Marconi to stop. Two days later he informed the press, and word of his accomplishment sped round the world. Communications on Planet Earth would never be the same.[70]

Debate continues over whether Marconi actually heard the Poldhu signals, and the doubters come well armed.[71] Since an inker would have left physical proof of a transmission, Marconi's decision to use a

---

[69] *Evening Telegram,* 9 Dec. 1901, p. 4.
[70] And not just on Planet Earth. The Search for Extraterrestrial Intelligence (SETI) employs radiotelescopes to monitor the sky for electromagnetic signals from other planets. If alien civilizations exist, first contact is more likely to be made this way than by space travel. A spaceship travelling one million miles per hour would take nearly 3,000 years to get from Earth to the nearest star system. See Timothy Ferris, *Coming of Age in the Milky Way* (New York, 1989), pp. 371-80.
[71] This discussion draws from material in Baker, *History of the Marconi Company,* pp. 67-73; Aitken, *Syntony and Spark,* pp. 264-65; John S. Belrose, "A Radioscientist's Reaction to Marconi's First Transatlantic Wireless Experiment – Revisited," *Institute of Electrical and Electronics Engineers/ Antennas and Propagation Society International Symposium* (Boston, 2001), Vol. 1, pp. 22–25; and, also by Belrose, "The Development of Wireless Telegraphy and Telephony, and Pioneering Attempts to Achieve Transatlantic Wireless Communications," in Tapan K. Sarkar *et al.* (eds.), *History of Wireless* (Hoboken, NJ, 2006), pp. 387-94.

telephone receiver meant that, other than his own notebook entry, no such proof existed. Instead, he and Kemp had to be taken at their word, and they were hardly unbiased observers. Likewise, reception of a prearranged signal was not as convincing as reception of an unknown message that Marconi would have had to decipher correctly. Viewed strictly as a scientific experiment, these lapses in method alone might suffice to disqualify the results. But there is more. After the loss of the original Poldhu antenna system, the replacement system was improvised so quickly that there was not enough time to match its diminished capacity with the generator's output. As a result, the frequency of the signals coming from the new antenna was a mystery. Not that it mattered, because Marconi was using an untuned receiver when he claimed to have detected the signals in Newfoundland. (He had brought a tuned receiver but found it a poor match for the wire antenna.) The attempt also took place in daytime, when because of ultraviolet radiation from the sun, the ionosphere is weak and thus more likely to absorb low frequency radio waves than to reflect them. Conversely, ionization is strongest at night, producing the "night effect" so favourable to wave propagation. This was borne out in January 1902 when Marconi returned to England (via New York) aboard the SS *Philadelphia*, which he had specially fitted with a Morse inker, a tuned receiver, and a fixed antenna instead of one flopping about at the end of a wind-tossed kite. Determined to get tangible evidence in front of an impartial observer (the ship's captain), Marconi endeavoured throughout the voyage to receive messages and signals (the letter "s" again) from Poldhu. At night the inker responded to signals at distances of up to 3,379 kilometres. During the day, however, it did not budge until the ship got within 1,126 kilometres. Signal Hill, it must be noted, was an additional 2,299 kilometres away. According to critics, the only clicking sounds that Marconi and Kemp could possibly have heard were ones that naturally occur in atmospheric noise.

During the Marconi centennial of 12 December 2001 two groups of Canadian, American, and British military radio technicians—one in Poldhu, one on Signal Hill—successfully sent and received the letter "s" at 12:30 p. m. Newfoundland time by using a spark transmitter and "primitive" receiving equipment. If nothing else, this suggests that Marconi *could* have succeeded in 1901. In his defence, it is well to remember that he had virtually no training and was not a scientist *per se*. He was, however, a businessman, and "the Big Thing" was as much or more a business gamble as a controlled, scientific experiment. Indeed, there were so many variables that control was out of the question. Accordingly, it may be unfair to judge the attempt solely from a scientific perspective. Even from that perspective, however, Marconi's claim is tenable. Interference from other wireless transmissions was probably non-existent—it has been suggested that "perhaps only" Nikola Tesla was transmitting at the time—and natural interference from thunderstorms in tropical or temperate latitudes would have been near an annual minimum owing to the approaching winter solstice.[72] Because of the time of year there were also fewer daylight hours, and thus the cumulative effects of solar radiation were minimal as well. While high frequency waves are certainly superior for daytime transmissions, low frequency waves perform well enough when sunspot activity—and thus ultraviolet radiation—is low. Incredibly, on 12 December 1901 sunspot activity was nil. Thus, despite all the obstacles, it seems that Marconi was the beneficiary of "a rare confluence of circumstances," otherwise known as a miracle. There is no denying that there was something miraculous about the achievement, but his every subsequent word and deed indicated that a miracle had occurred.

On 16 December 1901 Marconi revisited Cape Spear, which he now considered the most likely site for a new North American station. But he had no sooner returned to the city when he was slapped with a cease and desist order by lawyers for the Anglo-American Telegraph Company. In 1873 Anglo-American had merged with the New York, Newfoundland and London Telegraph Company and acquired the latter's fifty-year monopoly on transatlantic cable landings in Newfoundland, issued in 1854.[73] Even though wireless was a different medium, Anglo-American ingeniously claimed that the monopoly applied to it, and they were ready to go to court to prove so. As dire as things may have looked to Marconi, the order was a backhanded compliment, because no matter what he had heard on Signal Hill, the threat from wireless was all too real for Anglo-American. In business eyes, the Marconi miracle had happened.

Newfoundland itself was victimized by Anglo-American's legal gambit, because Marconi barely had time to collect his thoughts before a new offer dropped in his lap. William Smith, Secretary of the Canadian Post Office Department, happened to be in St. John's at the time and telegraphed news of Marconi's plight to W. S. Fielding,

---

[72] These technical arguments are from Lee, "Marconi's Transatlantic Triumph," pp. 81-96.
[73] Donard de Cogan, "Cable Landings in and around Newfoundland," *Newfoundland Quarterly*, Vol. 88, No. 2 (Winter 1992-93), p. 27.

Canada's Minister of Finance (and former Premier of Nova Scotia). On the twentieth Fielding invited Marconi to come to Canada and continue his work, no strings attached. Thus, on Christmas Eve Marconi and Kemp boarded a train in St. John's and began the journey that would take them across Newfoundland and into the embrace of the Canadian government. (Percy Paget had left by steamer for England the previous day with what remained of Marconi's tattered equipment.) This triggered a chain of events that would lead to the transmission of the first transatlantic wireless message (as opposed to a signal) from Glace Bay, Nova Scotia to Poldhu on 15 December 1902. However, the technical hurdles were still so numerous that it took almost five years before regular transatlantic wireless service commenced (between Glace Bay and Clifden, Ireland).

On 17 December 1901, a week before he left St. John's, Marconi welcomed Governor Sir Cavendish Boyle, Prime Minister Bond, and members of the cabinet to Signal Hill for a tour of his makeshift facilities.[74] Photographer James Vey, who had also been invited,

Fig. 46: Guglielmo Marconi with receiving equipment, Diphtheria and Fever Hospital, Signal Hill, 17 December 1901. Source: The Rooms Provincial Archives Division, B1-96/J. Vey. Despite this photograph and other incontrovertible evidence, a myth would emerge that Marconi was in Cabot Tower, not the Diphtheria and Fever Hospital, when he received the first transatlantic wireless signal.

---

[74] *Evening Telegram*, 17 Dec. 1901, p. 4.

rendered a service to posterity by photographing Marconi and his distinguished guests. Vey's images, some of which have become iconic, are important because of what they tell us about Marconi and the moment. One of the most revealing shows Marconi inside the Diphtheria and Fever Hospital. The receiving equipment sits on a table in the foreground, a deceptively simple array offering no hint of the magnitude of what happened there on the twelfth. A fire may have been burning in the stove behind him, because he is not wearing gloves, and we know it was cold, both from Kemp's diary and from newspaper accounts of skaters flocking to George's and Deadman's ponds on the fourteenth.[75] Marconi's hands are almost bird-like in their delicacy, but it is the face that truly commands attention. Of the legions who have tried to fathom it, one who came close thought it "pleasant enough, but the expression, even when smiling, is almost ineffably sad, disappointed, as though the great inventor, like Mithridates, had sipped a little poison every day of his life."[76] Close, but not close enough, because this photograph shows someone whose thoughts, like his gaze, are elsewhere—perhaps on the Anglo-American legal threat, or else on what in the world to do next. But maybe, just maybe, Marconi had already sat for so many photographs in his young life that the process had become a bore, because it is indifference rather than sadness that seems to radiate from this photograph, and from countless others of Marconi down through the years. Isolated as a child by heartless classmates and a bully of a father, the loner had come of age, only to find that it brought no escape. Instead, celebrity, a phenomenon as modern as wireless itself, engulfed him in all its nothingness.

A second noteworthy photograph shows Marconi with Kemp and Paget on the steps of Cabot Tower. It is a photograph for the ages. While his assistants gawk self-consciously into space, Marconi glares blankly into the camera. The only person who seems at ease is the oft-overlooked fourth individual, signalman Michael Cantwell, whose half smile suggests amusement, if not a slight impatience, toward the interlopers on the steps of his workplace. (Signalman Frank Scott had died on 2 September 1901, missing a date with destiny by three and a half months.) Whoever thought to include Cantwell deserves full marks, because the juxtaposition is extraordinary. Here was Marconi, a man able to communicate by invisible waves, in the company of someone who still used flags and a gun. James Vey had captured a

---

[75] *Evening Telegram*, 16 Dec. 1901, p. 3.
[76] Schueler, "Inventor Marconi," p. 132.

Fig. 47: Outside Cabot Tower, Signal Hill, St. John's, Newfoundland, 17 Dec. 1901. Source: Library and Archives Canada/Marchese Guglielmo Marconi collection/C-005941. Left to right: George Kemp, Guglielmo Marconi, Percy Paget, and signalman Michael Cantwell.

symbolic parting of the ways between old and new forms of communication. So close that they could touch, Marconi and Cantwell were worlds apart.

Marconi may have moved on, but not so wireless. In 1903 the Newfoundland and Canadian governments contracted separately with Montreal-based Marconi Wireless Telegraph Company of Canada to erect coastal wireless stations in Newfoundland and Labrador as soon as Anglo-American's monopoly expired.[77] Several of these stations, including five of Canada's, were already in place before the end of 1904. Most of the Newfoundland-sponsored stations were on the northeast coast and in Labrador, possessed limited range (roughly eighty kilometres), and operated seasonally as adjuncts to the seal hunt

---

[77] Bob Harding, "Wireless in Newfoundland, 1901-1933," *Newfoundland Quarterly* (Summer/Fall 2001), pp. 15-19; *Encyclopedia of Newfoundland and Labrador* (St. John's, 1981-1994), 5 vols., Vol. 5, "Navigational Aids."

and the Labrador fishery. The exception was Fogo, which not only had a range of some 400 kilometres, but also housed the all-important connection with the land-based telegraph system, by which telegraph messages from points south could be converted to wireless and sent north (and vice versa for wireless messages from the north). The presence of Canadian stations at Point Amour, Labrador and at Cape Race and Cape Ray, Newfoundland, reflected Newfoundland's dominance of the transatlantic shipping lanes and the two principal entrances (Cabot and Belle Isle straits) to the Gulf of St. Lawrence. No Canadian station was more powerful than Cape Race, which opened in November 1904 and had a range similar to Fogo's. The station became famous for its role in reporting the greatest peacetime marine disaster in history, the sinking of RMS *Titanic* on 14-15 April 1912.[78] That tragedy led to the International Conference on Safety of Life at Sea (1914), which made wireless mandatory on merchant vessels carrying fifty or more people. The cost—more than 1,500 lives—had been dear, but with wireless no longer optional, Marconi had been revealed as the seer he was when he envisioned a practical role for Morse code and electromagnetic waves.

Marconi was the latest in a long list of enemies of the Anglo-American Telegraph Company, which had been the envy of competing transatlantic cable companies ever since acquiring the monopoly. In 1902 fourteen transatlantic cables passed south of Newfoundland, most of them bound for Nova Scotia's Canso Peninsula, the part of mainland North America closest to Europe.[79] All were at a disadvantage compared with Anglo-American's cables, since transmission speeds were faster on shorter cables, something that would not change until the introduction of the repeater—an underwater amplifier that boosted signal strength—in the 1950s.[80] By bringing its cables ashore in Heart's Content and connecting with a cable laid in 1873 between Island Cove, Placentia Bay and Sydney, Nova Scotia, Anglo-American obtained the fastest possible transmission speeds across the Atlantic Ocean, and with that came more traffic and higher revenues.[81]

---

[78] Stephan Dubreuil, *Come Quick, Danger: A History of Marine Radio in Canada* (Ottawa, 1998), pp. 21-28; Baker, *History of the Marconi Company*, pp. 138-42.
[79] TNA:PRO, C. O. 194, Vol. 251, fols. 548-61, "Statement of Sir Robert Bond on the question of Imperial Defence," 5 July 1902, enclosure in Bond to Anderson, 5 July 1902.
[80] K. R. Haigh, *Cableships and Submarine Cables* (London, 1968), pp. 18-22. I thank Bill Burns for directing me to this reference.
[81] According to one estimate, transmission speeds via Newfoundland were thirty to thirty-five percent faster. See J. T. Meaney, "Communication in Newfoundland," in Smallwood (ed.), *The Book of Newfoundland*, Vol. I, p. 330.

Fig. 48: Landing the transatlantic cable at Cuckold's Cove, 12 July 1909. Source: Atlantic-Cable.com Website: Bill Holly Collection. Long overshadowed by Marconi and wireless, the Commercial Cable Company's linking of Ireland and New York via Cuckold's Cove was an important development in transatlantic communications history.

As soon as Anglo-American's monopoly expired, rival firms jockeyed to get permission from the Newfoundland government to divert their cables to the island. The first to succeed was the New York-based Commercial Cable Company, majority-owned by mining magnate John W. Mackay and *New York Herald* proprietor James Gordon Bennett, Jr.[82] Three of Commercial's existing cables looped all the way from Waterville, Ireland to Hazel Hill on the Canso Peninsula, and thence to New York; a fourth Waterville-Hazel Hill cable went via the Azores.[83] Although an agreement was reached in 1905, years of legal nitpicking and a change in government delayed implementation until 1909. On 12 July of that year a cable was brought ashore at Cuckold's Cove by the cable ship *Colonia*, whose work had only just begun.[84] From Cuckold's Cove *Colonia* paid out the cable to

[82] Bill Glover, "The Commercial Cable Company," from the Atlantic Cable website http://atlantic-cable.com/CableCos/CCC/index.htm, accessed on 27 Aug. 2009; and *Silver Anniversary of the Commercial Cable Company: Twenty Five years of Competitive Service* (New York, 1909), from the Commercial Cable Company website http://www.cial.org.uk/white/silveranniv/cover.htm, accessed on 27 Aug. 2009.
[83] Haigh, *Cableships and Submarine Cables*, pp. 257-58.
[84] Colin Preston, "The Commercial Cable Company Station in Cuckold's Cove, St. John's, Newfoundland" (Unpublished manuscript prepared for Parks Canada, 2004), pp. 15-22; Tarrant, *Atlantic Sentinel*, pp. 115-17.

Fig. 49: Commercial Cable Company station at Cuckold's Cove, 1909. Source: Atlantic-Cable.com Website: Bill Holly Collection. Known as "the Hut," the station was superseded in 1916 by a more elaborate one in the Water Street business district.

the Flemish Cap, where the crew of the cable ship *Mackay-Bennett* would later splice it to one of the Waterville-Hazel Hill cables. After returning to St. John's *Colonia* paid out the Cuckold's Cove-New York cable, which was landed at Coney Island on 2 August. Service between Waterville, St. John's, and New York began around mid-month. The exact date when the second Waterville-Hazel Hill cable was diverted to Cuckold's Cove is a mystery, but regardless, in November the *Mackay-Bennett* began paying out the cable from Cuckold's Cove to Hazel Hill, and the connection was up and running by January. Commercial was quick to tout its new position as "first amongst the Atlantic Cable Companies for speed, accuracy and reliability."[85]

Known as "the Hut," Commercial's humble station at Cuckold's Cove was superseded in 1916 by an imposing Classical Revival building at 95 Water Street. The cables were brought into town via Quidi Vidi Lake and trenched from there to Water Street. With or without the Hut, the cables linking Newfoundland with Ireland, the United States, and Canada still came and went through Cuckold's Cove, adding yet another page to Signal Hill's illustrious communications history, and taking some of the sting out of losing Marconi to Canada.

---

[85] *Silver Anniversary of the Commercial Cable Company*, p. 2.

KEEPING TIME

Despite the rivalry between their backers, cable and wireless had common, transformative effects on the related fields of timekeeping and navigation. In 1851 the Harvard Observatory became the first in the world to issue a telegraphic time signal, a service that proved immediately attractive to surveyors (for establishing longitude) and railway companies (for writing timetables and reducing accidents), although not yet to mariners.[86] The Harvard signal, which was distributed throughout the northeastern United States, was superseded in 1877 by a national time service based on a telegraphic signal from the United States Naval Observatory in Washington, D. C.[87] Britain's Royal Observatory launched a telegraphic time service one year after Harvard, and by 1855 ninety-eight percent of the country's public clocks were set to Greenwich mean time (GMT).[88] Moreover, from 1852 onward the Greenwich time ball dropped on receipt of the same telegraphic cue that went round the country. In the United States the Western Union Telegraph Company installed a time ball atop its New York office in 1877, the ball dropping daily at noon on receipt of the Washington signal. Six years later the Canadian government used the telegraph network to ensure that the time maintained by federal observatories in Toronto, Quebec, and Saint John was identical to the nearest tenth of a second.[89] In addition to providing a time-ball service to the port of Saint John, the observatory in that city relayed the signal to the rest of the Maritime Provinces. However, at the region's major centre, Halifax, the military authorities who operated the noonday gun ignored the signal and continued to base firing times on transit sightings by jeweller Robert Cogswell.[90] Not until 1904, when Halifax inaugurated a time-ball service of its own, did it heed the official Saint John signal.

By making underwater communication possible, cable proved beneficial not only to timekeeping, but also to marine navigation. In 1854 the Royal Observatory used the Channel cable to exchange time signals with the Paris Observatory, establishing the simultaneous time in London and Paris and, with it, the true longitude difference between the two cities. On a bigger scale, in the fall of 1866, mere

---

[86] Peter Galison, *Einstein's Clocks, Poincaré's Maps: Empires of Time* (New York, 2003), p. 103.
[87] Bartky, *Selling the True Time*, pp. 104-14. See also Bartky's "The Adoption of Standard Time," *Technology and Culture*, Vol. 30, No. 1 (1989), p. 30.
[88] Howse, *Greenwich time*, pp. 113-17.
[89] Thomson, *The Beginning of the Long Dash*, pp. xii-xiii.
[90] Thomson, *The Beginning of the Long Dash*, pp. 40-41.

months after the transatlantic cable had been laid, the United States Coast Survey dispatched time sentries to Heart's Content and Valentia Island in hopes of resolving the baffling longitude difference between Europe and the United States.[91] Chronometer-based longitude readings on ships travelling from Europe to North America were three seconds different than on ships going the other way, and no amount of head-scratching had been able to resolve the discrepancy. Now, based on transit sightings from makeshift observatories in Newfoundland and Ireland, the sentries exchanged time signals across the ocean via cable and put the matter to rest.

Canada's embrace of coordinated timekeeping in 1883 coincided with a decision by Canadian and American railways to adopt a system of four standard one-hour time belts based on a prime meridian through Greenwich. This was an outgrowth of an earlier trend in which regional railways adopted the local time of major cities.[92] Both systems were improvements over the old one in which local time varied by four minutes for every degree of longitude, which posed major challenges for train scheduling and safety. In 1884 pressure from mariners, astronomers, map makers, railway men, and other supporters of a standard global time system culminated with the International Meridian Conference in Washington, D. C. Delegates from twenty-five countries passed a resolution supporting a prime meridian of longitude through Greenwich, a sensible decision considering that nearly three-quarters of the world's ships already used Greenwich as the prime meridian—a reflection of Britain's position as the world's leading maritime nation—as did the British and mainland North American railways. Making it the international standard therefore promised to cause less disruption than any other option. Although the Washington resolution was not binding, by 1914 all major European nations had made Greenwich their prime meridian.[93]

Newfoundland did not send a delegate to Washington, but as a maritime nation with historic ties to the Royal Navy, it was already using Greenwich for navigation and timekeeping purposes. Still, even in Newfoundland longitude had shown its malleable character: as late as 1851 the *Newfoundland Almanac* gave two longitudes for St. John's Harbour, one based on "Meridian of Greenwich," the other on

---

[91] Galison, *Einstein's Clocks*, pp. 133-36; Bartky, *Selling the True Time*, pp. 16-18.
[92] Bartky, "The Adoption of Standard Time," pp. 27-28.
[93] Ian R. Bartky, *One Time Fits All: The Campaigns for Global Uniformity* (Stanford, CA, 2007), pp. 148-49.

"Meridian of Halifax."[94] By 1860, however, Greenwich had completely displaced Halifax. In 1890 the Colonial Secretary, Lord Knutsford, sent all colonial governors a memorandum by Sandford Fleming, former chief engineer of the Canadian Pacific Railway, in which Fleming argued the merits of a universal time system based on twenty-four hourly meridians, each comprising fifteen degrees of longitude and based on a prime meridian through Greenwich.[95] In an accompanying map Fleming placed Newfoundland, Nova Scotia, and Prince Edward Island in a time zone based on longitude sixty degrees West, or four hours behind GMT. There is no record of whether the Newfoundland government, then consumed by fishery disputes with Canada and France, gave any consideration to the idea. Eight years later, with the recently completed trans-Newfoundland railway on the verge of beginning operations, government engineer (and Nova Scotia native) Herbert C. Burchell cryptically reported that it "has been in contemplation to suggest to the Government the advisability of adopting ... the 60th Meridian time as the standard for the Colony thereby conforming with the general usage in Canada and in the United States."[96] Again, this would have put Newfoundland in the same time zone as Nova Scotia, to which it was about to be connected by a ferry service owned and operated, like the railway, by the Reid Newfoundland Company. That firm's principal, Robert Gillespie Reid, was a veteran of the North American railway industry that had pioneered standard time, and he may well have pitched the idea to Burchell.

If Burchell ever followed up with his employer, he found no takers, and local mean time in St. John's stayed right where it was. Technically, that was three hours, thirty minutes, and 49.5 seconds behind GMT, as determined from sextant and artificial horizon readings by watchmaker Joseph Roper, the self-styled "Successor to J. A. Whiteford," at whose feet Roper had learned his trade.[97] This had long been rounded off to a convenient three hours and thirty minutes, a practice that would not, however, become official until 1935. According to Burchell, St. John's time was "generally" used throughout Newfoundland but not at the Anglo-American Telegraph Company's

[94] *The Newfoundland Almanac for the Year of Our Lord 1851* (St. John's, 1850), p. 3.
[95] Canada. *Sessional Papers, 1891*, No. 44.
[96] TNA:PRO, C. O. 194, Vol. 240, fols. 12-13, Burchell to Colonial Secretary, 1 Jan. 1898; *The Newfoundland Almanac for the Year of Our Lord 1873* (St. John's, 1872), pp. 3-4.
[97] *Daily News*, 23 May 1906, p. 3; Suzanne Sexty, "The Whiteford Family: Irish and Methodist," *Newfoundland Quarterly*, Vol. 103, No. 2 (Fall 2010), pp. 26-27.

Heart's Content office, which based its time on a cable signal from head office in London (likely originating in Greenwich), putting it three hours, thirty-three minutes, and thirty-three seconds behind GMT.

While it would appear to have been desirable for government officials to coordinate the noonday gun with Anglo-American's more accurate signal, they stayed with Roper, even after Burchell maintained that his readings were seriously flawed.[98] Whiteford, whose services the government had mysteriously terminated in 1882, insisted afterward that he was still "the only Watchmaker in St. John's who by scientific observation can obtain true mean time and make at intervals the corrections for mean time which even the best chronometers require."[99] In December 1896 a complaint by James Adams, time-conscious captain of Anglo-American's cable ship *Minia*, lent weight to Whiteford's claim. Adams wrote to the editor of the *Daily News* to protest that the noonday gun had been fired three minutes and twenty-two seconds ahead of schedule.[100] That was fine, he allowed, for those who used it to know "when it is time to go to dinner," but "when one considers that an error of 3 minutes of time in a ship's chronometer means a corresponding error of 45 minutes of longitude, equivalent in this latitude, to a little over 30 nautical miles, it will be seen that a ship-master, taking the error of his chronometer, might find his vessel on the rocks when his longitude by observation put him 30 miles off."

Adams's diatribe provoked a fascinating follow-up letter in which a Mr. J. Haddon hinted at one explanation for the gun's unreliability. According to Haddon, the government had previously employed a friend of his "to give the correct time by signals from his house to the man on the hill for the firing of the mid-day gun."[101] Haddon claimed that his friend would occasionally signal at the wrong time, since otherwise mariners "could all rate their own chronometers by the gun" and thereby deprive his friend of business. Still, said Haddon, he would never have let the gap reach three minutes, which was "too large an error." If, incidentally, that friend was James A. Whiteford, he is more likely to have signalled from his shop at 224 Water Street than from his residence on Portugal Cove Road, which was then on the outskirts of town.

---

[98] TNA:PRO, C. O. 194, Vol. 240, fols. 12-13, Burchell to Colonial Secretary, 1 Jan. 1898.
[99] TRPAD, GN 2.22.A, Memorial of J. A. Whiteford, 22 Dec. 1885.
[100] *Daily News*, 16 Dec. 1896, p. 4.
[101] *Daily News*, 19 Dec. 1896, p. 2.

Fig. 50: View of Queen's Battery, harbour, and city of St. John's, Newfoundland, 1908. Source: Library and Archives Canada/Credit: William Notman and Son/C-23340. It was not noon in St. John's until the noonday gun (right foreground) said so.

Whether the noonday gun's erratic ways were the result of duplicity by Joseph Roper or carelessness by Frank Scott is immaterial. The bottom line is that mariners could no longer trust it. This was corroborated by the *Newfoundland and Labrador Pilot* of 1897, which perhaps because of the Adams complaint warned that the gun "is reported to be quite unreliable for the purpose of rating chronometers."[102] By 1907 the *Pilot* had downgraded its assessment of the gun to "useless," and it would repeat the injunction in subsequent editions.[103] The same caution appeared on the new Admiralty chart of St. John's Harbour that was published in 1914.[104] Those arbiters of so much in Newfoundland, the Anglo-American Telegraph Company, stepped into the breach in 1917, announcing that they would give the correct time to any mariner who asked at their St. John's office, provided they got twenty-four hours notice of the request.[105]

---

[102] William Frederick Maxwell, *The Newfoundland and Labrador Pilot* (London, 1897), p. 421. I am indebted to Bob Cuff for this reference.
[103] William Frederick Maxwell and Henry Saunders Penn, *The Newfoundland and Labrador Pilot* (London, 1907), p. 481.
[104] City of St. John's Archives (hereafter CSJA), Map A.014, "St. John's Harbour Surveyed by Captain J. W. F. Combe, R. N.," published by the Admiralty, 16 Jan. 1914.
[105] William John Nowell Baird, *The Newfoundland and Labrador Pilot* (London, 1917), p. 57.

Even as Anglo-American were coming to the rescue, newer technology was rendering chronometers and time guns obsolete. In 1905 the United States Naval Observatory issued the first regular wireless time signal for mariners, and in 1907 the wireless station at Camperdown, on the approaches to Halifax harbour, inaugurated a time signal for mariners using that port.[106] France and Germany joined the trend in 1910, issuing signals that were available "on a regular basis to much of Europe and broad sections of the Atlantic Ocean."[107] Three years later, when the United States Navy's Arlington, Virginia wireless station began emitting a powerful noon-hour signal that could be detected 1,600 kilometres seaward, reliable time information became even more widely available. By 1922 the trend was so widespread that the Admiralty saw fit to publish the first *Admiralty List of Wireless Signals*. The chronometer's days were all but over.

Whatever the noonday gun's limitations as timekeeper and aid to navigation, no one in St. John's seemed to mind, and if it was good enough for St. John's, then it was good enough for the rest of the island, Heart's Content excepted. Thus, in 1917, when Newfoundland became the first jurisdiction in North America to adopt Daylight Saving Time, section five of the enabling legislation duly advised that "The gun at St. John's shall be fired at noon, Newfoundland Time."[108] The act failed to mention that noon in Newfoundland, as proclaimed by the gun, was a decidedly flexible concept.

---

[106] Rebecca Robbins Raines, *Getting the Message Through: A Branch History of the U. S. Army Signal Corps* (Washington, 1996), p. 140; Arthur Eric Zimmerman, *In the Shadow of the Shield: The Development of Wireless Telegraphy and Radio Broadcasting in Kingston and at Queen's University: An Oral and Documentary History, 1902-1957* (Kingston, 1991), pp. 211-12, and, by the same author, "The First Wireless Time Signals to Ships at Sea," *Old Timer's Bulletin* [Antique Wireless Association], Vol. 43, No. 3 (Aug. 2002), pp. 57-60.
[107] Bartky, *One Time Fits All*, p. 139.
[108] 8 Geo. V, c. 9 (passed 7 June 1917).

CANADA'S FRONT DOOR

"Newfoundland lies across the sea-entrance to the Dominion of Canada and may well be described as Canada's front door, the stopper in the Canadian bottle, or in Mr. Churchill's picturesque language as 'an orange in the mouth of a sucking pig'." A. R. M. Lower in *Newfoundland: Economic, Diplomatic, and Strategic Studies* (Toronto, 1946)

RESERVISTS AND FRONTIERSMEN

Embracing a quarter of the earth's land mass and about the same proportion of its inhabitants, the late-nineteenth-century British empire was the largest and most powerful in human history. Because that power ultimately derived from economic superiority, it stood to reason that Britain's leadership would be challenged if rivals could close the economic gap, which they were busily trying to do.[1] The first tremors of change came in the mid-1880s when a French naval build-up and the related prospect of a Franco-Russian alliance raised questions about the Royal Navy's control of the Mediterranean. The ensuing reassessment of the navy's position led to adoption of the "two-power standard," by which Britain sought to maintain the same number of fighting ships as the next two biggest navies combined. The British government also began pushing the colonies to become more active in their own defence, and to support the Royal Navy through financial subsidies or by creating reserves of trained seamen from which the navy could draw. It opposed the creation of colonial navies, viewing them as a potential threat to unity of command under the Royal Navy.[2]

The Franco-Russian scare was superseded by a graver one from Germany, whose unification in 1871 ended French military dominance on the continent, and whose rapid industrial expansion was reflected in that of its navy, which would rise from sixth-largest in the world in 1898 to second-largest in 1914, trailing only the Royal Navy.[3] As German power grew, Britain accelerated the naval armaments race that had begun with the two-power standard, and courted new partners, forging an alliance with Japan (1902), settling the Alaska boundary

---

[1] Paul Kennedy, *The Rise and Fall of British Naval Mastery* (London, 1976), pp. 178-87.
[2] Donald C. Gordon, *The Dominion Partnership in Imperial Defense, 1870-1914* (Baltimore, 1965), pp. 78-79.
[3] Paul Kennedy, *The Rise and Fall of the Great Powers: Economic Change and Military Conflict from 1500 to 2000* (London, 1989), pp. 271-72.

dispute with the United States (1903), and concluding a series of conventions with arch-enemy France (1904) that were collectively known as the *entente cordiale*. It also abandoned all pretence of universal command of the seas, slashing the Royal Navy's overseas stations and concentrating the fleet in home waters, an initiative that brought the closure of Halifax's dockyard and the withdrawal of its imperial garrison (1905-06).[4] The latter was not only an acknowledgement that Canada was indefensible against the United States, but also that Britain no longer had anything to fear from its old foe.[5] The German menace, together with the rise of nationalist sentiment in the colonies, even led Britain to accept colonial navies, it being understood, however, that these would come under the Royal Navy's command in wartime.[6] In 1907 the new attitude toward the colonies, Newfoundland included, was reflected in Britain's abandonment of the pejorative "colony" in favour of the more neutral "dominion."[7] There was, however, no formal change in status, and London retained the right to conduct diplomatic relations with foreign countries and to sign treaties with them on behalf of its still junior partners.

Against this background of international realignment, Newfoundland's political leaders cleverly sought to curry favour with their overlords by emphasizing the island's role in the transatlantic cable system. Empires have always relied on the latest communication technology, and submarine cables, more so than telegraph lines, were the acknowledged "threads" that held the British empire together.[8] Even so, British awareness of cable's strategic value was not instantaneous, as was shown by the response in 1866-67 to rumours of Fenian plans to cut the transatlantic cable near Heart's Content. Endeavouring to soothe an agitated Newfoundland Governor Sir Anthony Musgrave, Colonial Secretary Lord Carnarvon acknowledged the cable's value to "the maintenance of immediate communication between the two continents," but concluded that its owners were "the parties primarily interested" in its security.[9] That kind of indifference

---

[4] Samuel F. Wells, "British Strategic Withdrawal from the Western Hemisphere, 1904-1906," *Canadian Historical Review*, Vol. 49, No. 4 (Dec. 1968), pp. 335-56.
[5] Bradford Perkins, *The Great Rapprochement: England and the United States, 1895-1914* (New York, 1968), p. 158.
[6] Gordon, *The Dominion Partnership in Imperial Defense*, pp 239-44.
[7] Ronald Hyam, "The British Empire in the Edwardian Era," in Judith M. Brown and Wm. Roger Louis (eds.), *The Oxford History of the British Empire: Volume IV: The Twentieth Century* (Oxford, 1999), p. 55.
[8] James Morris, *Farewell the Trumpets: An Imperial Retreat* (Harmondsworth, UK, 1981), p. 61; Harold A. Innis, *Empire and Communications* (Toronto, 1972 [originally published in 1950]), p. 5.
[9] TNA:PRO, C. O. 194, Vol. 175, fols. 339-42, Carnarvon to Musgrave, 8 Jan. 1867.

would soon become passé, thanks mainly to British concern for the security of telegraphic communication with its most valuable colony, India, to which it was linked by a maze of cables and land lines, many of the latter passing through countries that might not be so friendly in wartime.[10] Moreover, as the American Civil War had proven, land lines could be tapped or cut even when they did run through friendly territory. Undersea cables, however, were far less liable to sabotage, especially while the Royal Navy ruled the waves. Thus, after completion of the all sea cable route to India in 1870, the British gradually saw the wisdom of applying the concept to the empire as a whole. In 1902, when cables were laid between Australia, New Zealand, and British Columbia, Canada, the dream of an "all red" system—pinkish red being the colour of British possessions on word maps—was fulfilled. By then the British were masters of the medium, owning sixty-three percent of the world's submarine cables and twenty-four of its thirty cable ships, specialized craft without which no cable could be laid or repaired, regardless of who owned it.

Cable helped to restore Newfoundland to strategic significance for the first time since the demise of the migratory fishery, and simultaneously rekindled awareness of the island's value to Canada. During the 1887 Colonial Conference Prime Minister Sir Robert Thorburn insisted that Newfoundland's proximity to Cabot and Belle Isle straits and to transatlantic cables terminating in Nova Scotia made it worthy of inclusion in any British plans for Canada's defence.[11] Thorburn's insight was wasted on the Canadians, who would remain preoccupied with the spectre of American invasion until the eve of the First World War.[12] With the British, however, he had struck a nerve, or at least would in due course. British primacy in the transatlantic cable network was more or less assured so long as Anglo-American held the upper hand, but security concerns nonetheless began to mount as the push to complete the all red system gained momentum. In 1898 the

---

[10] P. M. Kennedy, "Imperial cable communications and strategy, 1870-1914," *English Historical Review*, Vol. 86, No. 341 (Oct. 1971), p. 731; Daniel R. Headrick, *The Invisible Weapon: Telecommunications and International Politics, 1851-1945* (Oxford, 1991), pp. 21-31.

[11] James E. Candow, "The Defence of Newfoundland, 1870-1918," in Shannon Ryan (comp.), *Newfoundland History 1986: Proceedings of the First Newfoundland Historical Society Conference* (St. John's, 1986), pp. 117-20.

[12] Roger Sarty, "Canada and the Great Rapprochement, 1902-1914," in B. J. C. McKercher and Lawrence Aronsen (eds.), *The North Atlantic Triangle in a Changing World: Anglo-American-Canadian Relations, 1902-1956* (Toronto, 1996), pp. 27-41; Michael L. Hadley and Roger Sarty, *Tin-Pots and Pirate Ships: Canadian Naval Forces and German Sea Raiders 1880-1918* (Montreal and Kingston, 1991), p. 24.

Colonial Defence Committee observed that, with four of five British-owned transatlantic cables being routed through Newfoundland, communication with the United States "could be seriously interrupted by a small party landed in Newfoundland from a hostile cruiser."[13] Colonial Office bureaucrats therefore grew worried when the Newfoundland government rejected their requests to raise a volunteer force to defend the cable landing sites, which it claimed it could not afford to do.[14]

At the 1902 Colonial Conference Prime Minister Sir Robert Bond further jangled British nerves by making a pitch for a new Royal Navy base in St. John's.[15] From such a base, said Bond, cruisers could patrol the cable zone south of the island and prevent "mischief" from St. Pierre. As a building block of Newfoundland nationalism, the anti-French card always went over well with voters, and it might have found favour with the British in a different time, but not now, only two years before the *entente cordiale*. Moreover, as an Admiralty official reminded Bond through Colonial Office channels, the existing Royal Navy base in Halifax—the same one that would be closed within four years—was adequate for all duties in the northwest Atlantic, cable defence included.[16] Bond likewise found no takers for his visionary suggestion that ships based in Halifax, St. John's, and Barehaven, Ireland would constitute "a chain right across the Atlantic," ensuring the safety of wartime food shipments from Canada to Britain. That scenario, which would entail cooperation between Newfoundland and Canada, would have to wait until the Second World War to be realized. Long before that, however, Bond endeared himself to the British by confirming arrangements for the creation of a Newfoundland branch of the Royal Naval Reserve.

Ever since the late 1880s the British had sought concrete help from the colonies. For Newfoundland, the timing could not have been worse. There was anger toward Britain for its failure to support aggressive action against French fishermen on the treaty shore, and for its refusal in 1891 to ratify a trade deal between Newfoundland and the United States after Canada objected to being left out of the talks.[17]

---

[13] TNA:PRO, C. O. 194, Vol. 246, fols. 368-69, "Newfoundland: Defence of Cable Landing-places," 2 Jan. 1900.
[14] TNA:PRO, C. O. 194, Vol. 245, fol. 12, Little to Chamberlain, 13 June 1900.
[15] TNA:PRO, C. O. 194, Vol. 251, "Statement by Sir Robert Bond on the question of Imperial Defence," 5 July 1902.
[16] TNA:PRO, C. O. 194, Vol. 251, fols. 101-03, Admiralty to Under-Secretary of State, Colonial Office, 11 Aug. 1902.
[17] Peter F. Neary and Sidney J. R. Noel, "Newfoundland's Quest for Reciprocity," in Mason Wade (ed.), *Regionalism in the Canadian Community 1867-1967* (Toronto, 1969), p. 212.

Fig. 51: Newfoundland Royal Naval Reservists alongside HMS *Briton* [formerly *Calypso*], between 1916 and 1922. Source: The Rooms Provincial Archives Division, NA 1529. Despite its contributions to home defence and to the British and Canadian navies in the First World War, the Newfoundland Royal Naval Reserve has long been overshadowed by the Royal Newfoundland Regiment.

The strained relations with the mother country revealed the contradictory nature of Newfoundland nationalism, which could be pro- and anti-British at one and the same time.[18] The disputes themselves were symptoms of the economic depression that struck Newfoundland in the late 1880s, and which was caused partly by declining average production as the fishery workforce reached unsustainable levels, partly by fierce competition and lower prices in saltfish markets—hence the animus toward France—and partly by a shift in consumer tastes in some market countries toward more modern fishery products.[19] In 1894 the economy hit rock bottom when the Union and Commercial banks closed their doors, plunging some of Newfoundland's largest firms into bankruptcy. It is noteworthy, however, that in the failed confederation talks between Newfoundland and Canada that followed the crash, Newfoundland's proposals

---

[18] James K. Hiller, "Status without Stature: Newfoundland, 1869-1949," in Phillip Buckner (ed.), *Canada and the British Empire* (Oxford, 2008), pp. 129-30.

[19] Ryan, *Fish Out of Water*, pp. 132-37; David Alexander, "Newfoundland's Traditional Economy and Development to1934," *Acadiensis*, Vol. 5, No. 2 (Spring 1976), pp. 61-63; Ernesto López Losa, "Institutions, Technical Change and the Development of the Spanish Fishing Industry (1858-1936)," in Bertil Andersson (ed.), *Swedish and International Fisheries* (Gothenburg, 1999), pp. 68-71.

included a request for a training ship "for the establishment of a naval brigade."[20] That concept took a new turn in December 1898 when Prime Minister Sir James Winter, anticipating an economic recovery based on the railway and growth in the mining and forestry sectors, advised the Colonial Office that he was willing to consider forming a local branch of the Royal Naval Reserve.[21] It is a mystery why Winter was open to a reserve but not to a volunteer force for cable protection, but it is indisputable that a reserve would cater to the British obsession with sea power. That it would also play to Newfoundland's loyalty and maritime traditions was icing on the cake.

The Newfoundland Royal Naval Reserve was unofficially born in November 1900 when fifty reservists left for a Caribbean training cruise aboard HMS *Charybdis*.[22] Despite a second cruise in 1901, the official start-up did not occur until 1902 when the Bond government pledged to spend £3,000 annually on a force of not less than 600 reservists. Although this was a pittance, the Admiralty was so enamoured of Newfoundland setting an example for the other colonies that it gladly assumed the lion's share of the costs, dispatching a commanding officer and instructors to St. John's, along with an old third-class cruiser, HMS *Calypso*, to serve as a stationary drill ship. Perhaps not coincidentally, British concerns about the vulnerability of Newfoundland's cable stations instantly ceased, suggesting that there may have been an understanding, tacit or otherwise, that the reservists would guard the stations if this were necessary.[23]

By forging a direct link between Newfoundland and one of the most hallowed British institutions, the reserve widened the pro-British streak of Newfoundland nationalism. It also quickly came to embody it, as shown by the presence of a reservist on the cover of the original sheet music for Governor Sir Cavendish Boyle's "Ode to Newfoundland," which was published in 1902 and became the national anthem two years later. In 1903 Newfoundland declared 24 May (the late Queen Victoria's birthday) as Empire Day, a national holiday

---

[20] A. M. Fraser, "Relations with Canada," in MacKay (ed.), *Newfoundland*, p. 453.
[21] TNA:PRO, C. O. 194, Vol. 245, fols. 370-71, Murray to Fisher, 20 Dec. 1898.
[22] Mark C. Hunter, *To Employ and Uplift Them: The Newfoundland Naval Reserve, 1899-1926* (St. John's, 2009), pp. 44-49; Bernard Ransom, "A Nursery of Fighting Seamen?: The Newfoundland Royal Naval Reserve, 1901-1920," in Michael L. Hadley *et al.* (eds.), *A Nation's Navy: In Quest of Canadian Naval Identity* (Montreal and Kingston, 1996), pp. 239-55.
[23] This interpretation would tie up a loose end in the work of Paul Kennedy, who claimed that "The open and undefended Newfoundland coast, where most of the Atlantic cables landed, was a problem which they [the Colonial Defence Committee] also never satisfactorily solved." See Kennedy, "Imperial cable communications," p. 746.

Fig. 52: Cover sheet to the first edition of "The Ode to Newfoundland," 1902. Source: The Rooms Provincial Archives Division, NA 1529. The juxtaposition of reservist and sealer on this historic document reveals the depth of national pride in the Newfoundland Royal Naval Reserve.

designed "to impress upon the minds of future generations— the children of the Empire—the necessity of co-hesion [sic] and union."[24] The fervour continued in 1904 when, as part of the *entente cordiale*, France relinquished its rights to land and dry fish on the treaty shore in return for financial compensation and territory in West Africa.[25] It was no great loss for France, as all but a handful of its fishermen had long since abandoned the shore in favour of the Grand Banks, but to Newfound-landers it marked the end of decades of resentment and frustration. With saltfish prices beginning to rise, iron ore production surging at the Bell Island mines (opened in 1895), and a deal about to be struck for a pulp and paper mill in what would become Grand Falls, the future seemed golden indeed.

As a stationary drill ship HMS *Calypso* was literally a fixture at her berth in the congested west end of St. John's Harbour. Because that setting precluded artillery practice from *Calypso*'s decks, the government offered the Admiralty the use of the old Narrows batteries for shore-based training. Although for a while it appeared that one of the Signal Hill batteries would be chosen, the Admiralty instead picked Fort Amherst, where in November 1905 the reservists began target practice with "heavy gun."[26] Signal Hill had to settle for use as a drilling ground by the Church Lads' Brigade and similar cadet corps.

---

[24] 3 Ed. VII, c. 5 (passed 20 May 1903).
[25] Hiller, "The Newfoundland Fisheries Issue in Anglo-French Treaties, 1713-1904," pp. 1-23. See also his "From 1713 to 3PS: The French Presence in Newfoundland," *Newfoundland Quarterly*, Vol. 96, No. 1 (Spring 2003), pp. 40-47, and "The 1904 Anglo-French Newfoundland Fisheries Convention: Another Look," *Acadiensis*, Vol. 25, No. 1 (Autumn 1995), pp. 82-98.
[26] *Evening Telegram*, 21 Nov. 1905, p. 4.

Fig. 53: "C. L. B. [Church Lads' Brigade] Drilling on Signal Hill, St. John's N. F.," ca. 1910. Source: The Rooms Provincial Archives Division, VA 33-71. The Church Lads' Brigade and other denominational cadet corps reflected Newfoundland's embrace of the era's martial spirit.

Sponsored by the Church of England, the brigade was part of an empire-wide movement that in Newfoundland spawned imitators among the major denominations.[27] The cadet corps may have lacked the reserve's cachet, but they reinforced Newfoundlanders' love of the empire and reflected the era's infatuation for all things military.

Signal Hill, The Narrows, and the Newfoundland Royal Naval Reserve would play mutual roles in the First World War, which began after the assassination of Archduke Franz Ferdinand of Austria on 28 June 1914 gave vent to tensions that had been stoked by the naval armaments race, the strident nationalisms of the period, and the various interlocking alliances that the global powers had forged while jockeying to advance their interests. Locally, the war is best remembered for the butchery of the Newfoundland Regiment at Beaumont-Hamel, France on 1 July 1916, at the start of the Somme Offensive. In a situation rich with irony, more than 20,000 British and empire troops died while fighting for French soil that day, including 324 of the 809 Newfoundlanders who were there.[28] Back home, the tragedy soon engendered a sense that, by the blood of its sons, Newfoundland had become a nation in its own right.[29] The British

---

[27] On the cadet corps, see Nicholson, *The Fighting Newfoundlander*, pp. 91-97.
[28] Patrick O'Flaherty, *Lost Country: The Rise and Fall of Newfoundland, 1843-1933* (St. John's, 2005), p. 461, n. 349. All but a handful of the regiment's 485 survivors were wounded.
[29] Robert J. Harding, "Glorious Tragedy: Newfoundland's Cultural Memory of the Attack at Beaumont Hamel, 1916-1925," *Newfoundland and Labrador Studies*, Vol. 21, No. 1 (2006), pp. 3-40.

connection remained important to the Newfoundland identity—the men, after all, had been part of a British brigade, and there was great pride in 1917 when, with the approval of King George V, the unit was officially renamed the Royal Newfoundland Regiment—but it was no longer as dominant. That, however, was more than could be said of the old nationalist mainstays of Cabot and Francophobia, which had become redundant and were shunted to the sidelines.

In the ensuing decades much became lost in the regiment's glare, not least the wartime contributions of 2,000 naval reservists—odd, given Newfoundland's maritime character and history as a nursery of seamen—and home defence, where events with immense long-term implications occurred. Shortly after Britain declared war against Germany on 5 August (by virtue of which Newfoundland and Canada were automatically in the war), Newfoundland naval reservists were dispatched to the Cuckold's Cove and Heart's Content cable stations, and to the Canadian-owned Cape Race wireless station.[30] This was a local manifestation of the wartime preoccupation with cable and wireless, which led the British to cut all German cables and to shut down all German-owned international wireless stations.[31] Indeed, the attack on a German wireless station in Togoland, Africa on 12 August was the first British land action of the war.[32] Because Anglo-American's monopoly had expired, the British were concerned that the prominence in Newfoundland of the American-owned Commercial and Western Union cable companies would render the island a weak link in the all red system. They need not have worried. British censorship measures and a requirement that cable messages to and from Britain had to be in plain language, thus making them longer and more expensive, reduced American cable capacity by half before the war was over.[33] Out of self-preservation, the United States Navy pursued new developments in wireless technology in order to offset the British stranglehold on cable.

---

[30] TRPAD, GN 2.5, file 379 (3), "Newfoundland in the Great War"/ F. A. Mackenzie [typescript], Office of the Colonial Secretary fonds, p. 14.
[31] Hugill, *Global Communications since 1844*, p. 46; Beauchamp, *History of Telegraphy*, pp. 323-24.
[32] Robert Holland, "The British Empire and the Great War, 1914-1918," in Brown and Louis (eds.), *The Oxford History of the British Empire: Volume IV: The Twentieth Century*, p. 114.
[33] Jonathan Reed Winkler, *Nexus: Strategic Communications and American Security in World War I* (Cambridge, MA, 2008), pp. 37-40; Hugh G. J. Aitken, *The Continuous Wave: Technology and American Radio, 1900-1932* (Princeton, 1985), pp. 250-301; Tarrant, *Atlantic Sentinel*, pp. 110-11.

The status of St. John's as a wartime communications hub was enhanced by its designation in fall 1914 as the Royal Navy's Naval Intelligence Centre for the northwest Atlantic, and, the following year, by the opening of His Majesty's Wireless Station, Mount Pearl, five kilometres west of the city. Built by Marconi's Wireless Telegraph Company, the Mount Pearl station was one of twenty that the firm erected for the Admiralty at strategic locations around the world, in the process making the navy "completely independent of existing commercial networks."[34] Like Cape Race and the Cuckold's Cove and Heart's Content cable stations, the Mount Pearl station was defended (initially at least) by Newfoundland naval reservists.

The reserve answered to the Commander-in-Chief of the Royal Navy's revived North America and West Indies station, which once again made Halifax the hub of regional naval activity. Since Halifax already had an intelligence centre and two powerful wireless stations, Canadian officials were baffled by the Admiralty's reliance on St. John's.[35] Little did they know that the Admiralty saw St. John's as a way of avoiding command and control issues with Halifax and Ottawa, one of many slights that Canada would have to endure at Admiralty hands as its neophyte navy began a tortuous rise to independent command. Despite the intelligence centre imbroglio, the war would feature a striking degree of cooperation between Canada and Newfoundland, lending credence to Sir Robert Thorburn's musings, although not yet to Sir Robert Bond's. One of the earliest signs appeared in October 1914 when the Canadians, unable to fill the 700-man complement of their lone east coast ship, HMCS *Niobe*, were saved from embarrassment by the transfer of an officer and 106 men from the Newfoundland Royal Naval Reserve.[36] But the relationship was truly consummated during the course of the war because of the impact of the submarine.

From the 1740s until the end of the age of sail, the Royal Navy's guiding principle in wartime was to concentrate the fleet in home waters, a deployment that provided insurance against invasion, protected British maritime trade, and disrupted enemy trade and naval operations, including possible forays to the Caribbean and North America.[37] As Ternay and Richery had proven, leakage was bound to

---

[34] Beauchamp, *History of Telegraphy*, pp. 322-23.
[35] Roger Sarty, *The Maritime Defence of Canada* (Toronto, 1996), pp. 65-66.
[36] Ransom, "A Nursery of Fighting Seamen?," pp. 247-48.
[37] N. A. M. Rodger, "Sea-Power and Empire, 1688-1793," in P. J. Marshall and Alaine Low (eds.), *The Oxford History of the British Empire: Volume II: The Eighteenth Century* (Oxford, 1998), pp. 169-83; Michael Duffy, "The Establishment of the Western Squadron as the Linchpin of British Naval Strategy," in Michael Duffy (ed.), *Parameters of British Naval Power 1650-1850* (Exeter, 1992), pp. 60-81.

occur, but rogue squadrons like theirs tended to have little ability to inflict lasting damage. Within this broader "strategy" (in English, the word dates only to 1810), the navy practised local strategies of close blockade and loose blockade, the former—much more demanding and therefore rarely used—in hopes of preventing an enemy from getting under way, the latter in hopes of drawing him out for a decisive encounter, failing which the fleet would happily settle for command of the seas. With the advent of steam-powered ships there was a shift to close blockade by light vessels supported by battleships, leaving cruisers free to prowl the trade lanes.[38] By 1914, however, new technologies such as mines, torpedo boats, and submarines posed so much risk to the Royal Navy's expensive modern battleships that close blockade became out of the question. During the First World War the navy opted instead for distant blockade, withdrawing the main battle fleet to Scapa Flow (the northern North Sea exit) and positioning flotilla vessels and older battleships across the Channel exit to contain the German navy and stifle German maritime commerce.[39]

The new strategy worked well against surface vessels. The Battle of Jutland, in which Newfoundland reservists participated as members of the Royal Navy, was the region's only significant naval engagement, after which the German High Seas Fleet by and large kept to its lair. But there was no way that "U-Boats" could be confined to the North Sea, and it was only a matter of time before they would also be capable of crossing the Atlantic. In May 1915 the Colonial Office warned Canada of this very possibility, and in October 1916, U 53 made it real by visiting Newport, Rhode Island in the then neutral United States, sinking five merchant ships (including Bowring Brothers' S. S. *Stephano*) before going home. In the broader North Atlantic the submarine threat forced Britain to adopt the convoy system in 1917 to protect Canadian and American food shipments. This favoured Halifax and Sydney, which were designated as convoy assembly ports, but not St. John's, which was only an emergency fuel depot for convoy escort vessels.[40] With this, as well, the Admiralty abolished the St. John's Naval Intelligence Centre and concentrated regional intelligence resources in Halifax. The submarine threat also prompted

---

[38] James Goldrick, "The Battleship Fleet: The Test of War 1895-1919," in Hill (ed.), *Oxford Illustrated History of the Royal Navy*, p. 280; Peter Padfield, *The Battleship Era* (London, 1975), pp. 203-09.

[39] On the blockade's economic dimensions, see Eric W. Osborne, *Britain's Economic Blockade of Germany 1914-1919* (London, 2004).

[40] Thomas G. Frothingham, *The Naval History of the World War: The United States in the War 1917-1918* (Freeport, NY, 1971 [originally published 1924-26]), 3 vols., Vol. 3, p. 135.

Fig. 54: W. F. Rendell, Newfoundland Legion of Frontiersmen, September 1914. Source: Dean Bruckshaw, History and Archives Section, Countess Mountbatten's Own Legion of Frontiersmen. Rendell would go on to play a significant role in Newfoundland's twentieth-century military history.

the creation of the Canada-Newfoundland Patrol, with the Royal Canadian Navy assuming responsibility for Newfoundland's south and west coasts—and thus Cabot and Belle Isle straits—and Newfoundland for the remainder of the island and the Labrador coast.[41] Discharged reservists manned the Newfoundland ships under the direction of the reserve's commanding officer, Commander Anthony MacDermott.

In St. John's the submarine menace provoked the first measures for harbour defence since the American Civil War. Coastal defence was completely neglected in favour of securing The Narrows, where in July 1916 Waldegrave Battery was reactivated and armed with a single 12-pounder gun from HMS *Briton*, as HMS *Calypso* was known after February 1916.[42] The battery was manned by members of the Newfoundland Legion of Frontiersmen, who answered to MacDermott. The frontiersmen were a local manifestation of an empire-wide volunteer movement founded in London in 1904 by Roger Ashwell Pocock, a Boer War veteran who had also served in Canada's North West Mounted Police.[43] Rooted in imperial idealism and a romantic concept of the frontier—Pocock saw the frontiersmen as scouts for British military intelligence—the

[41] TRPAD, GN 1.10.0, Correspondence, Sept. 1914 – Dec. 1917 [microfilm], Office of the Governor fonds, Davidson to Secretary of State, 2 March 1917; Patricia Ruth O'Brien, "The Newfoundland Patriotic Association: The Administration of the War Effort, 1914-1918" (Unpublished MA thesis, Memorial University of Newfoundland, 1981), pp. 227-28.
[42] TRPAD, MG 562 (Fort Waldegrave), Log Books, 1916-1918.
[43] *The History of the Legion of Frontiersmen: With particular reference to the Legion of Frontiersmen Canadian Division* (Regina, n.d.), p. 9; Robert H. MacDonald, *Sons of the Empire: The Frontier and the Boy Scout Movement, 1890-1918* (Toronto, 1993), pp. 31-61.

movement reached St. John's in 1912 after first being introduced into northern Newfoundland and Labrador by Dr. Arthur William Wakefield of the Royal National Mission to Deep Sea Fishermen. In 1914, when the Newfoundland government refused Wakefield's request for the frontiersmen to proceed to Europe as a unit, most of its 150 members, including Wakefield, joined the Newfoundland Regiment, although a few found their way into the reserve. Scarcely half a dozen remained when they were asked to serve at "Fort Waldegrave," the inflated name by which the battery was thereafter known.

The frontiersmen had company in The Narrows. In October 1916, in a move inspired by U 53's Rhode Island escapade, a boom made of timber and chain was placed across The Narrows between Chain and Pancake rocks from sunset to sunrise.[44] The contraption was the pride and joy of Minister of Marine and Fisheries Archibald Piccott, who took credit for its construction. An elaborate affair, it opened in the middle, one half moored during daytime on the north side of The Narrows, the other half on the south side; at night the two ends were drawn together by motorboat crews. In addition to the cover provided by Fort Waldegrave, the boom was backed by a searchlight on SS *Fiona*, and by a steam launch positioned inside the boom and armed with a machine gun. In 1917 the whaler SS *Port Saunders*, manned by discharged reservists and equipped with a 12-pounder gun, searchlight, and wireless, was detached from the Canada-Newfoundland Patrol and stationed outside the boom at night to ensure that it was opened only to authorized vessels or in emergency situations.[45] Night-time approaches to the harbour would have been difficult enough without such obstacles, given that the Fort Amherst light and the harbour's leading lights were extinguished, and the Cape Spear light reduced to a visibility of 19.3 kilometres.[46]

Early submarines were essentially surface vessels capable of submerging for brief periods. As such, they relied more on deck-mounted cannons than on torpedoes to attack their targets. It was therefore reasonable to expect that they might be sighted on the surface, to which end, and as a complement to the Narrows defences,

---

[44] TRPAD, GN 1.10.0, Davidson to Secretary of State, 23 May 1917, and Piccott to Bennett, 9 June 1917; TRPAD, GN 8, files 82-94, William Frederick Lloyd records, Office of the Prime Minister fonds, Squires to Piccott, 25 Oct. 1917.
[45] TRPAD, GN 1.10.0, Davidson to Long, 18 July 1917.
[46] TRPAD, GN 1.10.0, Davidson to Secretary of State, 23 May 1917, and Davidson to Long, 18 July 1917.

two watchmen were stationed at each of Cape Spear, Fort Amherst, and Signal Hill, plus one at King's Wharf.[47] According to Minister Piccott the Signal Hill watchmen stood duty in "the Blockhouse," by which he obviously meant Cabot Tower. If they saw suspicious activity they were to alert the local Admiralty Intelligence Officer or Piccott himself by phone. The phone lines likely began to hum in May 1918 when, in an effort to divert American naval resources from Europe, five powerful new German submarines crossed the Atlantic and began preying on targets between North Carolina and Newfoundland. Merchant ships bound to and from St. John's and Halifax were sunk, as were fishing schooners on the Grand Banks and the Scotian Shelf.

It was in this darkest hour on the home front that Newfoundland abruptly withdrew from the Canada-Newfoundland Patrol, ostensibly because it was a waste of money and because the puny guns on the patrol vessels were no match for those on the submarines, but in reality because, in a blatant case of profiteering, the private owners of the coastal fleet had sold off too many ships. As a result, the government was having trouble finding vessels to deliver food and medical services to communities in northern Newfoundland and Labrador.[48] In the age-old struggle between guns and butter, Newfoundland had chosen butter, doubtless hoping that Canada would supply the guns. Although the Royal Canadian Navy more than rose to the occasion, Canada, like Newfoundland, also needed help. The Admiralty, having already recommended that the Canadian contingent of the Canada-Newfoundland Patrol should be increased from twenty-two vessels to a breathtaking 108, now promised to donate thirty-six trawlers and thirty-six drifters that were already under construction in Canadian shipyards, and originally slated for use in European waters. Since the Admiralty could not comply with an additional Canadian request for six destroyers and six fast trawlers for convoy escort service, it suggested that Canada approach the United States for surface support and for the establishment of anti-submarine air patrols. Before the war ended, the United States Navy was conducting anti-submarine patrols off southwest Nova Scotia, had loaned ships to the Royal Canadian Navy as convoy escorts, and was flying anti-submarine air patrols from Eastern Passage (near Halifax) and North Sydney. Plans for an air patrol from Cape Race, which were scrapped when the war ended, were a portent of future American involvement in the defence of Newfoundland.

---

[47] TRPAD, GN 1.10.0, Piccott to Bennett, 9 June 1917.
[48] Candow, "The Defence of Newfoundland," p. 130; O'Brien, "Newfoundland Patriotic Association," pp. 238-39.

American assistance enabled the Canadians to assume sole responsibility for the naval defence of Newfoundland and Labrador, which included the addition of a minesweeping service for the port of St. John's. In a replay of the war's early months, Newfoundland redeemed itself through the participation of more than 300 naval reservists in Canada's expanded anti-submarine fleet.[49] In a further strengthening of the Canadian connection, the Royal Newfoundland Regiment supplied guards for the Bell Island iron ore mines, on which the Sydney, Nova Scotia steel plant had become dependent for supplies of iron ore.[50] Indeed, it was said at the time that "one shell in the boiler house or power house on Bell Island might stop production [in Sydney] for six months."[51]

Apart from the Canadian minesweeping service, the defence of St. John's was unsophisticated and inadequate. Governor Sir Walter Davidson admitted as much when he said of Piccott's boom that it was "not of great defensive value but it is considered to be better than nothing. It has a certain moral value and it is hoped that the enemy may not know its weakness."[52] He could have included Fort Waldegrave in that judgment, because its selection as the lone harbour defence did not make sense on any level except a symbolic one. As long ago as 1880 a British colonial defence report had identified a need for rifled artillery on Signal Hill to defend against enemy warships with similar weaponry.[53] The days when a ship—or now, a submarine—needed to make a run through The Narrows in order to fire on St. John's had passed, and The Narrows ought to have been relegated at best to a secondary role. Even so, the defence of The Narrows, including the use of a boom and the stationing of watchmen at Signal Hill and Fort Amherst, was a continuation of centuries of local military tradition. It was also a fitting complement to the presence of Newfoundland reservists in the British and Canadian navies, proving that the concept of the fisheries as a nursery of seamen was still valid.[54]

---

[49] Ransom, "A Nursery of Fighting Seamen?," p. 253.

[50] Newfoundland. *Journal of the House of Assembly*, 1919, Appendix, "Report of the Department of Militia" (1919), p. 558.

[51] Paul A. Bridle (ed.), *Documents on Relations between Canada and Newfoundland* (Ottawa, 1974), Vol. 1, 1935-49, Document 3, Memorandum by Joint Staff Committee, 22 March 1937.

[52] TRPAD, GN 1.10.0, Davidson to Long, 18 July 1917.

[53] TNA:PRO, C. O. 194, Vol. 199, fols. 20-31, "Report by Lieutenant Morgan, R. M., on the Batteries, Barracks, etc. at St. John's, Newfoundland," 25 Feb. 1880.

[54] On British fishermen during the First World War, see Robinson, "Effective Use of Scarce Resources," pp. 104-08.

There was one other continuity, which, paradoxically, heralded major change. Newfoundland had done its bit for the empire during the war, but as the least populous dominion there was a limit both to what it could contribute and what it could do to defend itself. It had long looked to the Royal Navy and the British Army for protection, but the scale and technology of modern war had begun to erode that connection, although not the paradigm of dependence. Combined with geography, these same factors had elevated Newfoundland's value to Canada, and it was Canada that filled Britain's shoes. Canada, however, was no less affected by Britain's diminished North American presence, and it, too, had to seek help elsewhere. The United States was to Canada as Canada was to Newfoundland.

CABLE, WIRELESS, AND THE WARDEN OF THE WATCH TOWER

Within three years of the end of the war, the Royal Newfoundland Regiment, the naval reserve, and the frontiersmen were all disbanded, and HMS *Briton* was sold. Nonetheless, the regiment's reputation lived on, for it had forged a new and significant chapter in the country's history. St. John's residents also continued to find room in their hearts for an older military symbol, the noonday gun. When signalman Michael Cantwell died on 3 January 1919 from injuries incurred in an accidental explosion just before noon on New Year's Eve, the press reverentially acknowledged that he had minded the gun for over a quarter of a century.[55]

Perhaps bad luck really does come in threes, because Cantwell's death was followed by two more mishaps on Signal Hill, both of them affecting remnants of the imperial garrison. Cantwell's successor, former assistant signalman John Bartlett, was in town on business on 18 February 1920 when he happened to glance at the hill and discovered to his horror that his house was on fire.[56] By the time he found a horse and sled and made his way up the hill it was too late to save anything. Fortunately for Bartlett, his wife and four children had been rescued by assistant signalman Eli Hayward, who after spotting the fire from his perch in Cabot Tower scurried down and helped them get out of the house. The house and an out-building that disappeared

---

[55] *Evening Telegram*, 2 Jan. 1919, p. 4; *Daily News*, 3 Jan. 1919, p. 3. The explosion allegedly happened when a spark from Cantwell's pipe ignited the gun's powder charge, which he was fetching from a locker in Cabot Tower. There is no doubt that the explosion occurred inside the tower, since it blew out all of the windows and doors, and caused so much damage to the interior that it had to be rebuilt.

[56] *Evening Telegram*, 19 Feb. 1920, p. 6.

Fig. 55: Robert William ("Bob") Gardner, Signal Hill, 1 July 1946. Source: Phyllis Fleuriau. Former naval reservist Bob Gardner was signalman from 1923 to 1946, a transitional period for Signal Hill and for Newfoundland. In many people's eyes, he *was* Signal Hill.

Fig. 56: Hotchkiss breech-loading gun from HMS *Briton*. Source: Parks Canada. This historic weapon served as the noonday gun from 1922 to 1949.

with it had been the main surviving components of the century-old armoury/artificers' complex. On 18 December 1920 another link to the imperial era was lost when Signal Hill Hospital went up in flames, also putting an end to the hill's use for medical purposes.[57]

Construction of a new signalman's house on ground close to the old one began in November 1922 and finished in June 1923.[58] In the interim Cabot Tower was fitted with rooms for Bartlett, which must have been quite cramped if his wife and children joined him there. It is not known if Bartlett ever set foot in the new, hip-roofed bungalow, but if he did his stay was short-lived, because in September 1923 Robert William Gardner became the new signalman.[59] Born in 1886 in Flower's Cove on the former French treaty shore, Bob Gardner grew up in Bareneed, Conception Bay, where he fished with his father from the age of ten.[60] In 1903 he trained as a naval reservist aboard HMS *Calypso* and took the requisite cruise on HMS *Charybdis*. During the First World War he joined the Royal Navy and served with distinction in the English Channel and the Dardanelles. As fate would have it, the new noonday gun as of October

---

[57] *Evening Herald* (St. John's), 20 Dec. 1920, p. 8.
[58] TRPAD,GN 4.1.C, Board of Works Journal, 1922-23.
[59] *Evening Telegram*, 9 July 1946, p. 3, and 10 July 1946, p. 3.
[60] Unless otherwise noted, details of Bob Gardner's life are from the following sources: *Evening Telegram*, 9 July 1946, p. 3, and 10 July 1946, p. 3; personal communications between the author and the late Phyllis (Gardner) Fleuriau (his daughter); personal communications between Douglas Gardner (his son) and Rose Veitch, former collections manager, Parks Canada, Newfoundland East Field Unit; personal communications between Douglas Gardner and the author. His birth date has been extrapolated from his *Evening Telegram* obituary, which stated that he was sixty years old when he died.

1922 was a three-pounder Hotchkiss breech-loader that had come from HMS *Briton*, and before that from HMS *Rowan*, on which, amazingly, Gardner had sailed during the war.[61] As a naval veteran with a personal attachment to the gun, Gardner took great pride in his work, paying monthly visits to Joseph Roper's shop to check the time of his American-made Waltham watch. Despite such fastidiousness, there continued to be lapses in the gun's timing. In January 1926 the editor of the *Evening Telegram*, tongue firmly in cheek, lamented: "Ten minutes slow last week, fired two minutes sooner on Saturday, and with about eight minutes in the alteration yesterday, the Signal Hill gun was responsible for making many people in the churches completely lose track of the discourses. Apparently it is back on schedule, since the time of firing to-day corresponds with that of yesterday, but there are even now many bitter complaints heard because of the ten minutes irretrievably lost."[62] As the editorial's humorous tone suggests, the gun had become part of the fabric of the city, and few really cared if it was fired exactly at noon. Affordable, mass-produced wristwatches were now widely available, and broadcast radio, with its regularly scheduled programmes and, in some cases, time signals, was slowly spreading in Newfoundland, and thus offering a new way of obtaining precise time.[63] But if the noon signal had entered the realm of nostalgia, other practical uses were being found for the gun itself, which was now fired to announce the start and end of Daylight Saving Time in spring and fall respectively, and to inform the community that the annual regatta was a go.[64] These uses may have deepened people's attachment to the gun, for when the government decided to discontinue it on 1 August 1931 as a depression-era economy measure, the outcry was so intense that it was quickly restored.[65] (The reprieve did not extend to Bob Gardner, whose salary was cut by ten percent, and especially not to assistant signalman Baxter Chaytor, whose position was eliminated.) History repeated itself when someone wrote a poem about the latest silencing, but it was a tedious effort that made people long for the genuine wit of Maurice Devine, who had died in 1915.

---

[61] *Evening Telegram*, 4 Oct. 1922, p. 4.
[62] *Evening Telegram*, 10 Jan. 1926, p. 6.
[63] Ernest Ash, "The Story of Radio in Newfoundland," in Smallwood (ed.), *The Book of Newfoundland*, Vol. 1, pp. 339-50.
[64] TRPAD, GN34/2, Department of Marine and Fisheries, Box 148, "Cabot Tower. Noon Gun."
[65] *Evening Telegram*, 3 Aug. 1931, p. 6.

While Gardner clung to the gun and the flags, modernity's noose grew steadily tighter. In 1926 the Commercial Cable Company diverted two Waterville-Hazel Hill cables to Quidi Vidi Harbour, doubling the number of cables that came ashore on or near the Signal Hill Peninsula.[66] This was a bold move at the time, because advances in wireless technology had put the cable firms under severe economic pressure. Wireless had been utterly transformed by the use of continuous wave transmitters and the resort to shorter wavelengths (or higher frequencies). Unlike spark-based systems, continuous wave transmitters sent waves of constant strength and frequency, thereby significantly reducing interference and improving tuning.[67] Since this also enabled wireless transmission of the human voice, broadcast radio was born in the 1920s. Short wave's superiority for daytime communication was discovered by accident after the *Titanic* disaster, when amateur operators were banished to this supposedly useless part of the electromagnetic spectrum to prevent interference with commercial transmissions.[68] By the early 1920s American amateurs were reaching their brethren across the Atlantic and Pacific oceans, and communication by long wave was beginning to look very silly indeed. In tandem, shorter wavelengths and continuous wave transmitters dramatically improved the range, ease, and reliability of long-distance wireless communication, and at a fraction of the cost of spark transmission. Even though Marconi was almost singlehandedly responsible for the spark transmitter/long wave model, it would have been business suicide to stay with it. As of 25 October 1926, the Canadian Marconi Company (as it had been renamed the previous year) no longer sent transatlantic messages via Glace Bay, but via its new short wave facility in Drummondville, Quebec.

By 1927 the cable companies had lost roughly half their business, their stocks had nosedived, and the end appeared to be near.[69] However, the British government was not about to let cable die. Whatever the merits of wireless, cable was more secure, and since secrecy would always be vital in wartime, the all red system was very much alive. Indeed, the government's unease over the growing number of American cable companies in Newfoundland had led it, in

---

[66] De Cogan, "Cable Landings," p. 32.

[67] Aitken, *The Continuous Wave*, p. 515. Of the competing means that were used to generate continuous waves, the vacuum tube had won out by 1925.

[68] Jerome S. Berg, *On the Short Waves, 1923-1945* (Jefferson, NC, 1998), pp. 10-11; Aitken, *The Continuous Wave*, pp. 514-17; Coe, *Wireless Radio*, pp. 41-42.

[69] Baker, *History of the Marconi Company*, pp. 229-33; Haigh, *Cableships and Submarine Cables*, pp. 152-53.

1920, to purchase the cables and Harbour Grace facilities of the Direct United States Cable Company.[70] In 1929, responding to the seemingly lethal threat from wireless, it forcibly merged a number of British and dominion cable and wireless firms, including Direct and, shockingly, the Marconi Wireless Telegraph Company, into what would become known as Cable and Wireless Limited. In a sign that strategic considerations were paramount, it reserved rights to the entire system in the event of a "national emergency" (that is, war). Despite some unavoidable consolidation after the merger, cable was alive and well, and Newfoundland's place in British transatlantic communications was assured.

In 1926 the Canadian Marconi Company maintained thirty-one wireless stations in Newfoundland and Labrador under contract to the Newfoundland and Canadian governments.[71] Because the paradigm shift in wireless created overcapacity, the Canadian government closed several of its stations, including, in 1930, Cape Race. That decision was based on the assumption that an adjacent radio direction finding station, opened in 1918, would suffice for marine safety.[72] A radio direction finder enabled an operator to establish the bearing of a passing ship by honing in on its radio signal, which information he would then relay to the ship. By 1920 the Cape Race radio direction finding station was giving bearings to an average of 385 ships a month. Useful though this was, it was no substitute for the greater all-round utility of a wireless station. The maritime community protested, and one year later the Cape Race wireless station reopened.

The temporary closure of Cape Race also incited demands for a wireless station in St. John's, which had inexplicably been without one since the Admiralty's Mount Pearl facility closed in 1924.[73] Signal Hill was the early favourite to host such a station, and although there were concerns that its soil cover might be unsuitable for grounding, there was much in its favour: its height, its coastal location, and the sheer force of its communications history, including its connection with Marconi, which had not altogether ended in 1901.[74] In July 1920 Montreal-based Marconi engineers had installed a temporary transmitter in Cabot Tower, from which they made wireless telephone

---

[70] Tarrant, *Atlantic Sentinel*, pp. 110-11.
[71] Harding, "Wireless in Newfoundland," p. 15.
[72] *Evening Telegram*, 2 Aug. 1930, p. 6; Dubreuil, *Come Quick Danger*, p. 28; *Encyclopedia of Newfoundland and Labrador*, Vol. 5, "Navigational Aids."
[73] *Evening Telegram*, 24 Oct. 1930, p. 6.
[74] *Evening Telegram*, 11 Oct. 1930, p. 15, and 13 Oct. 1930, p. 14.

contact with delegates of the Imperial Press Union en route from Liverpool to Montreal aboard RMS *Victorian*.[75] On the twenty-fifth Prime Minister Sir Richard Squires was the first of several dignitaries to talk with the ship; the others included the tower's old friend Sir Edgar Bowring, who had been knighted in 1915. Although the Cabot Tower-RMS *Victorian* affair was nothing more than a stunt to gain publicity for Marconi in the emerging field of wireless telephony, some Newfoundland authors have wrongly claimed that it was the first transatlantic wireless transmission of the human voice, and that wireless telephony was "an invention of Signor Marconi."[76] In fact, the first transatlantic wireless transmission of the human voice had occurred in 1915 (from Arlington, Virginia to Paris, France), and wireless telephony had been invented by Canadian Reginald Fessenden in 1906. If nothing else, however, the erroneous claims reflect an enduring attachment to Marconi and wireless in St. John's.

Just as the *Titanic* disaster was a turning point in global acceptance of wireless technology, so, too, it took a disaster to expose the shortcomings of wireless coverage in Newfoundland and Labrador, and to put Signal Hill back on the wireless map. The trigger was the loss of Bowring Brothers' SS *Viking* and the deaths of twenty-eight of its men after the aging sealing vessel was rocked by a series of explosions on 15 March 1931 as she lay jammed in the ice about thirteen kilometres east of the Horse Islands.[77] Because Horse Island itself had a wireless station, operator Otis Bartlett was able to get word to St. John's in the usual manner, that is, by wireless to Fogo and thence by telegraph. Two steamers bearing food and medical supplies for the 125 survivors set out from the capital on the sixteenth, but contact with the rescuers became complicated when a blizzard put the government telegraph line south of Fogo out of commission for three days.[78] A potential "second catastrophe" was averted when the resourceful Bartlett reached an amateur wireless operator in Port Albert, Notre Dame Bay, who in turn made contact with a fellow amateur in the

---

[75] Baker, *History of the Marconi Company*, pp. 184-87; Ash, "The Story of Radio in Newfoundland," p. 340.

[76] The myth that this was the first transatlantic wireless transmission of the human voice seems to have originated with Ernest Ash. See his "The Story of Radio in Newfoundland," p. 349. On this basis, it was perpetuated by the author in the *Encyclopedia of Newfoundland and Labrador*, Vol. 5, "Signal Hill." For the erroneous claim that Marconi invented wireless telephony, see Michael McCarthy *et al.*, *The Voice of Generations: A History of Communications in Newfoundland* (St. John's, 1994), p. 147.

[77] *Evening Telegram*, 17 March 1931, p. 1.

[78] *Evening Telegram*, 23 March 1931, p. 6; Ash, "The Story of Radio in Newfoundland," pp. 347-48.

Fig. 57: Cabot Tower, St. John's, Newfoundland, 1933. Source: Library and Archives Canada/Credit: Clifford M. Johnston/PA-056693. In a clash of modern and traditional communication technologies, one of the wireless station's two antenna towers stands to the left of the car, while the radio direction finder's loop antenna pokes up from Cabot Tower's deck, just below the yard of the main signal mast.

capital. For those still smarting from the ill-advised closure of the Cape Race wireless station, this was the final straw. Demands for a central wireless station in St. John's capable of reaching, directly or indirectly, any station in Newfoundland and Labrador, could no longer be ignored.[79]

The critics got their wish on 12 August 1933 when the Canadian Marconi Company, under contract to the Newfoundland government, opened a combined wireless and radio direction finding station on the second floor of Cabot Tower.[80] The station was staffed seven days a week by three men who worked alternating eight-hour shifts.[81] Since its continuous wave signals were powerful enough to reach a sister station in Battle Harbour, Labrador, the government was able to close the

---

[79] *Evening Telegram*, 23 March 1931, p. 6.
[80] There is a copy of the contract in TRPAD, GN 2.5, file 455, Wireless, 1914-1933, Deputy Secretary of State to Minister of Posts and Telegraphs, 4 May 1933.
[81] Interview with William J. Kelly, 14 Jan. 1978; personal communication, Douglas Gardner to Rose Veitch, 18 June 2005. This staffing arrangement seems to have persisted until confederation, after which round-the-clock staffing ceased.

Fogo station, formerly the junction of the wireless and telegraph systems. (Fogo manager E. J. Myrick was named manager of the Cabot Tower station.) Technically, those systems still intersected, but only by means of a modest telegraph line between Cabot Tower and the St. John's Post Office. The new station ensured that the wireless system would continue to be part of the invisible infrastructure of the seal hunt and the Labrador fishery, and to serve the needs of northern residents. In conjunction with the radio direction finder, it also enhanced marine safety. Operators gave ships their bearings, assisted them with entering or leaving port in poor visibility, monitored the airwaves for distress signals, and broadcast weather and ice conditions.[82] At one fell swoop the Cabot Tower station reinforced the noonday gun's irrelevance to marine navigation and undermined the role of flags in port signalling. Any merchant needing up-to-the-minute shipping intelligence could now get it via telegraph from the post office or by phoning the tower to speak with the duty operator, who, unlike the signalman, did not have to see a vessel to know it was approaching.

Amid the changes, Bob Gardner and his family soldiered on.[83] His wife Mary-Kate mended the mercantile house flags by hand, for which her husband resolutely billed the firms. Their children—two sons and a daughter—were equally industrious, and would, for example, pick wild flowers to sell to tourists. Gardner kept the tower shipshape, storing tools, paint, cleaning supplies, and other equipment on the building's first floor, which had become his workshop. He maintained a daily log in which he entered barometric and temperature readings at sunrise and 2:00 p.m.[84] He also recorded wind strength, although the entries under this heading—light, fresh, strong, or gale—were qualitative and idiosyncratic. Be that as it may, some fishermen and mariners considered Gardner an authority and would not put to sea without phoning the tower for his forecast. Although not a Canadian Marconi Company employee, he also minded the two steel towers that supported the station's antenna, sometimes risking life and limb to de-ice them and keep them from collapsing, as one eventually did. But his main informal duty, which took so much of his time that it came to define him, was that of tourist guide.

---

[82] Personal communication, Captain Harvey Adams, 7 April 2009. See also Sharon A. Babaian, *Radio Communication in Canada: A Historical and Technological Survey* (Ottawa, 1992), pp. 34-35.
[83] Personal communication, Doug Gardner to Rose Veitch, 8 Feb. 2008.
[84] TRPAD, GN 18.19.

Organized tourism came late to Newfoundland, and more so to St. John's than to the west coast, where the ferry connection with Nova Scotia gave that region a pronounced advantage.[85] In their wisdom, the St. John's-based Newfoundland Board of Trade decided that the indifferent state of tourism in the capital was entirely due to the dearth of first-class accommodations.[86] That shortcoming was more than rectified after businessman Walter Monroe became Prime Minister in 1924. Warmly remembered for repealing prohibition, Monroe also launched a series of initiatives to stimulate tourism, including financial assistance to the builders of an eight-story, 137-room hotel in St. John's.[87] The Newfoundland Hotel, which opened in 1926, proved too rich for such a small city (36,444 residents in 1921), and in 1931 the second government of Prime Minister Sir Richard Squires was forced to take it over.

Less spectacularly, Monroe extended government support to the fledgling Newfoundland Tourist and Publicity Commission. Formed in 1925 on the Board of Trade's initiative, the commission was funded (from 1927) by a tax on outgoing first-class steamship passengers.[88]

As described in the incorporating legislation, the commission's mandate was to "Discover, preserve, mark, restore or provide means of access to matters or places of sporting, scenic or historical interest." The emphasis on the sportsman and the nature lover was to be expected—these remain stock tourist types— but recognition that the island's past might interest visitors was a fairly new development. The only antecedents were the Cabot quatercentenary of 1897 and, in 1910, the tercentenary of the founding of Cupids, both of which were aimed at local audiences.[89] With the advent of the commission, Newfoundland's history began to be used to lure tourists to the island, and especially to the capital.

---

[85] On tourism in western Newfoundland, see James E. Candow, *Lomond: The Life and Death of a Newfoundland Woods Town* (St. John's, 1998), pp. 43-52. For Newfoundland generally, see James Overton, *Making a World of Difference: Essays on Tourism, Culture and Development in Newfoundland* (St. John's, 1996).

[86] Newfoundland. *Journal of the House of Assembly*, 1925, Appendix, "Sixteenth Annual Report of the Council of the Newfoundland Board of Trade," pp. 470-71.

[87] Great Britain. *Newfoundland Royal Commission 1933 Report* (London, 1934), p. 69. With thanks to Melvin Baker for the reference.

[88] TRPAD, GN 51.1, Executive minutes, 1925-1930, Newfoundland Tourist Development Board fonds, Minutes Provisional Committee, 29 May 1925.

[89] For the Cupids celebrations, see Melvin Baker and Hans Rollman, "The Cupers Cove (Cupids) Settlement in Historical Perspective" (Unpublished manuscript prepared for D. W. Knight Associates and the Cupids Historical Society, 2001). I am grateful to Bill Gilbert for sharing his copy of the report.

For various reasons—the commission's St. John's focus, Signal Hill's proximity to the Newfoundland Hotel, and the fact that the hill was already a tourist attraction—the commission looked to the hill to meet its need for a place of historical interest. Led by lawyer Brian Dunfield, who became chairman of the historical sub-committee in 1926, the commission urged owners of old smooth-bore cannons found about the city to donate them for mounting in Queen's Battery, which the commission insisted on calling by the imaginative name "The Queen's Own Fort." This stemmed from an erroneous belief that the battery dated from 1705 (during the reign of Queen Anne), as opposed to its actual commencement in 1796. A graduate of the University of London, Brian Dunfield was a brilliant man in the early stages of a distinguished legal career, but as a heritage pioneer he was crippled by the absence of professional historical support. Newfoundland lacked a national archive, and its first university had only opened its doors in 1925 (and would not offer a Newfoundland history course until 1943). As a result, amateurs roamed the land. This would not have mattered if, like Judge Prowse (who had died in 1914), they were competent amateurs, but men and women of this description were few and far between.[90] Placing too much faith in shaky sources, but principally an atrocious article by Deputy Minister of Customs H. W. LeMessurier, the commission embraced the Queen's Own Fort moniker and fed visitors a steady diet of misinformation.[91] In the same vein, the five guns that it managed to install in the battery by March 1930 were chosen solely on the basis of availability, not because they were appropriate to a particular period or told a certain story. Such were the foundations of Newfoundland's first historical restoration.

In March 1930 the manager of the Newfoundland Hotel informed a local newspaper that the Queen's Own Fort was "one of the first sights to be visited by almost every tourist."[92] His choice of words was instructive, because despite the commission's efforts, tourists were less interested in seeing the "fort" than in making a beeline for Cabot

---

[90] One of the rare good ones was William Howe Greene, who in addition to designing Cabot Tower wrote a fine account of the seal hunt, *Wooden Walls Among the Ice Floes: Telling the Romance of the Newfoundland Seal Fishery* (London, 1933).

[91] H. W. LeMessurier, "Forts and Places about St. John's of Historic Interest," *The Veteran*, Vol. 4, No. 2 (July 1924), pp. 63-67. For more on the subject, see James E. Candow, "A Structural and Narrative History of Queen's Battery, Signal Hill National Historic Park," *Manuscript Report No. 343* (Ottawa, 1980), pp. 28-36; and, by the same author, "The Myth of the Existence of Queen's Battery before 1796," *Research Bulletin No. 180* (Ottawa, 1982).

[92] *Evening Telegram*, 28 March 1930, p. 17.

Tower to meet Bob Gardner and soak up the view. Although the tower became a destination without the commission's involvement, once it did, the commission added it to the list of places it promoted. Given its incompetence in historical matters, this was a mixed blessing. Sure enough, the commission, which was renamed the Newfoundland Tourist Traffic Development Board in 1934, began to publicize the tower as the site of Marconi's "First wireless message."[93]

In 1929 the *Evening Telegram* acknowledged not only the tower's role in attracting tourists, but also Bob Gardner's: "The evidence of the popularity of Signal Hill is to be found in the visitors' book which is kept by the warden of the Watch Tower, Signalman Gardiner [sic]. No less than fifteen hundred names have been entered since June 15th. The courtesy of this official and the spic and span condition of Cabot Tower from top to bottom are not among the least of factors that add to the popularity of this vantage point. Resplendent in paint, the interior presents a striking contrast to the signs of neglect and dilapidation it formerly bore."[94] But Gardner was more than a caretaker, for he greeted visitors and made them feel welcome. In a world of historical make-believe, this touch of reality was a rare and wonderful thing.

It was ironic that the custodian of the official time signal, once the epitome of modern efficiency, had so much time on his hands that he could double as a tour guide. That he did is strongly indicative that his two formal responsibilities, the noonday gun and flag signalling, had outlived their usefulness. Truth be told, the gun was fired but once a day, and flag signalling had long ceased to be onerous. As Gardner's log reveals, only one or two ships entered port most days, and in late fall and dead of winter whole weeks might pass with no activity whatever.[95] Gardner's informal role was therefore a happy accident that suited the public, the government, the tourist board, and the man himself, who thrived on keeping active. Like Gardner, the Canadian Marconi Company operators discovered that working in the tower meant having two masters: the employer, to be sure, but also the visitor.

---

[93] *Daily News*, 28 July 1938, p. 1.
[94] *Evening Telegram*, 3 Sept. 1929, p. 6.
[95] It is possible that Gardner did not bother to record the movements of small sailing vessels that were not equipped with wireless. Still, as late as 1941, port activity in St. John's was said to be "moribund." See Bernard Ransom, "Canada's 'Newfyjohn' Tenancy: The Royal Canadian Navy in St. John's, 1941-1945," *Acadiensis*, Vol. 23, No. 2 (Spring 1994), pp. 55-57.

HANDS ACROSS THE WATER

Nearly 12,000 Newfoundlanders, Bob Gardner among them, came to Britain's aid in the First World War, with 1,570 paying the ultimate price.[96] This paled against the larger dominions—Canada lost 61,332 men—but Newfoundland's fatality rate of 20.3 percent was higher than the rest, exceeding even Britain's (14.1 percent).[97] It was therefore puzzling that the British government excluded Newfoundland from the rewards it handed out after the war. Unlike South Africa, New Zealand, Australia, Canada, and India, Newfoundland was not allowed to represent itself at the Paris Peace Conference, and thus was not a signatory to the Treaty of Versailles, or an original member of the League of Nations.[98] Stranger still that Ireland, which had used the distraction of the war as an opportunity to launch an armed rising against British power, was granted independence in 1922. Newfoundland's inferior stature was confirmed in the summer of 1931 when, as a condition of getting an emergency loan from a Canadian banking syndicate, it agreed to British monitoring of its financial affairs. This muted the joy when, later in the year, the Statute of Westminster established the principle of legislative equality between Britain and six dominions, Newfoundland among them.

The Great Depression spared no country from economic misery, but in Newfoundland it also had unique political consequences. Export earnings from the mainstays of fishing, mining, and paper-making (a second mill had begun production at Corner Brook in 1925) fell by nearly half, throwing tens of thousands out of work and onto government relief rolls. As personal incomes dwindled, so did demand for the imported goods on which government revenues, in the form of import tariffs, largely depended.[99] Bankruptcy loomed, and it did not matter to the British that more than a third of Newfoundland's debt was traceable to borrowing to finance the recent war effort.[100] When, in 1932, Prime Minister Frederick Alderdice proposed a partial default on interest payments, Secretary of State for

---

[96] Christopher A. Sharpe, "The 'Race of Honour': An Analysis of Enlistments and Casualties in the Armed Forces of Newfoundland: 1914-1918," *Newfoundland Studies*, Vol. 4, No. 1 (1988), p. 28, p. 49. The total number of Newfoundlanders who enlisted was 11,988, of whom 3,296 joined the Canadian Expeditionary Force.
[97] Sharpe, "Analysis of Enlistments and Casualties," p. 34. The Newfoundland fatality rate is for the Royal Newfoundland Regiment only.
[98] Hiller, "Status without Stature," pp. 134-35.
[99] S. J. R. Noel, *Politics in Newfoundland* (Toronto, 1971), pp. 188-209.
[100] Ian D. H. McDonald, *"To Each His Own": William Coaker and the Fishermen's Protective Union in Newfoundland Politics, 1908-1925* (ed. J. K. Hiller) (St. John's, 1987), Appendix II, "Newfoundland Public Debt from 1908-09 to 1931-32."

Dominion Affairs James H. Thomas forbade it for fear that it might impair both "the prestige of the Empire" and Canada's credit rating on the New York bond market.[101] As a stopgap, the British and Canadian governments arranged another short-term loan, but only after Newfoundland agreed to a royal commission to examine its finances.

In 1934, with a quarter of the country's 289,588 people (39,886 of them in St. John's) living on social assistance, and with no end in sight to the debt crisis, the Newfoundland government reluctantly swallowed the bitter medicine that the royal commission prescribed. It surrendered democracy and agreed to be ruled by a British-appointed "Commission of Government" until, as the royal commission report put it, "the Island's difficulties are overcome and Newfoundland is again self-supporting."[102] The commissioners—three Newfoundlanders and four Britons, including the governor, who was chairman— answered directly to the Dominions Office. The British commissioners settled into suites in the Newfoundland Hotel, which appropriately enough stood on the site of Fort William, the seat of imperial authority in bygone days. In the same vein, the governor for most of the commission's existence, Sir Humphrey Walwyn, was a retired Royal Navy officer. According to one cold-blooded British banker, Newfoundland had become "neither a Dominion nor a Colony, but just a place."[103]

It did not remain just a place for long. International events had contributed to its downfall, and international events would help it to regain its dignity. Japan's occupation of Manchuria in 1931 and subsequent rejection of a League of Nations resolution calling for it to withdraw were signs of worse to come. Germany's postwar economic collapse and resentment of the Treaty of Versailles fuelled the rise of Adolf Hitler and, with it, the country's re-emergence as a great power. It was in this context that in 1934 the Dominions Office asked Newfoundland Governor Sir Murray Anderson to "prepare, or have prepared, a Defence Scheme for the Island."[104] By 4 May 1936, when

---

[101] Noel, *Politics in Newfoundland*, pp. 190- 208; J. L. Granatstein, *How Britain's Weakness Forced Canada into the Arms of the United States* (Toronto, 1989), pp. 10-24. See also James K. Hiller, *Confederation: Deciding Newfoundland's Future 1934 to 1949* (St. John's, 1998), p. 3.

[102] *Newfoundland Royal Commission 1933 Report*, p. 197. Population figures are from the 1935 census.

[103] Cited in Peter Neary, " 'With great regret and after the most anxious consideration': Newfoundland's 1932 plan to reschedule interest payments," *Newfoundland Studies*, Vol. 10, No. 2 (Fall 1994), p. 253. Technically, Newfoundland was still a dominion.

[104] Bridle (ed.), *Documents on Relations between Canada and Newfoundland*, Document 1, Commissioner for Finance to Private Secretary, 4 May 1936.

a committee chaired by Commissioner for Natural Resources E. N. R. Trentham finished its work, German troops had occupied the Rhineland, and Italy, under the fascist Benito Mussolini, had invaded Ethiopia. With the League of Nations all but dead, another war looked inevitable.

The Trentham report underscored the influence of geography, technology, and resources.[105] It noted Newfoundland's command of the North Atlantic shipping lanes and the seaward approaches to Canada, and its role as "one of the principal nerve centres of the North Atlantic cable communication system." Fourteen transatlantic cables now came ashore on the island, four of them belonging to the Commercial Cable Company (two each in Cuckold's Cove and Quidi Vidi Harbour). The report identified the cable landing sites as potential military objectives, along with the Canadian- and Newfoundland-owned coastal wireless stations, and the Canadian-owned iron ore mines on Bell Island. It also cited as a new strategic factor Newfoundland's potential as "a stepping stone for an air service across the North Atlantic." Negotiations to this end had already begun, but for now the most the report's authors could say was that there was "every possibility" of Newfoundland's "developing into an important air base in the not far distant future."[106] This would prove to be an understatement.

Canadian defence planners were also busy, and Newfoundland caught their attention. In a 1937 memorandum on the defence of Sydney and its steel industry, the Canadian Joint Staff Committee (comprised of the military chiefs of the three armed services) stressed the Bell Island connection. Because smelting at Sydney was so geared to Bell Island ore, the chiefs warned that "the protection of the source of the ore supply is of no less importance than the security of the blast furnaces themselves."[107] From this it followed that the defence of the Atlantic coast was "intimately bound up with the defence of Newfoundland. The two problems are really one and no good purpose can be served by treating them separately." One person who did not share this view, at least not yet, was the inscrutable Canadian Prime Minister, Mackenzie King, whose aversion to military matters and foreign entanglements was legendary.[108] It was not until July 1938 that

---

[105] Bridle (ed.), *Documents on Relations between Canada and Newfoundland*, Document 2, Extract from Newfoundland Defence Scheme, 4 May 1936.
[106] On the negotiations, see Peter Neary, *Newfoundland in the North Atlantic World, 1929-1949* (Montreal and Kingston, 1988), pp. 110-12.
[107] Bridle (ed.), *Documents on Relations between Canada and Newfoundland*, Document 3, Memorandum by Joint Staff Committee, 22 March 1937.
[108] C. P. Stacey, *Canada and the Age of Conflict: A History of Canadian External Policies Volume 2: 1921-1948 The Mackenzie King Era* (Toronto, 1981), pp. 12-17.

King, at the behest of the Joint Staff Committee, reluctantly asked the Dominions Office "what measures, naval and air, for the defence of Newfoundland are contemplated in the event of war [?]"[109] In words that must have given cold comfort to the chiefs, the Dominions Office, apparently believing it was the seventeenth century and not the twentieth, repeated the old saw that "the general defence of the territory would rest on the cover provided by the Royal Navy."[110] Beyond that, the navy would send a few minesweepers and anti-submarine vessels and would maintain "trade protection units" in Halifax.

In contrast to British complacency, the United States was now beginning to realize that Canada would need help if threatened by foes as strong as Germany and Japan. On 14 August 1936, in a speech at Chautauqua, New York, President Franklin Roosevelt pledged that his country would defend both itself and its neighbours against foreign aggressors. Two years later, in Kingston, Ontario, he was more explicit, declaring that America would "not stand idly by" if Canada were threatened by a foreign power.[111] Far from alarming Canadians, Roosevelt's words reassured them. There were a mere 1,585 men (including officers) in the Royal Canadian Navy in 1939, with a paltry ten warships split between the Atlantic and Pacific coasts.[112] The only service for which King had any time, the air force, was relatively strong at 3,048 men, but it had only thirty-seven combat-ready aircraft. The Canadian Army, which at its peak during the First World War boasted over 600,000 troops, was down to a permanent strength of 4,261.

In January 1938 Canadian and American military officials met in Washington to discuss a coordinated approach to hemispheric defence.[113] The Americans, however, were exclusively concerned with the Japanese threat to the Pacific coast, and the Canadians, while mindful of the Atlantic, were hamstrung by King's policy of "avoidance of war rather than preparation for it."[114] King nominally changed his

---

[109] Bridle (ed.), *Documents on Relations between Canada and Newfoundland*, Document 14, Secretary of State for External Affairs to Dominions Secretary, 27 July 1938.
[110] Bridle (ed.), *Documents on Relations between Canada and Newfoundland*, Document 18, Dominions Secretary to Secretary of State for External Affairs, 21 Oct. 1938.
[111] Stanley W. Dziuban, *Military Relations between the United States and Canada 1939-1945* (Washington, 1959), p. 3.
[112] W. A. B. Douglas *et al.*, *No Higher Purpose: The Official History of the Royal Canadian Navy in the Second World War, 1939-1945: Volume II, Part I* (St. Catharines, ON, 2002), p. 28; J. L. Granatstein and Desmond Morton, *A Nation Forged in Fire: Canadians and the Second World War 1939-1945* (Toronto, 1989), p.7.
[113] Dziuban, *Military Relations between the United States and Canada*, pp. 3-4.
[114] David MacKenzie, *Inside the Atlantic Triangle: Canada and the Entrance of Newfoundland into Confederation, 1939-1949* (Toronto, 1986), p. 29.

tune after Britain declared war against Germany on 3 September 1939 (by virtue of which Newfoundland was automatically at war), two days after Germany attacked Poland. Speaking in the House of Commons on 8 September, he acknowledged that "The integrity of Newfoundland and Labrador is essential to the security of Canada."[115] At that point Canadian aircraft based in Sydney had already done a reconnaissance of Newfoundland's south coast at the request of the Royal Navy.[116] But Canada, like Britain and the United States, had no long-term plans for the island, and, initially at least, Newfoundland was virtually left to fend for itself.

During the war more than 12,000 Newfoundlanders served in various British and Canadian military and paramilitary units and in the merchant marine.[117] No separate regiment bearing the Newfoundland name went overseas, but the largest single group on active service were the 3,419 who joined the Royal Navy. As soon as the fighting began, First Lord of the Admiralty Winston Churchill asked for a contingent of Newfoundlanders, whom he considered "the hardiest and most skilful boatmen in rough seas who exist."[118] From the Newfoundland perspective the war was thus the culmination of the country's historic role as a nursery of seamen, even in the absence of a naval reserve. (There had been talk of forming one in the interwar years, but the idea foundered on Admiralty indifference and Newfoundland's straitened finances.)[119] Even fishermen who stayed home contributed, since in 1943 the Washington-based Combined Food Board took over the marketing of Newfoundland-caught fish as part of the coordination of Allied food production.

In the absence of a reserve, home defence initially devolved to the newly-created Newfoundland Militia, which numbered only twenty-two men by late September 1939. Its first commanding officer, Lieutenant-Colonel Walter F. Rendell, was a former member of the Newfoundland Legion of Frontiersmen and a veteran of the Royal Newfoundland

---

[115] Bridle (ed.), *Documents on Relations between Canada and Newfoundland*, Document 41, Extract from a Speech by Prime Minister, 8 Sept. 1939.
[116] W. A. B. Douglas, *The Creation of a National Air Force: The Official History of the Royal Canadian Air Force: Volume II* (Toronto, 1986), p. 380.
[117] The figure is based on LAC, RG 24 (Department of National Defence), Series G-3, Vol. 10995, File 290NFD.013 (D1), A. M. Fraser, "History of the Participation by Newfoundland in World War II" (Unpublished manuscript, 1951), graciously provided by Peter Neary.
[118] Winston S. Churchill, *The Second World War: The Gathering Storm* (Boston, 1948), p. 757.
[119] G. W. L. Nicholson, *More Fighting Newfoundlanders: A History of Newfoundland's Fighting Forces in the Second World War* (St. John's, 1969), pp. 520-30.

Regiment.[120] Small though it was, the militia's earliest duties included guarding the Commercial Cable Company's downtown station and the cable landing sites. Cable was still a British priority, hence the cutting of Germany's only two Atlantic cables on 3 September 1939.[121] The militia would achieve a maximum strength of 570 officers and men in 1943, the same year in which it acquired regimental status and was renamed the Newfoundland Regiment. By then it was also posting guards at the Bay Roberts and Harbour Grace cable stations, with the Newfoundland Constabulary minding Heart's Content.[122]

While cable defence had by now become standard fare, the war would feature much that was new. The negotiations that had been under way at the time of the Trentham report bore fruit in 1937 when flying boats belonging to Imperial and Pan-American airways began using the Botwood seaplane base, on the northeast coast, as a refuelling stop for transatlantic flights.[123] In May 1939 Botwood was joined by a state-of-the-art airfield in central Newfoundland called "Newfoundland Airport," which would eventually be known as Gander. Sensing that the two facilities could be used as leverage to defend the island at no cost to itself, the Commission of Government sought British permission to turn them over to Canada "for the duration of the war."[124] The Dominions Office refused, mainly for fear that if the Canadians became entrenched it might compromise British influence on postwar transatlantic aviation.[125]

British, Canadian, and American indifference was perhaps understandable while the "phoney war" persisted in western Europe, but everything changed after Hitler unleashed the *blitzkrieg* in the spring of 1940, culminating with the collapse of France and the Low Countries in May-June, and the rescue of 340,000 British, French, and Canadian troops from the beaches of Dunkirk. British grand strategy, which had been predicated on the French Army holding the Western Front, lay in tatters, and the nation faced an unexpected and uncertain fight for its very existence, with only the countries of the empire by its

---

[120] Robert L. Kavanagh, "W Force: The Canadian Army and the Defence of Newfoundland in the Second World War" (Unpublished MA thesis, Memorial University of Newfoundland, 1995), p. 82.

[121] Beauchamp, *History of Telegraphy*, p. 341.

[122] Tarrant, *Atlantic Sentinel*, p. 87, p. 102; Nicholson, *More Fighting Newfoundlanders*, p. 529.

[123] Neary, *Newfoundland in the North Atlantic World*, pp. 110-13.

[124] Bridle (ed.), *Documents on Relations between Canada and Newfoundland*, Document 44, Governor of Newfoundland to Dominions Secretary, 15 Sept. 1939.

[125] MacKenzie, *Inside the Atlantic Triangle*, p. 31.

side.[126] Almost overnight the prospect of enemy action against North America became something to be seriously considered, and Newfoundland, by virtue of geography and circumstance, loomed like a colossus on the strategic horizon. Aviation technology in particular enhanced its status, because German bombers based on the island would pose a threat to eastern Canada and the northeastern United States. Accordingly, there was relief in Ottawa when a besieged Britain reversed its earlier position and agreed to transfer the Botwood seaplane base and Newfoundland Airport to Canada's control for the rest of the war. On 17 June five Royal Canadian Air Force bombers alit at Newfoundland Airport; five days later SS *Antonia* arrived in Botwood with 900 men of the Black Watch (Royal Highland Regiment) of Canada, who were apportioned between the two air bases.[127] These were the vanguard of a Canadian presence in Newfoundland and Labrador whose peak strength in 1944 was roughly 15,000 men.[128] Because Botwood and Newfoundland Airport were the early priorities, the Canadian Army, in the form of some 800 infantry and artillerymen, did not arrive in St. John's until mid-November.[129] Like the British Army before 1870, the Canadians had no single base in the city. There were two main barracks—at Lester's Field and Shamrock Field—from which headquarters was about as remote as it could possibly be: in Winterholme, a Queen Anne Revival mansion owned by the family of the late Sir Marmaduke Winter.

After the fall of France the United States government gave urgent attention to the security of northeastern North America, and also sought ways to increase material aid to the Allies. In August 1940 President Roosevelt and Prime Minister King met in Ogdensburg, New York and agreed to create a Permanent Joint Board on Defence to "consider in the broad sense the defence of the north half of the Western Hemisphere."[130] This was the beginning of the end of

---

[126] Correlli Barnett, *The Collapse of British Power* (London, 1972), pp. 5-8.

[127] Neary, *Newfoundland in the North Atlantic World*, p. 131.

[128] Peak Canadian strength has long been underestimated, primarily because authors have taken C. P. Stacey's figure for "W" Force in mid-December 1943—5,692 all ranks —and mistakenly applied it to the whole. See, for example, MacKenzie, *Inside the Atlantic Triangle*, p. 80. Canadian naval personnel topped out at 5,000 in December 1944, and air force personnel at 4,760 in late 1943-early 1944. For the navy, see Gilbert Norman Tucker, *The Naval Service of Canada: Its Official History: Volume II: Activities on Shore during the Second World War* (Ottawa, 1952), p. 197. For the air force, I have used an estimate supplied by retired air force Colonel Ernie Cable of the Shearwater Aviation Museum.

[129] Kavanagh, "W Force," p. 86; Marc Milner, *North Atlantic Run: The Royal Canadian Navy and the Battle for the Convoys* (Toronto, 1985), pp. 32.

[130] Cited in MacKenzie, *Inside the Atlantic Triangle*, p. 45.

Canada's traditional reliance on Britain, and was no less momentous for Newfoundland, which was the subject of the board's first report and accounted for roughly half of its recommendations during its first year of existence.[131] Many of those recommendations stemmed from an Anglo-American agreement of 2 September that underscored just how desperate the British were, and how dependent they were about to become on American support. In exchange for fifty over-age American destroyers, they agreed to give the United States ninety-nine-year leases to base sites on British territory in the Caribbean Basin; as a gift, they threw in the right to put bases in Bermuda and Newfoundland.

Fig. 58: Men of Battery B, 62nd Coast Artillery Regiment (Antiaircraft) (Mobile) at Camp Alexander, spring 1941. Source: Angelo Gillotte. This regiment was one of two American units stationed on Signal Hill during the war.

The Leased Bases Agreement was not actually signed until 27 March 1941, just after Congress passed the Lend-Lease Act that made Britain financially dependent on the United States for the rest of the war. By this time American troops had already been in Newfoundland for a couple of months. On 29 January pilot George Anstey guided the United States Army Transport *Edmund B. Alexander* through The Narrows and into the harbour. It was no mean feat, for not only was there a dense fog, but the ship was the largest to have entered port up to that time.[132] Aboard it were 1,000 infantry, coast artillery, and

[131] Granatstein and Morton, *A Nation Forged in Fire*, p. 33.
[132] Maurice Burke, "Ship of Fate," *Atlantic Advocate* (March 1971), p. 57; Department of the Army, Center of Military History, Corps of Engineers, North Atlantic Division, "Historical Monograph: U. S. Army Bases Newfoundland" (New York, 1946, Manuscript on File), p. IV-2; Eric Seymour, "The Story of Pepperrell," *Newfoundland Quarterly*, Vol. 59, No. 2 (Summer 1960), p. 8.

anti-aircraft personnel commanded by Colonel Maurice D. Welty. Work had already begun on a permanent home for Newfoundland Base Command, but it was nowhere near ready. The *Edmund B. Alexander* therefore served as a floating barracks until 20 May, when the men were transferred to Camp Alexander, a temporary tent camp on Carpasian Road. They remained there until November 1941 when they finally began moving into Fort Pepperrell, named after Sir William Pepperrell, leader of the New England contingent against Louisbourg in 1745. What that had to do with Newfoundland is a good question, but at least there was poetry in the fort's location on the sloping ground north of Quidi Vidi Lake, once home to Grove Farm, across which Massachusetts Provincials had trod en route to liberating St. John's from the French in 1762. American armed forces in Newfoundland and Labrador would attain a maximum strength of 10,882 in 1943.[133]

For the first time since the American Revolutionary War, St. John's shared the spotlight with a host of other centres. With Botwood and Gander secured, Canada's next priority was Bell Island, defended from August 1940 by the 1st Coast Defence Battery (Royal Canadian Artillery).[134] After the Battle of Britain was won in the fall of 1940, Gander's standing rose because of its role in ferrying American-made bombers across the Atlantic. With deliveries escalating from twenty-six bombers in 1940 to 593 in 1941, Gander's limits were soon reached; to relieve the pressure, a new Canadian air base was opened in Goose Bay, Labrador in December 1941.[135] Goose Bay in turn became so important that, in the spring of 1942, the Canadians were joined by a United States army air force contingent. Incredibly, nearly 5,000 military aircraft were shipped via Gander and Goose Bay during the war.[136] In addition to Goose Bay and Fort Pepperrell, the Americans had a naval air station in Argentia, Placentia Bay, and an army air force base in Stephenville, Bay St. George, both of which began in 1941. Smaller groups of American and Canadian personnel were posted throughout Newfoundland and Labrador at an array of LORAN (*LOng RAnge Navigation*), radar, wireless, meteorological, and telephone repeater stations.[137] Wireless was now

---

[133] MacKenzie, *Inside the Atlantic Triangle*, p. 79.
[134] Kavanagh, "W Force," p. 79; Nicholson, *More Fighting Newfoundlanders*, p. 526.
[135] See Bridle (ed.), *Documents on Relations between Canada and Newfoundland*, Appendix D, "Aircraft Receipts and Deliveries by RAF Ferry Command and RAF Transport Command from September, 1940 to April 30, 1945."
[136] The exact number was 4,919.
[137] Kavanagh, "W Force," p. 134; John N. Cardoulis, *A Friendly Invasion: The American Military in Newfoundland 1940-1990* (St. John's, 1990), chapters 7 and 9.

standard in military communications, and the war was a spur to newer applications. Relying on a network of ground-based radio beacons, LORAN revolutionized air and sea navigation by enabling craft to fix their positions to previously impossible levels of accuracy. Radar (*RAdio Detection And Ranging*), which was crucial to victory in the Battle of Britain, was used both to detect targets and to guide projectiles to them.[138] Bristling with men and weapons of war, and surrounded by an electronic stockade, Newfoundland had become "a garrison country."[139]

Despite the vast military footprint and the relatively late arrival of Canadian and American forces in the capital, St. John's would attain greater strategic significance than at any time in its history. For this, geography and technology were largely responsible. As in the First World War, the Royal Navy employed distant blockade against the German surface fleet, but France's collapse allowed enemy submarines based in the Bay of Biscay to push their campaign against merchant shipping ever westward into the Atlantic.[140] The Royal Navy's need to send additional ships into the Mediterranean after Italy entered the war in June 1940, the diversion of many of its convoy escort vessels to anti-invasion duties in British waters, and the limited range of escort vessels on both sides of the Atlantic left gaps in convoy protection that German submarines were swift to exploit. In May 1941, in a bid to provide continuous support to convoys, the Admiralty decided to establish an advance base in St. John's for some sixty vessels belonging to a Newfoundland Escort Force (NEF).[141] Because Canada would supply the bulk of the ships, the Admiralty appointed Commodore L. W. Murray of the Royal Canadian Navy to head the operation. NEF would prove instrumental to the Canadian navy's heroic role in the Battle of the Atlantic and to its maturation as a fighting force.[142]

---

[138] On electronic warfare, see Van Creveld, *Technology and War*, pp. 267-71. On the Battle of Britain, see Michael Korda, *With Wings Like Eagles: A History of the Battle of Britain* (New York, 2009).
[139] Neary, *Newfoundland in the North Atlantic World*, p. 183.
[140] Eric J. Grove, "A Service Vindicated 1939-1946," in Hill (ed.), *Oxford Illustrated History of the Royal Navy*, pp. 354-56.
[141] Paul Collins, " 'First Line of Defence': The Establishment and Development of St. John's, Newfoundland as the Royal Canadian Navy's Premier Escort Base in the Second World War," *Northern Mariner*, Vol. 16, No. 3 (July 2006), pp. 15-32; Douglas *et al.*, *No Higher Purpose*, pp. 180-89; Roger Sarty, *Canada and the Battle of the Atlantic* (Montreal, 1998), pp. 63-64; Marc Milner, *The U-Boat Hunters: The Royal Canadian Navy and the Offensive Against Germany's Submarines* (Toronto, 1994), pp. 6-7; Ransom, "The Royal Canadian Navy in St. John's," pp. 45-71; Marc Milner, *North Atlantic Run: The Royal Canadian Navy and the Battle for the Convoys* (Toronto, 1985), pp. 41-44; MacKay, "Introduction," in Bridle (ed.), *Documents on Relations between Canada and Newfoundland*, pp. xlv-xlix; Tucker, *The Naval Service of Canada: Its Official History: Volume II*, pp. 188-89.
[142] Milner, *North Atlantic Run*, p. 32.

That summer, work began not only on naval facilities in St. John's Harbour, but also on a Canadian air base in nearby Torbay to offer anti-submarine air coverage for convoys. Torbay was up and running by the end of 1941, but the escort base, formally called HMCS *Avalon*, was not finished until the following year. Nonetheless, individual components (including a wireless station) were operational beforehand, and various Royal Navy stores, fuel, and depot ships filled in while the base was under construction. Upon its completion its berthage and repair facilities were still inadequate, so in 1942 work began on an auxiliary base in Bay Bulls. Until the latter was finished in 1944 the situation in St. John's remained "most acute," although the arrival of a United States Navy floating dry dock in September 1943 slightly eased the pressure.[143]

Convoys still originated in Halifax and Sydney, but their escorts yielded to NEF ships off Newfoundland, which accompanied them to a point south of Iceland, from where they completed the final leg of their journey with fresh escorts from the Hvalfjordur naval base. After a shake-up in January 1942 the NEF name disappeared and St. John's became part of the new Mid-Ocean Escort Force, with Londonderry replacing Hvalfjordur as the easternmost escort base.[144] Forty years earlier Sir Robert Bond had dreamed of a "chain right across the Atlantic," with Royal Navy bases in Halifax, St. John's, and Barehaven. Apart from the substitution of the Royal Canadian Navy for the Royal Navy, and of Londonderry for Barehaven, that dream had been fulfilled.

The coast defences of St. John's, although slow to develop, were ultimately something to behold. In a reminder of every conflict dating back to the Second Anglo-Dutch War, but with a modern twist, the very first element was a wire anti-submarine net strung between Chain Rock and a point forty-six metres west of Pancake Rock.[145] Even when raised, the net was no impediment to small craft, its purpose being "to foul propellers, etc., of any incoming submarine which it is thought would not be submerged on account of depth of water available." Mariners entering The Narrows were alerted to the net's presence by signals displayed from a flagstaff at Anchor Point, directly opposite Chain

[143] Bridle (ed.), *Documents on Relations between Canada and Newfoundland*, Document 624, PJBD, Journal of Discussions and Decisions, Report of Service Members, 24-25 Aug. 1943; Ransom, "The Royal Canadian Navy in St. John's," p. 66.
[144] Milner, *North Atlantic Run*, p. 91.
[145] Bridle (ed.), *Documents on Relations between Canada and Newfoundland*, Document 47, Governor of Newfoundland to Commander-in-Chief, America and West Indies, 19 Oct. 1939.

Fig. 59: Anti-torpedo baffles in The Narrows, 1943. Source: National Defence (Canada), 0-6550. Reproduced with the permission of the Minister of Public Works and Government Services, 2010. Developed in response to the submarine threat, anti-torpedo baffles were the latest twist on a centuries-old tradition of barrier defences in The Narrows.

Rock.[146] The net failed to impress Captain J. S. Bethell, Commanding Officer of HMS *Caradoc*, who compiled an intelligence report on Newfoundland harbours in August 1940.[147] In it he argued that a submarine attack via The Narrows was unlikely, "but, although a difficult shot, torpedoes might be fired up the channel to hit a vessel at anchor or alongside one of the main wharves." This being the case, he felt that "a modern anti-torpedo baffle net would be of much greater value." Bethell's views obviously carried weight, because by November removal of the net had begun.[148] Although materials for three pairs of anti-torpedo

---

[146] These were, by day, a large white ball with black band, and by night, three electric lights in a vertical line.
[147] Bridle (ed.), *Documents on Relations between Canada and Newfoundland*, Document 130, Commanding Officer, H. M. S. *Caradoc* to Commodore Commanding Halifax Force, 1 Aug. 1940.
[148] Bridle (ed.), *Documents on Relations between Canada and Newfoundland*, Document 144, Secretary of State for External Affairs to Governor of Newfoundland, 20 Nov. 1940.

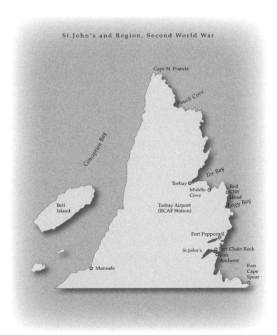

Fig. 60: St. John's and Region, Second World War.

baffles arrived in December, ice conditions delayed their installation until spring, when two pairs were set between Chain Rock and the Narrows entrance, and one between Chain Rock and the harbour entrance.[149] In 1943, by which time Bethell's logic had somehow lost its cachet, the baffles were supplemented with a new anti-submarine net.

Until the Canadian Army arrived in November 1940, the Newfoundland Militia guards and the original anti-submarine net were the sum total of the city's defences. It would be a while longer before all of the Canadians' artillery followed from the mainland, and by the time it did the Americans had more than chipped in with their own. The need for haste to complete the defences was heightened by the activities of the German battlecruisers *Gneisenau* and *Scharnhorst*, which penetrated the British North Sea blockade on 22 January 1941 and outraced their pursuers around the Atlantic before safely returning to Brest exactly two months later.[150] During their romp they sank twenty-

---

[149] Bridle (ed.), *Documents on Relations between Canada and Newfoundland*, Document 146, PJBD, Journal of Discussions and Decisions, Report of Service Members, 17 Dec. 1940; Canada. Department of National Defence, Directorate of History (hereafter DND, DH), War Diary, 103rd Heavy Battery, RCA, Vol. 40, Appendix D.

[150] Douglas *et al.*, *No Higher Purpose*, pp. 174-75; Douglas, *Creation of a National Air Force*, pp. 384-85.

two merchant vessels, most of them about 800 kilometres east of Newfoundland. Anyone who had still been blind to Newfoundland's strategic value to Canada could be blind no more.

The first armaments were a pair of 75-mm. field guns temporarily placed in Fort Amherst on 5 November and manned by a makeshift "Q" Battery (Royal Canadian Artillery), which in mid-May 1941 would be designated the 103rd Coast Battery.[151] Because of its forward position, Fort Amherst became (on 15 November) the examination battery, providing cover for an examination vessel whose captain was responsible for identifying merchant vessels and minor warships seeking to enter the harbour.[152] If the captain had any suspicions about a ship or its cargo he was to board, inspect, and detain it if necessary. Sometime in December an affiliated port war signal station (PWSS) was established in Cabot Tower to identify major warships and to coordinate their entrance into the harbour.[153] As with all such stations, it used a combination of wireless and visual signals (including Aldis lamps) to communicate with ships and shore installations.

The Canadians had originally planned to put two 4.7-in. coast defence guns on the hill, but those plans, like the Cabot Tower PWSS, did not last.[154] The problem was that Brigadier Philip Earnshaw, Commanding Officer of the Canadian Army in Newfoundland, did not think much of Signal Hill. In a letter of 27 December to the General Officer Commanding-in-Chief for Atlantic Command, Earnshaw expressed his bewildering reservations: (1) guns on the hill would be "a little too close" to Fort Amherst; and (2) the hill "is very high and comes as a consequence in a strata of low clouds which day after day prevent any signalling from the site."[155] Developments in the immediate future would show that Earnshaw's first point was baseless; the hill's history of nearly two and a half centuries as a signalling post

---

[151] Kavanagh, "W Force," p. 105; Bridle (ed.), *Documents on Relations between Canada and Newfoundland*, Document 143, PJBD, Journal of Discussions and Decisions, Report of Service Members, 14 Nov. 1940, and Document 147, Governor of Newfoundland to Secretary of State for External Affairs, 7 Jan. 1941.

[152] Tucker, *The Naval Service of Canada: Its Official History: Volume II*, p. 525.

[153] Tucker, *The Naval Service of Canada: Its Official History: Volume II*, p. 196; Bridle (ed.), *Documents on Relations between Canada and Newfoundland*, Document 144, Secretary of State for External Affairs to Governor of Newfoundland, 20 Nov. 1940.

[154] Bridle (ed.), *Documents on Relations between Canada and Newfoundland*, Document 222, Governor of Newfoundland to Secretary of State for External Affairs, 8 Oct. 1940.

[155] DND, DH, 321.009 (D378) (Correspondence... re Coast & AA ARTY Defs of St. John's, Nfld Oct 40/Oct 41), Earnshaw to General Officer Commanding-in-Chief, Atlantic Command, 27 Dec. 1940. Strangely, Earnshaw had been Director of Signals for the Canadian Army prior to being posted to Newfoundland. See Kavanagh, "W Force," p. 78, n. 68.

put the lie to the second. Nonetheless, work began in mid-January 1941 on preparing mounts for the 4.7-in. guns at Fort Amherst, which in addition to continuing as the examination battery assumed a new role as a close defence battery. This was followed in April by the commencement of work on a counter-bombardment battery at Cape Spear, and in May on an anti-motor torpedo boat battery at Chain Rock Point.

On 21 June the 4.7-in. guns went into service at Fort Amherst. Its original 75-mm. guns were transferred to Fort Chain Rock and were activated there on 9 and 15 October.[156] Although Fort Cape Spear was occupied in June, the installation of its 10-in. guns was so plagued by delays that the guns were not fully operational until 26 April 1942. The guns, which came from Fort Mott, New Jersey, had been built in 1894 and were the oldest to be used in the coast defence of St. John's during the war. On account of their age, their maximum range of 12.9 kilometres was less than that of smaller, more modern guns. Fort Cape Spear, Fort Amherst, and Fort Chain Rock were manned respectively by A, B, and C troops of the 103rd Coast Battery (Royal Canadian Artillery).[157] Another piece of the coast defence puzzle fell into place when the PWSS was transferred from Cabot Tower to Fort Amherst. The exact timing of the move is unknown, but it appears to have taken place in January 1941.[158] A secondary PWSS was later added at Fort Cape Spear.[159]

Earnshaw's misgivings about Signal Hill appear even stranger in light of his efforts to convince the Americans to occupy it, and given the alacrity with which they did. On 4 February 1941 he showed a group of senior American coast and anti-aircraft artillery officers around the hill as part of their general reconnaissance of the Avalon Peninsula.[160] He urged them to place their 155-mm. guns, which were then aboard the *Edmund B. Alexander*, on the hill as a complement to the two 75-mm. guns at Fort Amherst. He need not have worried, because in a conference aboard the troopship later that day, Colonel Welty gladly accepted the advice. Before the month was out, a four-gun 155-mm. mobile coast defence battery had been established along the eastern and southern faces of Ladies' Lookout.[161] Nicknamed

[156] DND, DH, 142.61B103.009 (D9), Fort Record Book, Fort Chain Rock.
[157] Kavanagh, "W Force," pp. 106-07.
[158] Power, *Fort Amherst*, pp. 94-95.
[159] Tucker, *The Naval Service of Canada: Its Official History: Volume II*, p. 196.
[160] DND, DH, 321.009 (D378), Earnshaw to General Officer Commanding-in-Chief, Atlantic Command, 6 Feb. 1941.
[161] National Archives and Records Administration (hereafter NARA) (Washington, D. C.), RG 338 (Newfoundland Base Command), Box 16, File 319.1, Welty to Commanding General, First Army, 28 Feb. 1941.

"Long Toms," the 155-mm. guns were the most sophisticated that Signal Hill had ever known, and with a range of 15.9 kilometres (versus 10 kilometres for the 75-mm. guns) covered not only the seaward approaches to St. John's, but even a portion of Conception Bay.[162] They were manned by the 57th Coast Artillery Regiment (155-mm. Gun) (Mobile), which on 16 February 1942 would be renamed Battery C, 24th Coast Artillery Separate Battalion.[163]

Welty had more in mind for Signal Hill than just coast defence. On 1 April 1941 work crews began preparing an area on the north side of George's Pond to accommodate four 3-in. anti-aircraft guns to provide air cover for the *Edmund B. Alexander* and the 155-mm. battery. In words that could have been spoken by a Royal Engineer a century earlier, an American officer complained that "the work has been slow because of the necessity of levelling the rock with sledges and crowbars." Manual labour yielded to dynamite, and on the seventeenth the guns, emplaced and camouflaged with netting, were inspected by Welty and Governor Walwyn. Supported by four .50 calibre machine guns for use against low-flying aircraft, the guns were manned by Battery B, 62nd Coast Artillery Regiment (Antiaircraft) (Mobile), which would be renamed the 421st Coast Artillery Battalion (Separate) on 1 August 1941, and further renamed the 421st Coast Artillery Battalion (Composite) (Antiaircraft) on 20 September 1941.

Exactly two weeks after the George's Pond anti-aircraft battery was up and running, two monstrous 8-in. railway coast defence guns—so called because they could be mounted on rail cars—arrived in St. John's from Fort Hancock, New Jersey. Their range of 22.8 kilometres was almost half as much again as the 155-mm. guns, whose reign was short-lived. The newcomers were slated for Cape St. Francis to cover the mouth of Conception Bay and the seaward approaches to Pouch Cove and Tor Bay.[164] However, with NEF about to come on stream and the Canadians still limited to two puny guns at Fort Amherst, Earnshaw implored Welty to retain the railway guns for the coast defence of St. John's. Once more Welty obliged, and before the end of May the guns

---

[162] NARA, RG 338, Box 19, File 660.22, Brant to Commanding General, Eastern Theatre of Operations, 31 Dec. 1941. On the ranges of American coast defences, see Mark Berhow *et al.*, "A Guide to the Weapons and Batteries of Modern American Harbor Defences," in Mark A. Berhow (ed.), *American Seacoast Defenses: A Reference Guide* (McLean, VA, 2004), p. 61. All ranges in this section are taken from Berhow. For my copy and guidance as to its use, I am indebted to Alex Holder of the Coast Defense Study Group.
[163] Shelby L. Stanton, *Order of Battle U. S. Army, World War II* (Novato, CA, 1984), p. 460.
[164] NARA, RG 338, Box 16, File 319.1, Welty to Commanding General, First Army, 3 June 1941; Bridle (ed.), *Documents on Relations between Canada and Newfoundland*, Document 593, Secretary, Chiefs of Staff Committee, to Secretary of Joint Service Committee, Atlantic Coast, 12 Feb. 1942.

Fig. 61: 8-in. guns on Signal Hill, 1941. Source: Provincial Resource Library, Newfoundland and Labrador Collection, Murrin Stockbook (288). These mammoth guns, which had a range of 22.8 kilometres, were later removed to Red Cliff Head.

were in place on the eastern edge of the summit between Cabot Tower and the first of the 155-mm. guns, on the understanding, however, that they would be moved to Cape St. Francis as soon as Fort Cape Spear's 10-in. guns were installed "and the battery demonstrates its value."[165] They were manned by Battery D, 52nd Coast Artillery Regiment (Railway 8-in. Gun), renamed Battery D, 24th Coast Artillery Separate Battalion on 16 February 1942. The area occupied by the Americans was designated Signal Hill Battery and was deemed an auxiliary station of Fort Pepperrell. Cabot Tower, the signalman's residence, and George's Pond, although all within its boundaries, were legally excluded from it.[166] The Americans clearly saw something in Signal Hill that Earnshaw did not, at least not at first, because his sudden eagerness to sell them on the hill in February 1941 had about it the zeal of the recently converted.

Sounding a familiar note, the American reconnaissance of the Avalon Peninsula had also revealed that St. John's was vulnerable to enemy forces that might land elsewhere along the coast.[167] As a result,

---

[165] NARA, RG 338, Box 16, File 319.1, Welty to Commanding General, First Army, 3 June 1941; NARA, RG 338, Box 19, File 660.22, Ramsay to Welty, 12 Nov. 1941.
[166] TRPAD, GN31/3/A, Department of Natural Resources, Box 46, File D26/21, Areas on Signal Hill.
[167] NARA, RG 338, Box 16, File 319.1, Welty to Commanding General, First Army, 3 April 1941.

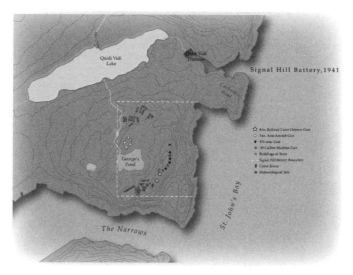

Fig. 62: Signal Hill Battery, 1941.

civilian "watchers" were enrolled to look for suspicious vessels, and Canadian and American observation posts were established at select locations along the Atlantic coast of the Avalon Peninsula and in Conception Bay.[168] The latter, already vital because of Bell Island, now became even more so because enemy ships could bombard the capital from there.[169] Thus, when army headquarters in New York ignored a request by Newfoundland Base Command for light artillery for beach defence, local officials decided to turn the 155-mm. guns on Signal Hill into a mobile coast defence battery.[170] Special 180-degree Panama mounts were built for the guns in Manuels, Conception Bay, and in Middle Cove, an inlet of Tor Bay.[171] Although the 8-in. guns were originally supposed to have gone to Cape St. Francis, the Americans put them instead on Red Cliff Head (formerly Red Head), between Logy Bay and Tor Bay, where they would cover both bays and serve as a second counter-bombardment battery to Fort Cape Spear.[172] In June 1942, with

---

[168] NARA, RG 338, Box 16, File 319.1, Welty to Commanding General, First Army, 3 June 1941.

[169] NARA, RG 165 (War Department, General and Special Staff, Operations Division), Box 782, File 320.2, Handy to Anonymous, 12 Dec. 1942.

[170] NARA, RG 338, Box 19, File 660.22, Brant to Commanding General, Newfoundland Base Command, 12 Nov. 1941; Bridle (ed.), *Documents on Relations between Canada and Newfoundland*, Document 593, Secretary, Chiefs of Staff Committee, to Secretary of Joint Service Committee, Atlantic Coast, 12 Feb. 1942.

[171] Personal communication, Alex Holder, 29 Oct. 2008.

[172] NARA, RG 338, Box 19, File 660.22, Brant to Chief of Staff, General Headquarters, U. S. Army, 4 Dec. 1941.

Fort Cape Spear finally working to everyone's satisfaction, preparations began at Red Cliff Head. The first of the 8-in. guns was installed there over the course of two days in mid-November, and the second on 15 December.[173] The Red Cliff Head counter-bombardment battery was manned by Battery D, 24th Coast Artillery Separate Battalion (Harbor Defense). Meanwhile, in the spring of 1942 the 155-mm. battery on Signal Hill had been partially compromised by the transfer of two of its four guns to Ernest Harmon Air Force Base in Stephenville.[174] The remaining guns continued to be based on Signal Hill, with their crews ready to move at a moment's notice to Manuels or Middle Cove.

With completion of the Red Cliff Head counter-bombardment battery, the coast defence of St. John's was close to its zenith, which technically would not be reached until the new anti-submarine net was placed in The Narrows in the summer of 1943. Despite the transfer of the 8-in. guns to Red Cliff Head and half of the 155-mm. battery to Stephenville, Signal Hill continued to play a coast defence role in keeping with what military planners had foreseen in 1880, but which had eluded it in the First World War. And while nobody in 1880 had predicted a role for the hill in anti-aircraft defence, the 3-in. battery at George's Pond was there for all to see. There was a further link with aviation technology when, on 1 February 1942, an American-operated aircraft recognition station began service from a position roughly 550 metres north of Cabot Tower.[175] In a system analogous to the port examination service, friendly aircraft entering local airspace had to identify themselves by approaching the station from the north at an altitude of 305 metres and on a course 270 degrees magnetic. The station was the responsibility of the duty officer in charge of the George's Pond anti-aircraft battery.[176]

Other changes on Signal Hill unintentionally evoked its history. In the hill's latest brush with wireless technology, a small radar installation was erected near George's Pond in the summer of 1944.[177] There were also reminders of the hill's unofficial role as a weather centre, first (in 1941) in the form of a makeshift meteorological station flush against the western face of Ladies Lookout, and later by a Rawin

[173] NARA, RG 407 (Adjutant-General's Office), Box 16887, File CABN-24-1.13, History of Battery D, 24th Separate Coast Artillery Battalion (Harbor Defense).
[174] Personal communication, Colonel Clarence T. Marsh, Jr. (Retired), 29 Jan. 1990.
[175] DND, DH, 355.019 (D12) (St. John's Anti-Aircraft Defences, Sept. 1941 – Feb. 1942), Earnshaw to General Officer Commanding-in-Chief, Atlantic Command, 3 Feb. 1942.
[176] NARA, RG 338, Box 17, File 373.2, Maxwell to Commander, Canadian Troops Newfoundland, 19 Dec. 1941.
[177] NARA, RG 338, Box 40, File 600.6, McDowall to Commanding General, Headquarters, Newfoundland Base Command, 24 June 1944.

Fig. 63: Aerial view of U. S. Army Barracks on Signal Hill, St. John's, Newfoundland, 10 Oct. 1941. Source: Library and Archives Canada/Canada. National Defence Collection/PA-135879. The barracks and other facilities in this photograph were those of the 57th Coast Artillery Regiment. There was a second such concentration at George's Pond belonging to the 421st Coast Artillery Battalion.

station that was functional by November 1944, and whose exact location remains unknown.[178] In meteorology a Rawin station determines wind speed and direction in the upper atmosphere by tracking a balloon-borne radio transmitter with radar or a radio direction finder. Since the aforementioned radar facility also dates from 1944, it is likely to have been part of the Rawin effort. In March 1945 the Regional Control Officer of the United States Army Air Corps, based in Manchester, New Hampshire, reported that observations by the Signal Hill Rawin station "are given a wide distribution and have proved very valuable not only to our own U. S. Army Air Forces Weather Service but to the Canadian and British Weather Services as well."[179]

---

[178] NARA, RG 338, Box 40, File 600.914, White to Engineer Officer, Fort Pepperrell, 30 Nov. 1944.
[179] NARA, RG 338, Box 47, File 000.93, Mereweither to Commanding General, Newfoundland Base Command, 19 March 1945.

Fig. 64: American soldiers horsing around on Signal Hill, ca. 1941. Source: Martin Zelenko. Note the flimsy construction of the buildings in the background, which enabled them to come down as easily as they went up.

Less exotic facilities on Signal Hill included eighteen barracks for 478 men, two mess halls, a tennis court, two recreation buildings, dispensary and post exchange, machine and carpenter shop, sewerage and refrigeration plants, and a pump house that drew water from George's Pond.[180] Except for two Armco steel ammunition igloos (commonly known as Quonset huts), all structures were of temporary frame construction, making them easy to put up and quick to tear down, hence the relative absence today of physical traces of the American presence. There were two main concentrations: (1) the sheltered area below Cabot Tower, then occupied by signalman Gardner's house and formerly home to the armoury and artificers' workshops; and (2) north of George's Pond along the "Burma Road," which was laid in late 1943 or early 1944 between George's Pond and Quidi Vidi as an alternative supply route from Fort Pepperrell to the Signal Hill gun sites, and as a way to reinforce or evacuate units on the hill if Signal Hill Road became impassable.[181] The road's unusual name

---

[180] Department of the Army, "Historical Monograph: U. S. Army Bases Newfoundland," p. II-37.
[181] NARA, RG 338, Box 41, File 600.96, McDowall to Commanding General, Newfoundland Base Command, 3 Feb. 1944; *Evening Telegram*, 23 June 1947, p. 24; Personal communication, Martin Zelenko, 29 April 1989.

was seemingly a play on that of the famous route by which the British supplied China before Burma fell to the Japanese in 1942.[182] Coincidentally or not, however, BURMA was also one of many postal acronyms used by soldiers to elude military censors and to send bawdy messages to wives and lovers back home. In that context, it was code for *Be Undressed, Ready, My Angel.*[183]

Hindsight, which was unavailable at the time, tells us that Newfoundland's anti-aircraft defences were redundant from the start. Only one German aircraft carrier was ever launched, but it was unfinished and never saw action. Likewise, the threat from surface vessels ended with the sinking of the *Bismarck* on 27 May 1941, and with it went the need for coast defences. Submarines, however, posed a real danger and brought the conflict to Newfoundland's doorstep. On the afternoon of 3 March 1942 an unidentified enemy submarine tried to fire two torpedoes up The Narrows in what was believed to be an attempt to hit an ammunition ship in the harbour.[184] The first torpedo exploded below Fort Amherst; two minutes later the second discharged harmlessly on North Head. That same year enemy submarines sank twenty-one ships in the Gulf of St. Lawrence, the St. Lawrence River estuary, and Cabot Strait, including, on 15 October, the Newfoundland-Nova Scotia passenger ferry SS *Caribou*, which cost 135 civilians and servicemen their lives.[185] Canadian fears for Bell Island's security were justified on 5 September when U 513 sank two ore carriers as they lay at anchor off the island, and again on 2 November when U 518 claimed two more, strikes that sent dozens of men to watery graves. If it were not for the Royal Canadian Navy, casualties in Newfoundland waters would have been catastrophic and the Battle of the Atlantic almost certainly would have been lost.

Ironically, by the time the new anti-submarine net was strung in The Narrows in mid-1943, the main submarine threat had permanently passed and the war itself was swinging the Allies' way. The Americans took this as a cue to start moving men to the European and Pacific theatres, and by year's end their strength in Newfoundland and Labrador had been halved.[186] On Signal Hill the first effects were felt

---

[182] Personal communication, Martin Zelenko, 29 April 1989.
[183] Jonathon Green and Dan Pearce, *Talking Dirty* (London, 2003), p. 292. Another variant of BURMA was *Be Upstairs, Ready, My Angel.* I thank Melvin Baker for alerting me to the naughty world of postal acronyms.
[184] DND, DH, War Diary, 103rd Heavy Battery, Vol. 8, 3 March 1942.
[185] MacKay, "Introduction," p. liii; Douglas *et al.*, *No Higher Purpose*, pp. 462-66. Other accounts put the casualties at 137. See, for example, Kavanagh, "W Force," pp. 116-17. The *Caribou* was sunk by U 69, which met its own end four months later.
[186] Dziuban, *Military Relations between the United States and Canada*, pp. 175-77.

in December with the departure from the summit of Battery C, 24th Coast Artillery Separate Battalion.[187] Battery B, 421st Coast Artillery Battalion, operators of the anti-aircraft guns at George's Pond, followed suit in mid-January 1944.[188] The Royal Canadian Artillery, on the other hand, clung to all of their coast defence positions until 31 May 1945, more than three weeks after victory in Europe was secured. The Americans were nonetheless last out the door. A Japanese threat was as likely as one from Mars, but that did not stop Battery D, 24th Coast Artillery Separate Battalion, from remaining at Red Cliff Head until 10 August 1945, one day after their comrades dropped a second atomic bomb on Japan, and four days before Japan surrendered.[189] Thus did the coast defence of St. John's come to an end.

For Signal Hill and The Narrows the Second World War was the final chapter in a saga that began with de Ruyter in 1665 and ran the gamut of Anglo-French rivalry before shifting focus in the twentieth century. Their use over such an extended period is noteworthy enough, but the fact that these 280 years witnessed such fundamental changes in weapons of war and communication technology is even more remarkable. The British had defended Newfoundland longer than anyone else, but with the Second World War their day was done. Geography, which formerly had made Newfoundland so attractive to Europe, now favoured North America, a shift in which technological change was also influential. The submarine and the airplane undermined the Royal Navy and simultaneously enhanced Newfoundland's value to Canada and the United States. These trends were reflected in the presence of American and Canadian soldiers on Signal Hill and in The Narrows, and in the resort to anti-aircraft and anti-submarine defences at the respective positions. The centuries-long parade of British, Canadian, and American defenders of the hill and The Narrows was also a reminder that, as a small entity, Newfoundland could never reliably defend itself, nor could it avoid the effects of conflict between the major powers, regardless of who they were or what period it was.[190] As with Canada, it needed the assistance of others.

---

[187] NARA, RG 165, Box 782, File 320.2, Arnold to Adjutant General, 6 Dec. 1943; and RG 338, Box 40, File 600.6, McDowall to Commanding General, Headquarters, Newfoundland Base Command, 24 June 1944.

[188] Stanton, *Order of Battle*, p. 498.

[189] NARA, RG 407, Box 16887, File CABN-24-1.13, History of Battery D, 24th Separate Coast Artillery Battalion (Harbor Defense).

[190] This was also true of 11 September 2001, when thousands of transatlantic air travellers were diverted to airports in Newfoundland and Labrador because of terrorist attacks against the United States. Terrorists are not powers in the traditional sense, but the threat they pose is no less real.

CHAPTER VIII

CONCLUSION: THIS VERY COMMENDABLE, NATIONAL MOVEMENT

"The Finance Committee of the Cabot Anniversary Committee met on Saturday afternoon to recommend to the Executive Committee that... it would be far better to give all citizens the immediate opportunity of associating with this very commendable, national movement which has as its object the recognition of the 450th anniversary of the discovery of this island by John Cabot." *Evening Telegram*, 16 June 1947

On Christmas Day 1944, as part of the British Broadcasting Corporation's "Journey Home" radio show, signalman Bob Gardner extended Newfoundland's greetings to the royal family and the empire from Cabot Tower.[1] Given that the tower had been built to honour the island's imperial ties, the setting was ideal, as was the choice of Gardner to speak for Newfoundland. Trained by British officers in the Newfoundland Royal Naval Reserve, he had served with the Royal Navy in the First World War, and his son Eric was now preserving Britain's lifeline by fighting the Battle of the Atlantic as a member of the Royal Canadian Navy. Gardner had also been profoundly affected by the torpedoing of the *Caribou*, for one of the victims was his wife Mary-Kate, who had been returning from a family visit to Montreal. It would have been difficult to find anyone who better symbolized Newfoundland's devotion to Britain, or its sacrifices on that account, than Bob Gardner.

Cabot Tower and the British connection were on the old sea dog's mind that Christmas Day, and he waxed poetic about both. The common denominator was the Atlantic Ocean, over which he looked every day and which, in his own words, "separates us from you in Britain and yet ties us closer together." He would, he said, have fought in the present conflict if not for his age, but he took comfort in the tower itself, which in a telling insight he described as "something like a ship with its signal masts and flags." He also declared that of all the signals he had flown in his twenty-one years on the job, the most memorable was on 17 June 1939 when he "dipped the Flag" during the visit of King George VI and Queen Elizabeth. "One day," he

---

[1] *Daily News*, 27 Dec. 1944, p. 3.

concluded, "when we've won the long battle, and peace is over the Empire again, I might dip my Flag to them again—who knows? Until then, for all Newfoundlanders, I send to Their Majesties our love and our respect. A Happy Christmas to them, and a Victorious New Year."

The New Year would indeed bring victory, but the price was empire itself. The Leased Bases Agreement, of which the Newfoundland and Labrador bases were as important as any, was a turning point in British history.[2] The war ravaged the British economy, enabling the United States and the Soviet Union to take the lead in the race for global supremacy. The dominions and the colonies, however, had been strengthened by their wartime experiences, and many now sought outright independence or membership in the more loosely structured "commonwealth." India's independence and the end of British rule in Palestine were the most glaring signs of the empire's meltdown, but Newfoundland was also part of the process.[3] It, too, had been transformed by the war, with base construction and demand for paper, minerals, and fishery products bringing full employment and economic conditions that one expert likened to "frontier days on the American continent."[4] Between 1935 and 1945 the population grew by 11.1 percent (to 321,819), and that of St. John's by 11.9 percent (to 44,603). Awash in budgetary surpluses from 1941 onward, the Commission of Government sent millions of badly needed Canadian dollars to Britain as outright transfers or interest-free loans, which the British used to buy Canadian munitions and food.[5] At war's end Newfoundland was more than carrying its weight, and that, according to the 1933 Royal Commission Report, entitled it to resume responsible government.

Postwar constitutional change in Newfoundland featured none of the bloodshed seen in some parts of the empire, but it still posed challenges to the British. They regarded the buoyant economy as a war-induced bubble and felt that true economic stability would come only through a costly reconstruction programme.[6] They had no desire to pay for that programme, but nor could they risk letting an independent Newfoundland slide back into an economic morass from which it might

---

[2] B. J. C. McKercher, *Transition of Power: Britain's Loss of Global Pre-eminence to the United States, 1930-1945* (Cambridge, 1999), p. 339.

[3] For Newfoundland in the broader context, see Robert Holland, "Newfoundland and the Pattern of British Decolonization," *Newfoundland Studies*, Vol. 14, No. 2 (1998), pp. 141-53.

[4] G. S. Watts, "The Impact of the War," in MacKay (ed.), *Newfoundland*, p. 221.

[5] Noel, *Politics in Newfoundland*, pp. 242-43.

[6] Neary, *Newfoundland in the North Atlantic World*, pp. 220-29.

have to be rescued at even greater expense. On top of this dilemma there was the possibility that a free Newfoundland might cosy up to the United States, adding to its formidable strength and causing unforeseeable complications, especially for Canada. Accordingly, their preferred option was for Newfoundland to join Canada, a known quantity with solid British connections and a proven sensitivity to American intentions. For their part, the Canadians were indeed leery of the American presence in Newfoundland and Labrador, something that those ninety-nine-year base leases suggested would not be ending any time soon. They also wanted a return on their investments in Gander, Torbay, and Goose Bay airports, and a say in intercontinental aviation and defence, which union with Newfoundland would give them in spades.[7] And, in late 1945, a Dominions Office emissary to Ottawa reported that Canadian officials noticeably perked up when he floated the idea that adding Newfoundland would constitute "the rounding off of the Confederation."[8]

After the British had gauged Canadian sentiment, they proceeded to do everything possible to smooth confederation's path. This included ignoring a key resolution of the Newfoundland National Convention, an elective body formed in 1946 "to make recommendations to His Majesty's Government in the United Kingdom as to possible forms of future government to be put before the people at a national referendum."[9] That resolution, if followed, would have kept confederation with Canada off the referendum ballot. Despite such blatant manoeuvring, the war and the Great Depression had whetted an appetite for change among many Newfoundlanders, and it was the people, not British or Canadian politicians and bureaucrats, who would have the final say. On 22 July 1948, in the second of two hotly contested referenda, voters narrowly chose confederation over responsible government "as it existed in 1933."[10] With that it was immaterial that Newfoundland might have been, as one historian of the empire later claimed it was, "the most thoroughly British of all the Dominions."[11] As of 31 March 1949, it was a province of Canada.

---

[7] MacKenzie, *Inside the Atlantic Triangle*, pp. 80-86; Neary, *Newfoundland in the North Atlantic World*, pp. 303-06.
[8] Neary, *Newfoundland in the North Atlantic World*, p. 232.
[9] Cited in Neary, *Newfoundland in the North Atlantic World*, p. 285.
[10] Three options appeared on the first ballot on 3 June, but as no one of them got over fifty percent of the votes, the third-place option—five more years of commission government—was dropped from the second ballot. The final result was 78,323 votes for confederation, 71,344 for responsible government. The essential account of the referenda campaigns is Neary's *Newfoundland in the North Atlantic World*. Noel's *Politics in Newfoundland* is still useful, while Hiller's *Confederation* booklet is a good short summary.
[11] Morris, *Farewell the Trumpets*, p. 215.

Fig. 65: Newfoundland 9¢ Cabot Tower, Signal Hill, St. John's, 3 January 1928. Source: © Canada Post Corporation {1985}. Reproduced with Permission. The stamp's caption was an early example of the erroneous claim that Marconi received the transatlantic wireless signal in Cabot Tower.

Bob Gardner did not live to see the new order of things. On 1 July 1946, the thirtieth anniversary of the Battle of Beaumont-Hamel—and thus the most revered date in the Newfoundland calendar—he donned a suit and tie, pinned his medals to his jacket, and strode downtown to join the Memorial Day ceremony and parade.[12] Eight days later he dropped dead of a heart attack in Cabot Tower, from which he had represented Newfoundland to the empire less than two years ago. Curiously enough, his beloved tower had also died a death of sorts, because Cabot's flame had all but gone out after the slaughter of the Royal Newfoundland Regiment shattered the old nationalist paradigm. With Cabot displaced by the regiment in the public's affections, there was, figuratively speaking, a vacuum in the tower, and into that vacuum came Guglielmo Marconi.

Exactly when the tower began to be perceived as the site of Marconi's reception of the first transatlantic wireless signal is unclear, but the myth had taken root at least by 1928, when the Newfoundland government issued two postage stamps of the tower, each bearing the caption "Cabot Tower, Signal Hill, St. John's. First Trans-Atlantic Wireless Signal Received 1901." Three years later, journalist Joseph Roberts Smallwood touted the claim as fact in his book *The New Newfoundland*.[13] Strangers to truth that they were, the Newfoundland

---

[12] Personal communication, Phyllis Fleuriau, 29 April 1984.
[13] J. R. Smallwood, *The New Newfoundland* (New York, 1931), p. 165.

Tourist Traffic Development Board promoted the tower in the 1930s as the place where Marconi received the "First wireless message." Aspiring journalist Michael Harrington joined the chorus in an article for Smallwood's influential *Book of Newfoundland*, published in 1937.[14] And on the occasion of Bob Gardner's empire-wide speech, the *Evening Telegram* lauded the tower's selection as the broadcast venue, because "it was there in 1901 that Marconi received the first wireless message across the Atlantic."[15]

When the Marconi myth arose is not as important as why. James Vey's photographs showing Marconi in and around the tower doubtless helped foster the myth, as did the loss of the former Diphtheria and Fever Hospital by fire, which removed the actual building Marconi had used. This, however, still does not answer the question: Why Marconi? Although there is probably no definitive answer, the myth can be seen as a function of Newfoundlanders' embrace of modernity.[16] It was no coincidence that most of the Newfoundland stamps from 1928 featured modern symbols, among them the Newfoundland Hotel; the Newfoundland Express; the SS *Caribou* ("9 Hours To Sydney, N. S."); Heart's Content ("First Trans-Atlantic Cable Landed 1866"); Alcock and Brown's biplane ("First Airplane To Cross Atlantic (Non-Stop) Leaving St. John's 1919"); and Labrador's Grand Falls. While the last-named stamp did not have a caption, it practically begged for investors to unleash Labrador's hydro-electric potential, a wish that would come true in 1971 with completion of the Churchill Falls mega-project. Nor was it coincidence that the Marconi myth jelled in the Great Depression, when the loss of democracy caused an agony of national self-doubt. In such a poisonous atmosphere, signs of modernity would have reassured Newfoundlanders that, their political shackles notwithstanding, they still had things in common with people who were free.

In a revealing speech at the official opening of the Cabot Tower wireless station on 5 August 1933, Prime Minister Alderdice assessed the technology's impact.[17] Conflating wireless telegraphy with broadcast radio, he acknowledged "the revolution it has wrought in

---

[14] Harrington, "Buildings and Monuments," p. 242.
[15] *Evening Telegram*, 23 Dec. 1944, p. 16.
[16] Although scholars continue to split hairs over what modernity means, I am guided here by the *Oxford English Dictionary* definition: "The quality or condition of being modern."
[17] "350th Anniversary of Landing of Sir Humphrey Gilbert: Prime Minister Alderdice Opens Marconi Signal Hill Station," *Newfoundland Quarterly*, Vol. 33 (Autumn 1933), p. 37. The official opening was for show only, as the station did not begin operations until a week later.

the social life of people throughout the world. Through its medium all that is best in the cultural development of the great centres of art, literature, science and music is brought into our homes." He went on to imply that the stakes were higher for Newfoundland, and he left no doubt as to who he felt was responsible: "For a people isolated as we are from the leading cities of the world, this is an inestimable boon, and in commemorating here to-day [sic] the remarkable achievements of Marchese Marconi we must not forget that it is to him we primarily owe the discovery that led up to these remarkable developments."[18] Alderdice had overlooked the earlier impact of cables and telegraphs, and had exaggerated—as many still do—Marconi's role in the invention of wireless (or radio).[19] But his words were proof that Marconi was synonymous with one of the most modern of all technologies, and that this meant something special to Newfoundland. By claiming Marconi through the medium of Cabot Tower, Newfoundlanders were claiming to be modern themselves.[20]

Broadly defined, modernization is the process by which traditional cultures—ones that are rural, religious, and autocratic—are transformed into modern cultures—ones that are urban, secular, and democratic.[21] Certain forces can speed the process, and as Newfoundland history proves, few are more influential than war.[22] The French Revolutionary and Napoleonic Wars essentially ended the British migratory fishery, paving the way for colonial status and self-government. Judge Prowse was at his perceptive best when he said that colonial status marked the beginning of "the modern period of our history."[23] Similarly, the Second World War accelerated Newfoundland's recovery from the Great Depression and made restoration of self-government imperative. As it was with war, so it was with technology. The successful laying of the transatlantic cable put

---

[18] Marconi had become a noble in 1924.

[19] Wireless would not have been possible without the contributions of others. In this regard, it is significant that when Marconi received the 1909 Nobel Prize in physics for "contributions to the development of wireless telegraphy," he shared the award with Germany's Karl Braun.

[20] How people perceive themselves is no minor point, for according to one of the leading scholars of modernity, "an essential part of being modern is thinking you are modern." See C. A. Bayly, *The Birth of the Modern World 1780-1914* (Oxford, 2003), p. 10.

[21] As the ensuing discussion will show, I do not believe in a sharp distinction between traditional and modern cultures.

[22] According to Eugen Weber, *Peasants into Frenchmen: The Modernization of Rural France 1870-1914* (Stanford, CA, 1976), p. 475, war is "less a cause of change than a precipitant of changes already under way." This judgment is echoed in Jeff A. Webb, "Gate Keeping and Newfoundland Popular Culture," in Steven High (ed.), *Occupied St. John's: A Social History of a City at War, 1939-1945* (Montreal and Kingston, 2010), pp. 191-219.

[23] Prowse, *History of Newfoundland*, p. xx.

Newfoundland on the cutting edge of modern communications. Marconi's miracle on Signal Hill was another giant step in modernity's march, not just for Newfoundland, but also for the world. Newfoundland and Labrador missed an opportunity when Marconi went to Glace Bay, but their coastal wireless and radio direction finding stations, including Cabot Tower, were vital to local and international shipping. And as further evidence of the closeness of the military and communications themes, the upgrades by the Canadian and American militaries left Newfoundland and Labrador with a communications infrastructure that by 1945 was second to none.[24]

In the course of helping Newfoundland to modernize, communications and war drew it closer to mainland North America, straining the British connection and favouring union with Canada.[25] This is not to say that they were dominant factors in confederation, or that they made it inevitable. But, to borrow a concept from quantum physics, they did make it more probable. The confederate leader, former journalist Joseph Smallwood, understood modernity's appeal and milked it for all it was worth. The triumph of his cause, and his lengthy political success after 1949—he won every provincial election until 1971—confirmed his reading of the spirit of the times. Still, the narrowness of the confederate victory reflected the weight of traditional forces, and thus the underlying duality of Newfoundland culture.[26] That quality was writ large on Signal Hill, where flags and the noonday gun wrestled with cable, wireless, and the telephone, and where Cabot and tradition did battle with Marconi and modernity.[27]

Events in 1947, the 450th anniversary of Cabot's "discovery" of Newfoundland, revealed the stunning degree to which Cabot's stock had fallen, and Marconi's risen. The seeds of that year's festivities were sown at a council meeting of the Newfoundland Historical Society on 7 November 1946.[28] The society's ideas to mark the anniversary included modest ones such as issuing a commemorative postage

---

[24] This story has yet to be written, but a modest start has been made in Cardoulis, *A Friendly Invasion*.

[25] Other influential forces, including cultural and economic ones, are not our concern here.

[26] For a masterly account of duality's persistence in Newfoundland culture, see Gerald L. Pocius, *A Place to Belong: Community Order and Everyday Space in Calvert, Newfoundland* (Montreal and Kingston, 2000), pp. 272-99.

[27] It is true that the noonday gun itself had once been a symbol of modernity, but those days were over.

[28] TRPAD, GN2/5, File 885.1 (Cabot Celebrations), Resolution of the Council of the Newfoundland Historical Society, 7 Nov. 1946, and Memorandum for Commission of Government, 10 Jan. 1947.

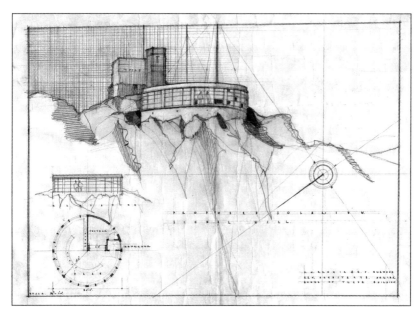

Fig. 66: "Proposed Solarium, Signal Hill," June 1947. Source: The Rooms Provincial Archives Division, GN2.5, File 885.1. Designed to commemorate the 450th anniversary of Cabot's "discovery" of Newfoundland, the proposal fell victim to a perfect storm of bad timing, inept fund-raising, and public indifference to the anniversary.

stamp—which the government already had in the works—and commissioning a painting of Cabot's departure from Bristol, and a model of his ship, the *Matthew*. Infinitely more ambitious was a bizarre proposal—bizarre, that is, for a heritage group—that would have put even Judge Prowse to shame: a paved "Cabot Highway" that would start at Cabot Tower, traverse the summit, swoop into Cuckold's Cove, wrap around North Head, and plough through The Battery before exiting via downtown *en route* to its final destination, Cape Bonavista, where a cairn would be erected as a Cabot memorial. As this was well beyond the society's means, a delegation led by its president, educator Vincent Patrick Burke, met with Commissioner for Home Affairs and Education Herman W. Quinton on 9 January and 10 February 1947 to obtain government backing. The outcome was both good and bad. Quinton would not commit to financial support, and instead urged the society to seek funding from the general public and "probably" St. John's City Council.[29] The delegates took heart, however, when he

---

[29] TRPAD, GN2/5, File 885.1, Quinton to Bartlett, 7 June 1947.

agreed that the highway "should be regarded as separate from the plans for the Celebration," which contained the hint of a suggestion that the government might build the highway. At some point after the February meeting—there are gaps in the records so the timing is vague—the society gave way to a new entity known as the Cabot Celebration Committee. This was largely window dressing, since the committee was chaired by Vincent Burke and was the society in all but name. Significantly, after concluding that a piece of the puzzle was missing, the committee determined to augment the Bonavista cairn with something more elaborate in St. John's, namely, a solarium on the old Duke of York's Battery site, immediately south of Cabot Tower. Excluding the highway, the estimated cost of the amended vision was $12,000, of which $9,000 was for the solarium.

Known as the Cabot Lookout, the solarium became the centre of attention. Architects Graham Rennie and Robert Horwood drew a plan and elevation of the proposed building, which was half spaceship and half sailing vessel, and thus a striking hybrid of modern and traditional elements. According to the celebration committee's publicity, the solarium would offer "all the advantages of a scenic coach on a modern train," with its glass roof and walls enabling visitors "to look over the magnificent panoramic view of the city... without the inconvenience of the usually prevailing winds."[30] The committee's selection of Signal Hill as the solarium's home was one of many nods to the 1897 celebrations. Cabot Tower's progenitor, Sir Edgar Bowring, had died in 1943, but the committee found room in its ranks for Bowring Brothers' new director, Geoffrey Milling. Bishop Howley was long gone, having died in 1913, so arrangements were made for the Roman Catholic Archbishop of St. John's, Edward Patrick Roche, to lay the solarium's cornerstone. Amid the mimicry, at least one thing was new. The festivities on 24 June were to include Governor Sir Gordon Macdonald's declaration of Signal Hill as a national park, a tourism initiative of the Commission of Government.[31] The Commission had assumed the tourism mantle after 15 November 1946, when the entire executive of the Newfoundland Tourist Traffic Development Board resigned in protest against years of neglect— although why tourism should have been a priority during the war is anyone's guess.

---

[30] *Evening Telegram*, 16 June 1947, p. 6.
[31] TRPAD, GN 38, S 5-8-1 "A Report on Newfoundland's Tourist-Trade Position,"/Douglas R. Oliver (typescript: Toronto, 1946), Department of Public Utilities, Commission of Government fonds, pp. 21-22.

Time would prove that Vincent Burke was no Daniel Prowse, and Geoffrey Milling no Edgar Bowring. Convinced that the government would assume the entire cost because of the "national character" of the celebrations, the Cabot Celebration Committee could not be bothered with fund-raising.[32] By early June, however, sensing that something was wrong, they decided to share their fantasy with Herman Quinton, who disabused them of it in a bluntly worded letter to their secretary, lawyer Rupert W. Bartlett, on the seventh, and again on the fourteenth after an incredulous Bartlett begged him to reconsider. Quinton advised that the Commission was prepared to give at most $3,000 toward the original components, but nothing toward the solarium. For that, money would have to come from the sources he had recommended back in February. The upshot, therefore, was that the committee did not launch the Cabot Celebration Fund until 16 June, only eight days before the ceremony. To cover their tracks, they claimed they had planned all along to seek public support after the cornerstone was laid, but now realized "it would be far better to give all citizens the immediate opportunity of associating with this very commendable, national movement...."[33] That explanation was belied by the air of panic in the first public appeal, which informed potential donors that "subscriptions of all sizes are most acceptable and they would be more appreciated if forwarded immediately."

The dubious organizational skills of Burke and his colleagues were compounded by desperate timing. Nineteen forty-seven was also the golden jubilee of Archbishop Roche's ordination to the priesthood, and Catholics had been fund-raising for months to pay for an extension to St. Clare's Hospital in his honour. That campaign was an unqualified success, raising nearly eighty thousand dollars, but it seems to have left Catholics with little desire to back the Cabot Celebration Fund; given that they comprised nearly half the city's population, this did not bode well.[34] Also, the main event to mark Roche's jubilee, a community mass, was scheduled for the morning of 24 June, the very day on which he was supposed to lay the solarium's cornerstone. This, however, was the least of it. The biggest problem was that the celebration fund was launched just as a National Convention delegation was preparing to leave for Ottawa to discuss possible terms of union with Canada.[35] Interest in the trip was

---

[32] TRPAD, GN2/5, File 885.1, Bartlett to Quinton, 3 June 1947, and Quinton to Bartlett, 7 and 14 June 1947.

[33] *Evening Telegram*, 16 June 1947, p. 1.

[34] *Evening Telegram*, 25 June 1947, p. 17. Of the city's 44,603 residents in 1945, 46.8 percent were Roman Catholics.

[35] The delegation left on 19 June.

feverish, and understandably so, because if confederation succeeded, Newfoundlanders would be embarking on a completely new experience. Seen in this light, a "commendable, national movement" based on a fossil like Cabot was neither commendable nor national. It was irrelevant.

As it became obvious that Protestants were no more inclined to support the fund than Catholics, the organizers went into full panic mode. Interviewed on the nineteenth, Vincent Burke allowed that the committee was "exceedingly anxious to have a reasonable amount of funds in hand to defray immediate expenses in connection with the ceremonies and urgently invites business firms and others who are in sympathy with this memorial, to send in a subscription today...."[36] Public displays of weakness are never a good omen, and this one was no exception. When the celebration took place on the afternoon of the twenty-fourth, there was no mention of Signal Hill becoming a national park, the Commission having deferred it to a later date. Going through the motions, Governor Macdonald cut a ribbon to open the Cabot Highway, a phantom that was never built.[37] In an unforeseen twist that was strangely reminiscent of 1897, when Bishop Howley was a last-minute replacement for Sir Herbert Murray, Archbishop Roche wore himself out at the community mass and had to send a substitute, Coadjutor Archbishop of St. John's T. J. Flynn, to lay the Cabot Lookout cornerstone. There was no need for spectators to crane their necks to glimpse the dignitaries on the reviewing stands, because the crowd was only a few hundred strong. The celebration fund eventually topped out at a paltry $1,510 (one-third of it from a single donor), and the solarium died an ignominious death, in the process ensuring that Cabot Tower would remain the city's most dominant and recognizable building.[38] Nor did the Commission revive its plan to turn the hill into a national park, which was dropped along with much else as Newfoundland descended into the maelstrom of the referenda campaigns.[39]

While the Cabot celebrations were imploding, the wizard of wireless emphatically re-entered public consciousness. Back in the

---

[36] *Evening Telegram*, 20 June 1947, p. 3.
[37] *Evening Telegram*, 25 June 1947, p. 2. It was never built as such. The Cabot Highway name was given to the "highway" that opened in 1947 from Clarenville to Lethbridge, and thence along the shore to Bonavista. It was described in the mid-1950s as "a narrow dirt road, often blocked in winter and not suitable for heavy traffic." See W. C. Wilton and H. S. Lewis, "Forestry Problems of the Bonavista Peninsula Newfoundland," *Forest Research Division Technical Note No. 26* (Ottawa, 1956), p. 10. Today's Route 230 on the Bonavista Peninsula still bears the nickname. Personal communication, Patrick Carroll, 3 Sept. 2009.
[38] *Evening Telegram*, 27 June 1947, p. 3.
[39] The apathy was not confined to St. John's, as the Cape Bonavista cairn was never erected. Personal communication, Don Johnson, 21 Jan. 2011.

Fig. 67: Stonemason Luke Madden in front of the Marconi monument, Signal Hill, ca. 1947. Source: Jerry Pennucci. Commemorating Marconi's reception of the first transatlantic wireless signal, this monument was unveiled on 16 July 1947 to immense public interest.

spring of 1939, less than two years after Marconi had passed away in Rome, the Commission of Government gave the Canadian Marconi Company permission to erect a memorial on Signal Hill. In early September a three-metre-high stone monument crafted by Luke Madden of Muir's Marble Works was placed, according to the public notice, "on the exact spot on which the first wireless signal was received," and an official unveiling was scheduled for the twelfth.[40] An attached plaque explained that the monument marked "an outstanding event in the history of Newfoundland and a new era in world communications. The first transatlantic wireless signal was received by Guglielmo Marconi on December 12, 1901 on this spot." (Despite the claims to exactitude, the monument was not on the hospital ruins but on a concrete platform only six metres north of Cabot Tower, where it was bound to encourage the Marconi myth.)[41] The planning went for nought, as the unveiling was cancelled when the war broke out. The Canadian Marconi Company, however, did not lose sight of their monument, and in October 1946 General Manager Stuart M. Finlayson wrote from Montreal to see if a new ceremony could be scheduled.[42] The Commission was still warm to the idea, and after further correspondence the parties agreed to a date of 16 July 1947, hard on the heels of the Cabot Day farce.

---

[40] TRPAD, GN31/3B, Department of Natural Resources, Departmental Files, Double Alphabetical Series, Box 23, File FM1, Marconi Memorial Signal Hill, Public Notice, 2 Sept. 1939.
[41] This, at least, was its location at the time of the official unveiling in 1947. It is possible that the monument was correctly situated in 1939, was removed to make way for one of the 8-in. guns, and was re-established in the wrong place in 1947. The monument is no longer on Signal Hill, although the plaque sits on a wall next to the hospital ruins.
[42] TRPAD, GN2/5, File 885.1, Finlayson to Roddis, 28 Oct. 1946.

Fig. 68: Cabot Tower with Marconi monument in foreground, 1959. Source: Parks Canada. The monument's placement so close to the tower fanned the flames of the Marconi myth.

When the sixteenth arrived, it was as though the Fates themselves had made the arrangements. The city was slammed by thunder, torrential rains, and the worst electrical storm in thirty years, a timely electromagnetic display that also evoked the young Marconi and the kite experiment that presaged his career.[43] Miraculously, the rain paused in the early afternoon and the ceremony went ahead as planned at 3:15 p. m., albeit as lightning continued to flicker and streak in the simmering sky. Forty-five minutes after the ceremony ended, the heavens erupted anew and an awesome lightning bolt shot into the harbour, striking the south-side generating station and plunging the city into watery darkness for nearly two hours. Only then did the dazed residents begin to return to normal.

Stuart Finlayson's address to the crowd, which the *Daily News* described as "huge," went a long way toward explaining why so many had braved the elements "to honour Marconi and wireless."[44] According to Finlayson, Marconi's efforts on Signal Hill constituted "the most momentous experiment in the history of communications." Well aware of the advances achieved in the war years, he further asserted that Newfoundland had "developed communication by wireless to a greater extent than any other country in the world," a

---

[43] *Evening Telegram*, 17 July 1947, p. 1.
[44] *Daily News*, 17 July 1947, p. 5.

staggering claim, but one he was eminently qualified to make. His words were not lost on the audience, whose very presence acknowledged the modernity for which Marconi and wireless were such powerful symbols. Fittingly, the ceremony was heard live over local radio station VONF and was taped and rebroadcast in Canada and overseas by the Canadian Broadcasting Corporation. As for the fourth estate, the *Daily News* reporter was joined by his *Evening Telegram* counterpart, whose adherence to the party line was strengthened by the monument's improper placement. Once more with feeling, the paper solemnly and wrongly reminded its readers that Marconi's receiver had been "located in Cabot Tower."[45]

The Marconi myth was the latest addition to Signal Hill's evolving canvas of the imagination. The Royal Engineers spent half a century chasing a citadel concept that proved to be a chimera, but which nonetheless fostered a group identity. With Cabot Tower's arrival as a symbol of the British connection, identity ascended to the national level. Not all that long afterward, when the Royal Newfoundland Regiment burned itself into the national psyche, Cabot became disposable. The impulse behind the attachment to Marconi was genuine enough, but since the Marconi myth rested on a false historical foundation, it was only a matter of time before it toppled as well. The late 1940s were probably its heyday, because it was soon swept aside by the next big thing.

Within months of confederation the Newfoundland government began pressuring Ottawa to designate Signal Hill as a national historic park, a cause that was joined after 25 January 1950 by the Province's newest man in Ottawa, Senator Vincent Patrick Burke.[46] Since protocol stipulated that designations must start with a ministerial recommendation by the Historic Sites and Monuments Board of Canada, the torch was passed to the Board's first Newfoundland appointee, C. E. A. Jeffery. Like Burke, Jeffery had been a Signal Hill booster for years—as editor (since 1923) of the *Evening Telegram*, as an executive member of the Newfoundland Tourist Traffic Development Board, and as one of the Newfoundland Historical Society delegates who pitched the 1947 Cabot celebrations to an unsuspecting Herman Quinton. The Board's minutes do not reveal how Jeffery convinced his colleagues of Signal Hill's relevance, but he seems to have played on Anglo-French conflict, a theme that resonated deeply in

---

[45] *Evening Telegram*, 17 July 1947, p. 1.
[46] LAC, R5747-7-0-E, Terra Nova National Park – History – Establishment – Boundary Revision, Part 1, Carter to Gibson, 30 Nov. 1949, and Tuck to Lewis, 27 Jan. 1950.

Newfoundland and Canadian history. This has been inferred from the text of the plaque that the Board produced in 1959 to explain the hill's significance. It dealt solely with the Battle of Signal Hill, which it described in florid prose as "the last phase of the battle in North America between the forces of Great Britain and France," thus ignoring both the recapture of Fort William, to which the Battle of Signal Hill was but the prelude, and Richery's raid of 1796, the last hostile action by French forces against British subjects in North America.[47] As debatable as the wording was, it could have been worse, because Jeffery had also been a driving force behind the Marconi myth.

Jeffery's approach succeeded, and in 1951 the Board recommended "that steps be taken to create a National Historic Park on Signal Hill, St. John's, Newfoundland." Despite ministerial approval, the National Parks Branch of the Department of Resources and Development could not accept title to the land until ownership of George's Pond—still part of the city's standby water supply—was resolved, and until the Province removed some fifty families who were squatting on the western extremity of the intended park area.[48] The ensuing bureaucratic stalemate began to break in 1954 when the federal Department of Transport levelled the nineteenth-century lighthouse and fortifications at Fort Amherst to make way for a new lighthouse. Since the Board had also declared Fort Amherst to be of national historic significance, the loss provoked angry demands to finish the job on Signal Hill.

On 26 May 1956 the Province transferred 105.3 hectares (260 acres) of the Signal Hill Peninsula to the federal Crown. Although the fringe where the squatters lived had been excluded, it was understood that the Province would transfer this, too, once the squatters were gone. (The squatters were eventually removed, but the land in question was never transferred.) George's Pond now became the focus, and when the federal Crown officially accepted the transfer on 22 May 1958, it took 98.6 hectares (243.4 acres), the City having retained the pond and some adjacent land. Thus did Signal Hill become Newfoundland's first national historic park, and thus did the hill and Cabot Tower begin new careers as symbols of Canadian national identity.

Officials of the National Parks Branch quickly resumed firings of the noonday gun, which had lain silent since running out of

---

[47] In 1998 the Board revisited the original designation and concluded that Signal Hill was of national historic significance because it was "importantly associated with Canada's defence and communications history [sic]."

[48] CSJA, MG 56 (Cindy Snow Collection), "Title to Signal Hill National Historic Park, St. John's, Newfoundland," 1999.

ammunition in mid-March 1949. By the 1980s its operation had become fitful, and in recent years it has been fired, if at all, in conjunction with seasonal performances of the military pageant known as the Signal Hill Tattoo.[49] After confederation the federal Department of Transport became responsible for flag signalling and the Cabot Tower wireless station. In 1958 it ended flag signalling on grounds it was obsolete, as it had been for decades, and the Branch opted not to revive it. The wireless station remained in Cabot Tower until 1960, when its employees were transferred to Torbay Airport. In a case of "out of sight, out of mind," no one seems to have paid any heed to the cables at Cuckold's Cove and Quidi Vidi, but even these stopped working in 1961 when the Commercial Cable Company closed its St. John's office. Business had been in free fall since the advent of transatlantic telephone cables in the 1950s, the first two of which came ashore in Clarenville, Trinity Bay.

Shorn of most of its customary roles, Signal Hill reverted to being the people's hill, and so it remains today. In an echo of the excitement formerly reserved for the comings and goings of the sealing fleet, spectators will occasionally gather on the hill to watch the arrival or departure of cruise ships. However, crowds of the old magnitude are usually seen only on the first of July, when thousands make their way to the summit for the annual Canada Day sunrise ceremony, which falls, ironically, on the same date as Memorial Day, Newfoundland's pre-confederation national anniversary. Otherwise, people come to learn about the hill's past or for sundry other reasons, including, as any resident will tell you, romantic liaisons.[50] Mostly, though, they come for the views, which is easy to understand once you have been to the hill. Except from the air, there is no better place from which to observe the sprawling city, admire the majestic coastline, scan the ocean for whales or icebergs or vessels big and small, or simply to marvel at the same, immutable horizon over which Ternay and the Whiteboys went waltzing in 1762. Another view, invisible to the naked eye, is the one within, because there is something about the hill's grandeur that encourages introspection. In that sense, there are as many views from Signal Hill as there are people who go there.

That people do go for the views is a challenge to the staff of Signal Hill National Historic Site of Canada (as it is known today), whose job, after all, is to share the hill's history with visitors. But the role is an apt

---

[49] Personal communication, Paula Morgan, 19 Jan. 2010.
[50] On people's motives for visiting the hill, see Patrick Carroll, "Mixed Meanings: Messages from Signal Hill" (Unpublished paper, Department of Folklore, Memorial University of Newfoundland, 2001).

one. The hill was originally The Lookout; the soldiers who defended it looked out for the enemy; the signalmen as well as the stations where they worked were lookouts; and the Cabot Tower wireless operators were lookouts, maintaining not an eye but an ear for mariners in distress or, literally, needing direction. In this as in so much else, Signal Hill was a microcosm, because Newfoundland and Labrador had long been lookouts for northeastern North America. That is why they were the first point of contact by the Norse, and by the hordes of fishermen who came after Cabot. That is why their waters gave rise to the first European industry in Canada. That is why they acquired strategic significance. And that is why they were intrinsic to transatlantic communications and aviation. Out on the edge, where the continent welcomes the ocean, the lookout was a bridge between safety and peril, the past and the future, the familiar and the unknown.

ABOUT THE AUTHOR

JAMES E. CANDOW

A graduate of Memorial and Dalhousie universities, James E. (Jim) Candow has worked in Parks Canada's Atlantic Service Centre in Halifax, Nova Scotia since 1977. His books include *Of Men and Seals: A History of the Newfoundland Seal Hunt* (1989) and *Lomond: The Life and Death of a Newfoundland Woods Town* (1998).

ACKNOWLEDGEMENTS

I am happy that Catherine Dempsey, past Executive Director of the Historic Sites Association of Newfoundland and Labrador, and the association's Board of Directors chaired by Joan Ritcey, saw the value in a history of Signal Hill, and happier still that they asked me to write it. There would have been no book, however, if Creative Publishers had not seen fit to publish it, and I thank them, and especially Donna Francis, for their support. I must also acknowledge Paul Johnson, who in 1989 partnered with Parks Canada on the Lookout Project, an interpretive trail atop the summit. Paul subsequently established the Johnson Geo Centre farther down the hill, providing additional proof that Newfoundland's natural and cultural heritage has no greater friend. It is to Paul that I owe the inspiration for the book's title.

My biggest debt is to my colleague Don Parsons, Interpretation Specialist with Parks Canada's Newfoundland East Field Unit. Don has been my right hand, my left hand, and sometimes my brain itself. I can never thank him enough. My former colleague Marilyn Dawe, who was the field unit's Cultural Resource Management Specialist before her retirement, was a constant source of energy and ideas. Many of the topics explored in these pages grew out of working with her on the visitor centre exhibit at Signal Hill National Historic Site of Canada. Rose Veitch, also retired but formerly the field unit's Collections Manager, built a relationship over the years with Doug Gardner, son of long-time signalman Bob Gardner. I learned much from Rose's e-mail exchanges with Doug, and subsequently from my own correspondence with him. For administrative help, I thank Karen Malone and Pat Power, also of the Newfoundland East Field Unit, and Bernadette Samson of Parks Canada's Atlantic Service Centre. I would also like to salute Field Unit Superintendent Bill Brake and former Service Centre Director Rob Thompson, who unfailingly backed my research over the years.

Historians are nothing without their sources, and for access to them we lean heavily on archivists and librarians. None bore a heavier burden than Margo Page, Administrative Assistant with the Service Centre Library, who cheerfully withstood an avalanche of interlibrary loan requests. Much of my primary research took place at the old Provincial Archives of Newfoundland and Labrador, which has since given way to the Provincial Archives Division of the Rooms Corporation. I would like to acknowledge the assistance of retired archivists Howard Brown, Tony Murphy, and Cal Best, and of active ones Melanie Tucker, Jessie Chisholm, and Sandra Ronayne. Mark

Ferguson of the Provincial Museum Division supplied useful material on Fort Townshend and St. George's Hospital, and as a bonus showed me the museum's chronometer collection. Thanks are also due to John Griffin of the Provincial Resource Library; Joan Ritcey of the Centre for Newfoundland Studies, Memorial University Libraries; Linda White of Archives and Special Collections, Queen Elizabeth II Library, Memorial University of Newfoundland; Helen Miller of the City of St. John's Archives; and Helen Gillespie of Library and Archives Canada.

I did most of my research on the Second World War in the late 1980s, and was privileged to visit the National Archives in Washington, D. C. and the Washington National Records Center in Suitland, Maryland. That led to an article for the *Newfoundland Quarterly* in 1993, and I thank the *Quarterly's* current circulation manager Linda Jackman for kindly allowing me to exploit it for present purposes. The late John Cardoulis put me in touch with American veterans who served on Signal Hill. Although I have since lost contact with them, Angelo Gillotte, Gerry Pennucci, and Martin Zelenko sent photographs and reminiscences. More recently, Alex Holder of the Coast Defense Study Group helped me to grasp the coast defence role of the 155-mm. guns on Signal Hill. Peter Neary of the University of Western Ontario generously shared his statistics on Newfoundlanders' participation in the war, and Ernie Cable of the Shearwater Aviation Museum in Dartmouth, Nova Scotia made what I believe is the first reliable estimate of the Royal Canadian Air Force's wartime strength in Newfoundland and Labrador.

My introduction to cable technology came via the superb Atlantic Cable website maintained by Bill Burns of FTL Design, in Long Island, New York. What I could not glean from the site I learned from Bill himself, who patiently fielded my enquiries and corrected some of my early musings. For wireless time signals in Canada, I profited from e-mail exchanges with private researcher Arthur E. Zimmerman. On the interrelated worlds of timekeeping and navigation, my most valuable contact was Frederick R. Smith, Dean of Science at Memorial University, who commented on relevant portions of the manuscript and opened my eyes to new vistas. And not only had he heard of official timekeeper James A. Whiteford, but his wife's grandparents once owned Dunluce, Whiteford's old home on Portugal Cove Road, St.

John's. Dave Heffler, formerly of the Geological Survey of Canada, and Captain Harvey Adams, now retired from the Canadian Coast Guard, offered corrections and comments on longitude and radio direction finding. Historian Bob Cuff of Gerald Penney Associates recommended important sources on longitude and timekeeping, was a font of knowledge for port history, and knew great places to eat in St. John's.

As shown by Frederick Smith's Whiteford connection, we are never far from the past wherever we live, although the distances often seem shorter in Newfoundland and Labrador. With input from Gerry Cantwell and, as always, Don Parsons, I was able to establish that Michael Cantwell was the mysterious fourth person in the photograph of Marconi, Kemp, and Paget on the steps of Cabot Tower. Finding confirmation after the fact in Irene Collins's Cantwell genealogy was embarrassing but nonetheless welcome. For details on signalman Bob Gardner, I am deeply thankful to his children, the late Mrs. Phyllis Fleuriau and, again, Doug Gardner.

That sage of the Newfoundland past, Melvin Baker of Memorial University, rescued me from several dead ends and never ceased to amaze. Olaf Janzen of Sir Wilfred Grenfell College, Roger Sarty of Wilfrid Laurier University, my colleague Monica MacDonald, and my supervisor Ron McDonald read all or parts of earlier drafts and offered constructive criticism, for which I thank them profusely. Any remaining errors of fact or interpretation are mine, not theirs.

My wife Grace Warner endured endless talk about Signal Hill, and by asking questions forced me to clarify what I was trying to say. In the process, she shaped things for the better. Lastly, and still with family, I dedicate this book to my mother, and to the memory of my late father.

James E. (Jim) Candow
Halifax, Nova Scotia

BIBLIOGRAPHICAL NOTE

The best general introductions to the history of Newfoundland and Labrador are Patrick O'Flaherty's companion volumes *Old Newfoundland: A History to 1843* (St. John's: Long Beach Press, 1999) and *Lost Country: The Rise and Fall of Newfoundland, 1843-1933* (St. John's: Long Beach Press, 2005). (*Leaving the Past Behind: Newfoundland History from 1934* will follow in 2011.) The standard military texts continue to be G. W. L. Nicholson's *The Fighting Newfoundlander: A History of the Royal Newfoundland Regiment* (St. John's: Government of Newfoundland and Labrador, 1964) and *More Fighting Newfoundlanders: A History of Newfoundland's Fighting Forces in the Second World War* (St. John's: Government of Newfoundland and Labrador, 1969). Cable history is well served by D. R. Tarrant, *Atlantic Sentinel: Newfoundland's Role in Transatlantic Cable Communications* (St. John's: Flanker Press, 1999). Nothing comparable exists for wireless, but Bob Harding has made a solid start in "Wireless in Newfoundland, 1901-1933," *Newfoundland Quarterly* (Summer/Fall 2001), pp. 15-19.

Anglo-French conflict in Newfoundland and Labrador awaits comprehensive treatment. That being said, Peter E. Pope, *Fish into Wine: The Newfoundland Plantation in the Seventeenth Century* (Chapel Hill, NC: University of North Carolina Press, 2004) reveals the economic reach of the early English fisheries; that it is a classic of Newfoundland literature in any genre is so much the better. For strategic considerations, Gerald S. Graham, "Newfoundland in British Strategy from Cabot to Napoleon," in R. A. MacKay (ed.), *Newfoundland: Economic, Diplomatic, and Strategic Studies* (Toronto: Oxford University Press, 1946), pp. 245-264, has yet to be superseded. Laurier Turgeon has written extensively and brilliantly on France's northwest Atlantic fisheries, but see especially his "Le temps des pêches lointaines: permanences et transformations (vers 1500 – vers 1850)," in Michel Mollat (ed.), *Histoire des Pêches Maritimes en France* (Toulouse: Bibliothèque historique Privat, 1987), pp. 133-181. Translated by Aspi Balsara, the same article is available in booklet form as *The Era of the Far-Distant Fisheries: Permanence and Transformation (circa 1500-1850)* (St. John's: Memorial University of Newfoundland, 2005). The best account of French military objectives, and their limitations, is James Pritchard, *In Search of Empire: The French in the Americas, 1670-1730* (Cambridge: Cambridge University Press, 2004). For the general history of Plaisance, Nicolas Landry, *Plaisance (Terre-Neuve), 1650-1713: Une colonie française en Amérique* (Sillery, QC: Septentrion, 2008) is meticulous and essential. Alas, early St. John's awaits a study of similar rigour.

Guy Frégault, *Iberville le conquérant* (Montréal: Société des Éditions Pascal, 1944) is still valuable for Iberville's Newfoundland campaign. English-only readers will do fine with Nellis M. Crouse, *Lemoyne d'Iberville: Soldier of New France* (Ithaca, NY: Cornell University Press, 1954) and Bernard Pothier's entry on Iberville in Volume Two of the *Dictionary of Canadian Biography* (Toronto: University of Toronto Press, 1969). Be forewarned, however: Pothier's thoughts on violence in North America are Eurocentric, and his conclusion that Iberville is "beyond doubt the first truly Canadian hero" is also blinkered. Despite a disorganized text, Alan F. Williams, *Father Baudoin's War: D'Iberville's Campaigns in Acadia and Newfoundland 1696, 1697* (St. John's: Memorial University of Newfoundland, 1987) will reward those with the patience to slog through it.

The best accounts of the loss and recapture of St. John's in 1762 (and with contrasting views on Ternay) are Olaf Uwe Janzen, "The French Raid upon the Newfoundland Fishery in 1762: A Study in the Nature and Limits of Eighteenth-Century Sea Power," in William B. Cogar (ed.), *Naval History: The Seventh Symposium of the U.S. Naval Academy* (Wilmington, DE: Scholarly Resources, 1988), pp. 35-54; Maurice Linÿer de la Barbée, *Le Chevalier de Ternay: Vie de Charles Henry Louis d'Arsac de Ternay Chef d'escadre des armies navales 1723-1780* (Grenoble: Les Éditions des 4 Seigneurs, 1972), Volume 1; and Evan W. H. Fyers, "The Loss and Recapture of St. John's, Newfoundland in 1762," *Journal of the Society for Army Historical Research*, Vol. 11 (1932), pp. 179-215. There are no equivalents in French or English for Richery's raid of 1796.

Context for nineteenth-century military developments in Newfoundland, including the withdrawal of the imperial garrison, can be found in J. Mackay Hitsman, *Safeguarding Canada 1763-1871* (Toronto: University of Toronto Press, 1968). For the First World War, Michael L. Hadley and Roger Sarty, *Tin-Pots and Pirate Ships: Canadian Naval Forces and German Sea Raiders 1880-1918* (Montreal and Kingston: McGill-Queen's University Press, 1991) is indispensable. For the Second World War, so are Gilbert Norman Tucker, *The Naval Service of Canada: Its Official History: Volume II: Activities on Shore during the Second World War* (Ottawa: King's Printer, 1952) and W. A. B. Douglas *et al.*, *No Higher Purpose: The Official History of the Royal Canadian Navy in the Second World War, 1939-1945: Volume II, Part I* (St. Catharines, ON: Vanwell Publishing, 2002). On the political accompaniments to military developments, two works stand out: David MacKenzie, *Inside the Atlantic Triangle: Canada and the Entrance of Newfoundland into Confederation, 1939-1949* (Toronto: University of Toronto Press, 1986) and Peter Neary's *magnum opus, Newfoundland in the North Atlantic World, 1929-1949* (Montreal and Kingston: McGill-Queen's University Press, 1988).

Superb introductions to wireless and telegraphy exist in Lewis Coe, *Wireless Radio: A History* (Jefferson, NC: McFarland and Company, 1996) and Ken Beauchamp, *History of Telegraphy* (London: The Institution of Electrical Engineers, 2001). W. J. Baker, *A History of the Marconi Company* (New York: St. Martin's Press, 1971) succeeds as business and personal history, as does W. P. Jolly, *Marconi* (London: Constable, 1972). Also rewarding is Gavin Weightman, *Signor Marconi's Magic Box: How an Amateur Inventor defied Scientists and began the Radio Revolution* (London: Harper Collins, 2003). Donald G. Schueler takes the man's measure as father and husband in "Inventor Marconi: brilliant, dapper, tough to live with," *Smithsonian Magazine,* Vol. 12, No. 12 (March 1982), pp. 126-47, and finds him sorely lacking.

While Baker, Jolly, and Weightman are competent enough on technical matters, they should be augmented by Sungook Hong, *Wireless: From Marconi's Black-Box to the Audion* (Cambridge, MA: MIT Press, 2001). In *Syntony and Spark—The Origins of Radio* (New York: John Wiley and Sons, 1976), Hugh G. J. Aitken raises serious doubts as to whether Marconi heard the Poldhu signals on Signal Hill. In the end he hedges his bets, but not so John S. Belrose, who flatly rejects the Marconi miracle in two important articles: "A Radioscientist's Reaction to Marconi's First Transatlantic Wireless Experiment – Revisited," *Institute of Electrical and Electronics Engineers/Antennas and Propagation Society International Symposium* (Boston: IEEE/APS, 2001), Vol. 1, pp. 22–25; and "The Development of Wireless Telegraphy and Telephony, and Pioneering Attempts to Achieve Transatlantic Wireless Communications," in Tapan K. Sarkar *et al.* (eds.), *History of Wireless* (Hoboken, NJ: John Wiley and Sons, 2006), pp. 349-420. Bartholomew Lee provides an ingenious defence in "Marconi's Transatlantic Triumph—A Skip into History," *Antique Wireless Association Review,* Vol. 13 (2000), pp. 81-96.

INDEX

Acadia, 11, 13, 31, 32, 31, 33, 36, 41, 47, 66.

Alderdice, Frederick, 223-224.

Allemand, Zacharie-Jacques-Théodore, 77-78.

Allied Forces Food from Newfoundland Fisheries, 199.

Americans in Newfoundland and Labrador, 202, *202*, 207, 215, *215*, 217.

Amherst, Jeffrey, 48, 49-51, 62-63.

Amherst, William, 49-56, 62, 73.

Amherst's Tower, image, 64.

Amulree Report. *See* Royal Commission (Amulree) Report. 1933.

Anderson, Murray, 196.

Anglo-American Telegraph Company, 155, 157, 158, 160, 164-167, 171, 177.

Anstey, George, 202.

Aquaforte, 45.

Argentia, 203.

Army Barracks, Signal Hill, 1941 aerial view, 214.

Arsac de Ternay, Charles-Henri, Louis d'. 42, 43-48, *43*, 50-51, 53, 54, 56, 57.

Artifacts, 193.

Auger de Subercase, Daniel d', 28, 30-31.

Aviation, 200, 213, 216, 221, 235. *see also* Military Operations – Air Force.

Bankruptcy (1894), 173.

Banks, Joseph, 62.

Bannerman, Alexander, 118.

Barracks. *see* St. John's – Fortifications *and* St. John's – Harbour – Narrows – Fortifications *and* Troops on Signal Hill.

Bartlett, John, 183, 185.

Bartlett, Otis, 189.

Bartlett, Rupert W., 228.

Bases, Military, 202, 203, 205, 211, 220, 221.

Basque Country, 9.

Basques in Newfoundland, 10.

Batteries. *see* St. John's – Fortifications *and* St. John's – Harbour – Narrows – Fortifications.

Battle of Signal Hill, 52-54, 55.

Baudoin, Jean, 21, 22, 23.

Bay Bulls, 17, 21, 22, 28-29, 48, 66, 67, 68, 77, 85.

Bay Roberts, 200.

Beauty of Signal Hill. *see* Tourism.

Belcher, Jonathan, 48, 49.

Bell Island, 175, 183, 197, 216.

Bellecombe, Guillaume de, 53, 54.

Bermuda, 96,

Bethell, J.S., 206.

Boes, Nicholas, 16.

Bonavista, 31.

Bond, Robert, 151, 152, 156, 172, 178.

Bonnycastle, Richard Henry, 103-106, 109-111.

Botany of Signal Hill, 2.

Botwood, 200, 201.
Bowring, Edgar R., 123-124, 131, 133-137, *135*, 139, 189, 227.
Boyle, Cavendish, 156, 174.
Bristol, England, 139.
British empire, 97, 114, 132-133, 135, 169-171, 174-175, 176, 184, 196, 200, 219-221.
Brouillan *see* Monbeton de Brouillan.
"Brown, Wynn C." *see* Devine, Maurice.
Browne, Arthur H., 136.
Burchell, Herbert C., 164, 165.
Burke, Johnny, 132.
Burke, Vincent P., 226, 228, 229, 232.
Burma Road. *see* Signal Hill Roads.

Cable Building, St. John's, 161.
Cabot, John, 7, 133, 177, 232.
Cabot Celebrations (1897 and 1947), 131-139, 192, 219, 225-232.
Cabot Lookout or Solarium. *see* Summit of Signal Hill.
Cabot Tower, *see* Summit of Signal Hill – Tower.
Campaigns. *see* Military Operations.
Canada, Defence of, 171, 178, 179-180, 184, 197, 199.
Canada, Dominion of, 122.
Canada-Newfoundland Patrol. *see* Military Operations – Navy – Canada-Newfoundland Patrol.
Canada-Newfoundland Relations, 171, 172, 173-174, 184, 196.
1865-1895, Proposed Union with Canada, 121,122,173, 228-229.
1949 Union with Canada, 5, 221, 225, 228, 232, 234.
Canadian Marconi Company, 187, 188, 230.
Canadians in Newfoundland (to 1949), 201, 203, 205, 207, 217.
Cantwell, Michael, 130, 157, *158*, 184.
Cap Rouge, French Fishing Station, c.1860 image, 94.
Cape Bonavista, 132, 133, 226, 227.
Cape Breton Island, 36, 38, 40, 41, 42, 48, 49, 58, 71, 89, 133, 156, 179, 225.
Cape Broyle, 44, 56.
Cape Race, 152, 159, 178, 182, 188.
Cape Ray, 159.
Cape St. Francis, 131, 139, 210, 211.
Cape Spear, 108, 109, 131, 139, 155, 181, 211, 212.
Carbonear, 22, 38, 40, 47.
Carbonear Island, 23.
Chain Rock *see* St. John's – Harbour – Narrows *and* St. John's – Harbour – Narrows – Barriers.
Chamberlain, Joseph, 135.
Chaytor, Baxter, 186.
Choiseul, Etienne-François de Stainville, 42, 44, 48, 57.
Church Lads' Brigade on Signal Hill, 1910 image, 176.
Churchill, Winston, quotes regarding Newfoundland, 169, 199.
Civilian Purposes, Use of Signal Hill for, 106, 107, 108-109, 110, 114, 123, 129.
see also Tourism.
Clarenville, 234.
Clifden, Ireland, 156.

Clonard, (Capt.) *see* Sutton, (Capt.).

Cochrane, Thomas, 100, 101.

Collins, John, 33.

Colonization. *see* Settlement.

Colvill, Alexander, 45, 48-53, 56.

Commercial Cable Company, 160-161, 177, 187, 197, 200, 234.

Commissariat Store, 103, 105.

Commission of Government. *see* Government – 1934-1949.

Communications, 4, 191, 203-204, 224-225.

Postal Service, 109, 191, 225-226; Stamps, 132, 135, *222*, 223, 226.

Radio, 186, 187, 223, 224, 232.

Signalling, 29-30, 39, 72, 74, 90-91, 102, 107-112,116, 117, 124, 129, 130, 131, 136, 138, 139, 146-147, 157, 184, 185, 186, 191, 194, 234, 235 ; PWSS, 108-209.

Telegraphy, Cable, 3, 122, 145-146, 149, 160-163, 170-172, 174, 177, 178, 187-188, 191, 200, 234; Cable Linkages, Canada, 146, 159-161, 172, 187, ; Ireland, 146, 156, 160, 161, 172, 187, ; United States, 161.

Telegraphy, Wireless, 3, 148-159, 167, 177, 178, 187-191, 194, 203-204, 213, 222-223 , 224, 231-233, 235; Myth of Cabot Tower as Site for First Transatlantic Wireless Signal, 222-223, 230, 232.

Telephone, 139, 146, 147, 188-189, 191, 234.

Timekeeping, 87, 110-114, 116, 117, 130-131, 140-145, 162-167, 184-186, 187, 191, 194, 233-234.

Conception Bay, 22-23, 49, 210.

Confederation with Canada. *see* Canada – Newfoundland Relations.

Cook, James, 3, 48.

Corner Brook, 195.

Costebelle, Philippe Pastour de, 32.

Crowe, Josiah, 33.

Cuckold's Cove, 51, 68, 72, 73, 77, 80, *160, 161*, 177,197, 234.

Cuckold's Cove Commercial Cable Company Station, image, 160.

Cuckold's Cove, Landing of Transatlantic Cable, image, 160.

Cupids, 192.

Customs and Revenue. *see* Trade and Commerce.

Darling, Charles, 95.

Davidson, Walter, 183.

Dawe, Eli, 143.

Dawson, Samuel E., 131.

Deadman's Pond, 123.

Debbieg, Hugh, 62-63, 67.

Denys de La Ronde, Louis, 31-32.

Deportations, 32, 36, 41, 47, 48, 66, 71.

Devine, Maurice, 143-144, *143*, 186.

Direct United States Cable Company, 187.

Dominion Status. *see* Newfoundland, Dominion Status of.

Douglas, Charles, 45, 48, 51, 52, 53.

Duckworth, John, 90.

Dunfield, Brian, 193.

Durnford, Elias Walker, 86-92.

Earnshaw, Philip, 208-209, 210-211.
Easton, Peter, 14.
Economy - 1855-1918, 173, 174, 175.
Economy – 1918-1934, 186, 195.
Economy - 1934-1949, 196, 199, 220-221, 224.
England – France Relations, 9-11, 17, 23, 27. *after 1707 see* Great Britain – France Relations.
English, Edward, 143.
English Shore, 11, 13, 16, 25-26, 33, 37, 57, 69.
Entente cordiale (1904), 170, 172, 175.
Europe – History to 1713, 7-9.
Europe – History - 1713-1763, 37.
Europe, International Rivalries, 9, 11, 27, 37-38, 40, 41, 42, 44, 71, 121, 169-170. *see also names of individual countries; see also* International Military Events.

Fencible Infantry. *see* Military Units - Royal Newfoundland Regiment of Fencible Infantry.
Fenians, 121-122, 170.
Fermeuse, 21, 24.
Ferryland, 18, 21, 24, 33, 38, 40, 41, 66.
Fessenden, Reginald, 189.
Fielding, W.S., 155-156.
Finlayson, Stuart M., 230-231, 230.
First World War, 3, 176-185, 195, 198.
Fisheries, 7-9, 94, 159, 164, 199; Bait, 93; Fisheries Convention of 1818, 97.
Fisheries – England, 9, 14, 26-27, 28.
Fisheries – France, 9-10, 23, 27, 31, 36, 37, 41-42, 57, 59, 61, 65, 69, 70, 93, 175.
Fisheries – Great Britain, 36-37, 40-42, 57, 61-62, 66, 69, 70, 71, 93, 96, 173.
Fisheries – Sealing, 95, 109, 124, 158, 189.
Fisheries – United States, 69, 70, 97.
Flags, 109-110, 136. *see also* Communications – Signalling.
Fleming, John Ambrose, 150.
Fleming, Sanford, 164.
Flynn, T.J., 229.
Fog Gun. *see* Communications – Signalling.
Fogo Island, 159, 191.
Fort Impregnable. *see* Summit of Signal Hill.
Fort Pepperrell. *see* Bases, Military.
Fort William Bombardment, image, 55
France – History, 71.
Francophobia, 95, 172, 173, 177, 232-233.
French – British Relations *see* Great Britain – France Relations.
French – English Relations *see* England – France Relations.
French and English Fishery Shores, map, 10.
French Campaign of 1696-1697, map, 20.
French in Newfoundland, 12, 21, 23, 28, 47, 133.
French Shore, 10-11, 31, 35-36, 58, 69, 93, 94, 95-96, 97, 172, 175.
French Treaty Shores, map, 35.

Gander, 200.

Gardner, Robert "Bob", 185-187, *185*, 191, 194, 195, 219-220, 221, 223; Family, 191.

Garrett, Samuel, 137-138.

Garrisons *see* St. John's, Defence of *and* St. John's – Fortifications.

Geography of Signal Hill, 1-5, 55, 85, 125, 217, 235.

Geology of Signal Hill, 1-2, 100, 105, 138, 139.

George's Barracks, c. 1870 image, 115.

George's Pond, 80, 104, 105, 106, 115, 116, 210, 213, 214, 217, 233.

George's Valley, 104.

Gibbet Hill, 2, 54, 72-73, 74, 100, 138.

Gilbert, Humphrey, 23.

Gibson, John, 24, 26.

Glascock, William, 111.

Gledhill, Joseph, 38, 40.

Government to 1713, 17, 33.

Government – 1713-1763, 37.

Government – 1763-1832, 61, 95.

Government – 1855-1918, 96, 114, 119, 122, 123, 132, 134, 135, 140-144, 151, 152, 156, 160, 164, 170, 172, 174, 182.

Government – 1918-1934, 192, 195.

Government - 1934-1949, 196, 200, 220, 223, 224, 226, 228.

Government – 1949-1971, 233.

Governors. *See* Government.

Governors' Residences, 64, 100, 101, 110.

Gower, Erasmus, 85.

Grand Banks, 42, 70, 93, 175, 182.

Graves, Thomas, 45, 48, 76.

Graydon, John, 27.

Great Britain – Canada Relations, 170, 178, 182, 198, 200, 201.

Great Britain – France Relations, 41, 58-59 93, 97-98, 114, 170, 172.

Great Britain – Newfoundland Relations, 95, 119, 121, 132-133, 170, 172-173, 188, 195, 200, 220-221.

Great Britain – United States Relations, 69, 89-90, 96-98, 114, 118, 121, 169-170, 201 202, 221.

Greene, Daniel J., 144.

Greene, William Howe, 131-135, 137.

Guns on Signal Hill, images, 185, 211.

Halifax, 40, 71, 96-97, 98, 118, 119, 162, 164, 167, 170, 172, 178, 179, 198.

Harbour Grace, 47, 188, 200.

Harrington, Michael F., 223.

Harvey, John, 104, 105, 110, 111.

Haussonville, Joseph-Louis-Bernard de Cléron d', 44, 46, 54-55, 57.

Hay, David, 68.

Hayward, Eli, 184.

Heart's Content, 146, 159, 163, 178, 200.

Hertz, Heinrich, 148-149.

Historic Park, Signal Hill. *see* Tourism.

Historical Facts, 193, 222-223, 230, 232-233.

History of Newfoundland and Labrador, 4.

History of Newfoundland and Labrador to 1713, 7, 9-30, 32-34, 78, 217, 234.
History of Newfoundland and Labrador – 1713-1763, 31, 35-56, 73, 193, 203, 217.
History of Newfoundland and Labrador – 1763-1832, 57-59, 61-92, 94-101, 108, 110, 111, 114, 193, 233.
History of Newfoundland and Labrador – 1832-1855, 94, 102-117, 124, 217, 224.
History of Newfoundland and Labrador – 1855-1918, 95, 106, 107, 108-109, 116, 118-122, 124-167, 169-192, 195, 217.
History of Newfoundland and Labrador – 1918-1934, 139, 150, 184-195, 198, 224.
History of Newfoundland and Labrador – 1934-1949, 191-217, 219-223, 225, 228-232.
History of Newfoundland and Labrador – 1949-1971, 94, 234.
History of Newfoundland and Labrador – 1979-1989, 234.
Hoar, Jonathan, 53.
Holloway, John, 85.
Horse Islands, 189.
Horwood, Robert, 227.
Hospitals, 101, 102, 104, 105, 106, 121, 125-127, *126*, 134,138, 152, 157, 185, 223.
Howley, James P., 132-133.
Howley, Michael F., 131, 134-135.

Iberville. *See* Le Moyne d'Iberville.
Iceland, 205.
Île St.-Jean. *See* Prince Edward Island.
Impressment, 13, 14, 15, 29, 40, 48, 66, 89, 93.
Intelligence, Military, 178, 179, 180, 182, 206.
International Military Events, 38, 57-58, 89, 114, 169, 177, 179, 196-198, 200, 204, 207, 217.
Ireland, 82, 163, 195, 205. *see also* Communications – Cable *and* Communications – Wireless.
Irish in Newfoundland, 38, 40, 44-47, 48, 54, 82-83, 91, 122.

Jackson, John, 30.
Jeffery, Charles E.A., 232-233.
Judge, William, 129-130.

Keen, William, 32.
Keats, Richard, 90.
Kemp, George, 151,152, 156, 157, *158*.
King, Mackenzie, 197-198.
Kirke, David, 11, 15.

La Ronde, Louis Denys de. *see* Denys de La Ronde, Louis.
Labouchere, Henry, 1857, 95.
Labrador Coast, 66, 77, 78, 95, 97, 133, 159, 180, 190.
Labrador Fishery, 159.
Ladies' Lookout. *see* Summit of Signal Hill.
Latham, Robert, 30.
Le Moyne d'Iberville et d'Ardillières, Pierre, *19*, 19-20, 22-24, 31, 47, 78.
Leake, John, 27.
LeMessurier, H.W., 193.
Lend Lease Act. *see* Bases, Military.

Lighthouses, 102, 108, 112, 139, 181, 233.
Lilly, Christian, 18.
Lloyd, Thomas, 29, 32.
Longitude, 112-113, 162-166.
The Lookout, 30, 52, 235.
LORAN Stations, 203-204.
Louisbourg. *see* Cape Breton Island.

MacDermott, Anthony, 180.
Macdonald, Gordon, 229.
Macdonnell, Charles, 49, 53-54, 56.
Madden, Luke, 230.
Maine, 11.
Mainwaring, Henry, 14.
Manuels, 212, 213.
Marconi, Guglielmo, 3, 147-159, *156, 158,* 161, 187-189, 194, 222-224, 225, 230, 232.
Marconi Centennial 2001, 154.
Marconi Monument on Signal Hill, 230-231, *230, 231.*
Marconi Wireless Telegraph Company of Canada, 158.
Martin, Christopher, 16.
Massachusetts, 48, 49, 53, 150-151.
Maxwell, John, 49, 56.
Mermaid, 7.
Merchants, English, 24. *See also* Trade and Commerce.
Merchants, British. 38, 40, 45, 94. *see also* Trade and Commerce.
Methodist Church, 140.
Middle Cove, 213.
Military Operations, 4. *see also* Military Units.
Air Force (British), Ferry Command, 203.
Air Force (Canadian), 198, 199, 201, 203.
Army (American), 202-203, 215; Army Air Force, 203, 209, 210, 211, 212, 21-215, 217.
Army (British), 25, 31, 48-56, 63, 72, 97, 108, 115, 118, 119, 233.
Army (Canadian), 178, 198, 201, 203, 207, 208, 209, 217.
Army (French), 21-22, 27-29, 30-31, 42, 44-48, 57.
Army (Newfoundland Regiment/ Royal Newfoundland Regiment in First World War), 176-177, 181, 183, 184, 199-200, 207, 232.
Cadet Corps, 175-176, *176.*
Navy (American), 134, 182; Navy Air Patrol, 182, 205.
Navy (Canadian), 178-181, 182-183, 198, 216.
Navy (Canada-Newfoundland Patrol), 180, 181, 183.
Navy (Convoy Escort Service), 179, 182, 204, 205, 210.
Navy (French), 18, 19-21, 25-26, 30, 31-32, 42, 44-46, 57, 58, 61, 65, 76-78.
Navy (German), 179, 180-181, 182, 216.
Navy (Royal), 13, 17, 19, 24-25, 27, 31,33, 40, 44-46, 48-51, 56, 57, 63, 66, 90, 96-97, 170, 174, 175, 178-179, 180, 198, 199, 204, 217.
Navy (Royal Naval Reserve), 172-174, *173,* 176, 177, 178, 179-180, 182, 184, 199.
Newfoundland Militia. *see* Army – Newfoundland Regiment.
Newfoundlanders in British and Canadian Forces, 183, 199.
Military Units. *see also* Military Operations.

1st Royal (1761), 49.
15th Regiment (1761), 49.
45th Regiment (1761), 50.
62nd Regiment (1861), 118.
66th Regiment (1800), 83, 84.
77th Regiment (Montgomerie's), 48.
78th Regiment (Fraser's Highlanders), 49.
Black Watch (Royal Highland Regiment) (Canada), 201.
Coast Artillery Separate Battalions (U.S.), 210-211, 213, 217.
Coast Artillery Regiments (U.S.), 210-211.
Beauvaisis, Marine, Pethièvre, Montrevel (French Regiments), 44.
French Grenadiers, 54.
Hoar's Massachusetts Regiment, 53.
Independent Company (English), 29
Massachusetts Provincials, 49, 52, 203.
Newfoundland Legion of Frontiersmen, 180-181, 184.
Newfoundland Regiment of Foot, 69.
Nova Scotia Regiment of Fencible Infantry, 85.
Royal Artillery, 75, 82, 85, 87, 115, 119, 120.
Royal Canadian Artillery, 203, 209.
Royal Canadian Rifle Regiment (1862), 120.
Royal Engineers, 30, 85, 101, 232.
Royal Military Artificers, 83, 87.
Royal Newfoundland Companies, 115, 117-118, 120.
Royal Newfoundland Regiment of Fencible Infantry, 72, 75, 83, 85.
Royal Newfoundland Veteran Companies, 98.
Royal Newfoundland Volunteers, 72.
Royal Sappers and Miners, 91.
Volunteer Rifle Companies, 121.
Watchmen, 182, 183, 212.
Milling, Geoffrey, 227-228.
Mines and Mining, 183, 197.
Minesweeping. *see* Military Operations – Navy (Canadian).
Modernity, Appeal of, 173, 187, 223-225, 232.
Monbeton de Brouillan, Jacques-François de, 20-22.
Monbeton de Brouillan *dit* Saint-Ovide, Joseph de, 31, 32.
Monroe, Walter, 192.
Montigny, Jacques Testard de. *see* Testard de Montigny, Jacques,
Moody, John, 29, 30.
Morris, H. Charles, 143.
Mouat, Patrick, 46.
Mount Pearl, 178, 188.
Murray, Herbert, 135.
Musgrave, Anthony, 170.
Mutiny (1798). *see* Troops at Signal Hill.
Myrick, E.J., 191.

Narrows *see* St. John's – Harbour – Narrows.
The Narrows, 1910 image, 119.
National Park. *see* Tourism.

Nationalism, 5, 95, 132-133, 135-136, 139-140, 170, 173, 174-175, 176-177, 193, 222-223, 224, 228-229, 232, 233, 234.
Nationalism – Canadian National Identity and Signal Hill, 5, 233, 234.
Native Peoples, 18, 19, 23, 28, 30, 89.
Naval Reserve *see* Military Operations – Navy – Royal Naval Reserve.
Navigation, 113-114, 162-163, 166, 188, 204.
Nescambiouit, Chief, 20, 28, 30.
Nesmond, André de, 25, 26.
Netherlands, 15-16.
New England, 38, 40, 61, 66.
New France, 12, 13, 23, 58.
New Hampshire, 214.
New Jersey, 210.
Newfoundland and Labrador, Defence of, 37, 38, 172, 180, 182, 184, 196, 197, 198, 200, 210-212, 216.
Newfoundland and Northeastern North America, map, 4.
Newfoundland Constabulary, 122, 200.
Newfoundland, Dominion Status of, 170, 195, 221.
Newfoundland Historical Society, 225-229, 232.
Newfoundland Hotel, 192.
Newfoundland Regiment. *prior to First World War see* Military Units; *after First World War see* Military Operations – Army (Newfoundland Regiment).
Nicolls, Gustavus, 98-99.
Noonday Gun. *see* Communications – Timekeeping.
Noonday Gun Poem. *see* Poems about Signal Hill.
Norris, John, 24-26.
North America, Defence of, 1, 3, *4*, 13, 41, 49, 58, 98, 172, 179, 197, 201, 208, 217, 235.
Northeastern North America, map, 4
Nova Scotia, 48, 56, 85, 97, 131, 183.

"Ode to Newfoundland", cover sheet, 175.
Oldfield, John, 101.
Outport-St. John's Rivalry, 132.

Paget, Percy, 151, 156, 157, *158.*
Palliser, Hugh, 49, 62.
Pancake Rock *see* St. John's – Harbour – Narrows.
Parson's Pond. *see* Deadman's Pond.
Pesche des morues vertes et seches, c. 1698 image, 8.
Perry, David, 52, 55.
Petty Harbour, 21, 29, 50.
Phillpotts, W., 123.
Piccott, Archibald, 181-182.
Piracy and Privateering, 14-15, 18, 21, 27-28, 31, 33, 48, 66, 68, 70, 90.
Placentia, 35-36, 37, 38, 40, 41, 47, 48, 66, 96. *before 1713 see* Plaisance.
Placentia Bay, 159.
Placentia Harbour, image 12.
Plaisance 12, 17, 18, 21, 22, 23, 27, 28, 31, 32, 33, 36. *after 1713 see* Placentia.
Poems about Signal Hill, 123, 140-145, 186; (Fame of Noonday Gun Poem, 144-145).

Poldhu, Cornwall, England, 150-151, 153-154, 156.
Police *see* Newfoundland Constabulary.
Population of Newfoundland and Labrador. *See* Settlement.
Population of St. John's. *see* St. John's – Population.
Portugal, 9.
Postal Service. *see* Communications – Postal Service.
Pouch Cove, 210.
Prince Edward Island, 58.
Pringle, Robert, 68, 69, 72.
Prisons, 104, 106, 107, 116, 120, 121.
Protestant Churches, 229.
Prowse, D.W., 127-128, 131-140, *128*, 193, 224.

Queen's Battery, images, 124, 166.
Quidi Vidi Harbour and Quidi Vidi Battery area, 50-51, 52, 53, 54, 63, 68, 72, 73, 80, 89, 98, 100, 117, 161, 178, 187, 197, 203, 234.
Quidi Vidi Lake area, 52, 53, 105.
Quinton, Herman W., 226, 228, 232.

Radio Direction Finding Stations, 188, 190.
Radar Stations, 203-204, 213, 214.
Red Head/ Red Cliff Head, 91, 212, 213, 217.
Regimental School, 121.
Regiments at Signal Hill. *See* Military Units *and* Troops at Signal Hill.
Reid, Robert Gillespie, 164.
Reid, W.D., 128.
Religion, 140, 228, 229.
Rendell, W.F., *180*, 199.
Renews, 21, 66.
Rennie, Graham, 227.
Richery, Joseph de, 76, *76*, 77-78.
Riot at St. John's (1861), 18.
Roads. *see* Signal Hill Roads.
Robe, Alexander Watt, 105.
Roche, Edward P., 227, 228, 229.
Roman Catholic Church, 102, 106, 228.
Roope, John, 29.
Roosevelt, Franklin D., 198.
Roper, Joseph, 164, 165, 166.
Rose, Thomas, 140-143, 145.
Ross, George, 85, 86.
Ross, Walter, 45, 46, 87.
Ross's Valley, 2, 87, 126.
Royal Commission (Amulree) Report. 1933, 196, 220.
Royal Newfoundland Regiment. *see* Military Operations – Army (Newfoundland Regiment).
Royal Visits, 123, 119.
Ruyter, Michiel de, 16.

St. John's – The Battery (community), 128.
St. John's – Council, 226.

St. John's – Economy, 36, 61-62, 94-95.

St. John's – Fires, 75, 81, 106, 111, 116, 125, 126, 127, 128, 130, 131, 132, 184, 185.

St. John's – Fortifications, 16-17, 25, 85-86, 90, 100, 117, 119, 211-213, 233. *see also names of sites on Signal Hill, e.g.* Gibbet Hill, Summit of Signal Hill, etc.

St. John's – Fortifications – Carronade Battery, 80.

St. John's – Fortifications – Fort Mary, 18, 22.

St. John's – Fortifications – Fort St. George/Fort George/George's Battery/Lower Fort, 38, 39.

St. John's – Fortifications – Fort Townshend, 64, 67, 72, 78, 80, 82, 86, 87-88, 99, 100, 101, 102, 105, 110, 115, 117, 120.

St. John's – Fortifications – Fort William/King William's Fort, 18,22, 26, 29, 30, 32-33, 39, 46, 50, 52, 53, 55, 62-63, 69, 78, 80, 81, 86, 87, 88, 91, 98, 100, 101, 102, 104, 105, 110, 111, 115, 117, 120, 233.

St. John's – Fortifications – New Fort, 32, 46, 210.

St. John's – Fortifications – Signal Hill Battery, 211, *212*, 215, 217.

St. John's – Harbour, 3, 36-37, 51, 67, 75, 78, *96*, 119, 127, 128, 175, 183, 205, *207*, 216, (torpedo attack), 217. *see also* St. John's – Fortifications.

St. John's – Harbour – Narrows – Barriers, 15, 18, 26, 29, 32, 40, 46, 51, 54, 77, 181, 183, 205-207, 209, 213, 216.

St. John's – Harbour – Narrows – Fortifications –

103rd Coast Battery, 208.

Amherst's Battery/ Amherst's Tower/ Fort Amherst, 64, 68-69, 72, 74, 77, 86-87, 88, 100, 102, 105, 108, 117, 120, 139, 175, 182, 208-209, 233.

Anchor Point, 16-17.

Chain Rock Point, 16-17, 40, 64, 68, 72, 73, 74, 120.

Duke of York's Battery, 74, 77, 80, 91, 227.

Fort Townshend Grand Sea Battery, 90.

Fort William Narrows Battery, 90.

Frederick's Battery, 68, 100, 102, 105, 110, 117.

North Battery, 40.

North Fort, 16-17, 18.

North Head, 100.

North Point Battery, 104.

Old Fort, 18.

Pigg's Point, 18.

Queen's Battery/"Queen's Old Fort", 74, 75, 80, 86, 89, *99*, 100, 101, 111, 120, 140, *166*, 193.

South Battery/ South Castle, 29, 30, 32, 39.

South Head, 16-17, 63-64.

South Fort, 16, 18.

Waldegrave Battery/ Fort Waldegrave, 81, 89, 100, 117, 120, 180, 181, 183.

Wallace's Battery, 74, 81, 98, 117.

St. John's – Harbour – Traffic, 108-109.

St. John's – Land Ownership, 233.

St. John's – Population, 13, 27, 32, 40, 41, 61, 70, 94-95, 106, 125, 196, 220, 228.

St. John's – Water Supply, 106, 233.

St. John's 1762 recapture, map, 51.

St. John's as Capital City. *see* St. John's, Importance of.

St. John's, Defence of, 15-18, 22-26, 29, 30, 31-33, 38, 40, 42, 45-57, 62-63, 67-68, 72, 74, 75, 77-78, 80, 81, 84-85, 87, 88, 90-91, 96-97, 98-100, 104, 105, 117, 118-120, 172, 177, 180-183, 199, 201, 204-213, 216-217, 233.

St. John's Entrance, image by J. Hall, 81.

St. John's Harbour and Town, image by W. Eagar, 99.

St. John's Harbour, map, 25, 39, 67, 79.

St. John's Narrows, 1943 image, 206.

St. John's, image by C. Lilly, 18.

St. John's, image by P.C. Le Geyt, 96.

St. John's, Importance of, 1, 33, 36, 37, 40, 62, 63, 95, 96, 97, 122, 132, 134, 167, 178, 197, 204, 214, 235.

St. John's, map, 16, 17, 207.

St. John's, Signal Hill and Area, map, 1

St. Mary's, 66.

Saint Ovide. see Monbeton de Brouillan *dit* Saint-Ovide.

St. Pierre and Miquelon, 59, *65*, 69, 71, 77-78, 93-94.

St. Pierre, Vue de la Rade, image, 65.

Scott, Frank, 130, 157, 166.

Second World War, 3, 199-217, 219-220, 222, 224, 225, 227, 230, 231.

"Séguiran, M. de", 46.

Settlement, 11-14, 24, 27, 28, 40-41, 61, 62, 66, 69, 70-71, 93, 95.

Shipping – Safety, 108-109, 111-113, 131, 134, 149, 152, 159, 162, 165, 187, 188, 191, 225, 235.

Ships -

ANTELOPE, 45, 48.

ANTONIA, 201.

AVALON, 205.

BISMARCK, 216.

BRITON, 180, 184, 186. *before 1916 see* Ships - CALYPSO.

CALYPSO, 174, 175, 185. *after 1916 see* BRITON.

CARADOC, 106.

CARIBOU, 216, 219.

CHARYBDIS, 174, 185.

COMTESSE DE GRAMMONT, 46, 54, 57. *see also* GRAMONT.

COLONIA, 160-161.

EDMUND B. ALEXANDER, 202-203, 209, 210.

ENTERPRISE, 56.

FANNY, 56.

FIONA, 181.

GARONNE, 44, 45.

GOSPORT, 48.

GRAMONT, 45, 46. *see also* COMTESSE DE GRAMMONT

JAMES, 49, 56.

KING GEORGE, 48.

MACKAY-BENNETT, 161.

MAGDALENA, 119.

NIOBE, 178.

NORTHUMBERLAND, 48, 50, 51.

PORT SAUNDERS, 181.

PROFOND, 21.

ROWAN, 186.

SARDINIAN, 151.

SPY, 68.

SQUID, 45.

STEPHANO, 179.
SYREN, 45, 46, 47, 51-52.
TAMAR, 122.
TITANIC, 159, 187.
VENUS, 31-32.
VICTORIAN, 189.
VIKING, 189.
Sightseeing at Signal Hill. *see* Tourism.
Signal Code, image, 107.
Signal Hill and Area, map, 1.
Signal Hill Battery 1941, map, 212.
Signal Hill Buildings 1851, image, 116.
Signal Hill, Place Name, 1, 52.
Signal Hill Plan, map, 88.
Signal Hill Roads, 55, 74, 75, 86, 128, 215, 226, 227, 229.
Signal Hill Tattoo, 234.
Skelton, George, 144-145.
Skerrett, John, 82-83, 88.
Skinner, Thomas, 72-75, 78, 80-86, 92.
Smallwood, Joseph, R., 222-223, 225.
Smith, Thomas, 38.
Smith, William, 155.
Solarium. *see* Summit of Signal Hill.
Solarium, 1947 image, 126.
Southwood, Henry, 16, 17.
Spain, 9, 27, 29, 35, 37. 40, 42, 77, 97. *see also* Europe – International Rivalries.
Squires, Richard, 189, 192.
Stamps *see* Communications – Postal Service – Stamps.
Stephenville, 203, 213.
Strategic Importance of Newfoundland and Labrador. *see* North America, Defence of.
Strategic Importance of Signal Hill. *see* St. John's, Importance of.
Subercase, Daniel d'Auger de. See Auger de Subercase, Daniel d'.
Summit of Signal Hill, 2, 30, 39, 73-75, 78, 80, 81-82, 83-84, *84*, 86, 87-88, 90, 91-92, 99-100-102, *102*, *103*, 103-104, 108, 110, 116-117, 120-121, 129, *129*, 130, *130*, 131, 152-153-154, 156-157, 185, 193-194, 209-211, 213, 214, 215, 217, *226*, 227-230, *230*, 233.
Summit of Signal Hill – Cabot Tower, 5, 132-140, *136, 137, 138, 158*, 182, 184-185, 188, 190-191, *190*, 194, 208, 219, 222-223, *231*, 232, 234.
Supplies, 9-10, 17, 26, 33, 37, 41, 46, 47, 66, 71, 102, 103, 172, 182, 205. *see also* Trade and Commerce.
Sutton, (Capt.), 44, 45, 46, 54.

Taylor, Joseph, 32.
Technology, New, 117, 119-120, 145-146, 148-149, 153, 158, 167, 179, 187, 191, 217, 223-224.
Temperance, 140.
Ternay, Charles-Henry-Louis d'. *see* Arsac de Ternay, Charles-Henry-Louis d'.
Testard de Montigny, Jacques, 28-31.
Thomas, Aaron, 109.
Thomas, Henry J., 137.

Thomas, James H., 196.
Thorburn, Robert, 171, 178.
Time Zones, 162-165,167,186.
Tor Bay, 51-52, 210, 212.
Torbay, 63, 66, 68, 85.
Tourism, 123-125, 128, 191-192, 194, 223, 227, 229, 232, 233, 234-235. *see also* Civilian Purposes, Use of Signal Hill for.
Trade and Commerce, 24, 33, 35, 37, 41, 42, 57-58, 61, 66, 82, 85, 94-95, 108-109, 111, 130-131, 132, 172, 182, 220.
Treaty of Paris. *see* History of Newfoundland and Labrador - 1763-1832.
Treaty of Utrecht. *see* History of Newfoundland and Labrador - 1713-1763.
Treaty of Versailles 1783. *see* History of Newfoundland and Labrador – 1763-1832.
Trentham, E.N.R., 197, 200.
Trepassey, 66.
Trinity, 38, 40, 41, 47, 66.
Trinity Bay, 23.
Troops at Signal Hill, 13, 25-26, 29, 30, 38, 40, 44, 45, 46, 50, 52, 53, 57, 67, 67-69, 74, 75, 78, 80-81, 82-85, 89, 97, 98-101, 103, 104, 105, 106-107, 110-111, 115-118, 120-121, 122, 123, 124, 125, 183, 201, 202-204, 214-216; Mutiny (1798), 82-83..

United States – History, 65, 69, 89, 115, 118, 121. *see also* International Military Events.

Vey, James, 156-158, 223.
Vicars, Richard, 92.
Victoria, Queen of Great Britain – Anniversaries, 131, 134-135.
Voltaire quote regarding Seven Years' War, 58.

Waldegrave, William, 78.
Wallace, James, 74, 77, 78.
Walwyn, Humphrey, 196, 210.
War of 1812. *see* Great Britain – United States Relations *and* History - 1763-1832.
Watson, Ellis Cornish, 143.
Weather Stations, 130, 131, 135, 136, 139, 191, 203, 213-214.
Welty, Maurice, D. 203, 209, 210.
West Country Merchants. *see* Merchants, English *and* Merchants, British.
Western Union Telegraph Company, 146-147, 162, 177.
Wheatley, George, 143.
Wheler, Francis, 17, 18.
Whitbourne, Richard, 7.
White, Richard, 143.
The Whiteboys. *see* Irish in Newfoundland.
Whiteford, J.A., 164,165.
"Who Stopped the Gun", 141-143 (words of poem); 144-145 (fame of poem).
Winter, Marmaduke, 201.
Wireless Stations, 158-159, 167, 177, 178, 188, 189, 199-191, 223, 234.
Wood, William, 45.